ADOBE PHOTOSHOP LIGHTROOM 3

CLASSROOM IN A BOOK®

The official training workbook from Adobe Systems

CD-ROM Included for Windows and Mac OS

WHAT'S ON THE DISC

Here is an overview of the contents of the Classroom in a Book disc

The *Adobe Photoshop Lightroom 3 Classroom in a Book* disc includes the lesson files that you'll need to complete the exercises in this book, as well as other content to help you learn more about Adobe Photoshop Lightroom 3 and use it with greater efficiency and ease. The diagram below represents the contents of the disc, which should help you locate the files you need.

Lesson files

Each lesson has its own folder inside the Lessons folder. You will need to copy these lesson folders to your hard drive before you can begin each lesson.

Online resources

Links to Adobe Community Help, product Help and Support pages, Adobe certification programs, Adobe TV, and other useful online resources can be found inside a handy HTML file. Just open it in your Web browser and click on the links, including a special link to this book's product page where you can access updates and bonus material.

Adobe Press

ADOBE PRESS Find information about other Adobe Press titles, covering the full spectrum of Adobe products, in the Online Resources file.

CONTENTS

4   REVIEWING   114

5   ORGANIZING AND SELECTING   138

9 PUBLISHING YOUR PHOTOS 268

GETTING STARTED

Adobe® Photoshop® Lightroom® delivers a complete workflow solution for the digital photographer—from importing, reviewing, organizing, and enhancing digital images to publishing photos, producing client presentations, creating web galleries, and outputting high-quality prints. The user interface is highly intuitive and easy to learn, yet Lightroom has all the power and versatility you would expect from an Adobe application, utilizing state-of-the-art technologies to manage large volumes of digital photographs and to perform sophisticated image processing tasks. Whether you're a home user, a professional photographer, a hobbyist, or a business user, Lightroom enables you to stay in control of your growing digital photo library and to easily produce good-looking pictures and polished presentations for both web and print.

If you've used an earlier version of Lightroom, you'll find that this Classroom in a Book® will teach you advanced skills and covers the many new innovative features that Adobe Systems has introduced in this version. If you're new to Lightroom, you'll learn the fundamental concepts and techniques that will help you master the application.

About Classroom in a Book

Adobe Photoshop Lightroom 3 Classroom in a Book is part of the official training series for Adobe graphics and publishing software developed with the support of Adobe product experts. Each lesson in this book is made up of a series of self-paced projects that give you hands-on experience using Adobe Photoshop Lightroom 3.

Adobe Photoshop Lightroom 3 Classroom in a Book includes a CD attached to the inside back cover. On the CD you'll find all the image files used for the lessons in this book, along with additional learning resources.

Prerequisites

Before starting on the lessons in this book, make sure that you and your computer are ready by following the tips and instructions on the next few pages.

Requirements on your computer

You'll need about 400 MB of free space on your hard disk for the lesson files and the work files that you'll create as you work through the exercises.

Required skills

The lessons in this book assume that you have a working knowledge of your computer and its operating system. Make sure that you know how to use the mouse and the standard menus and commands, and also how to open, save, and close files. Can you scroll (vertically and horizontally) within a window to see content that may not be visible in the displayed area? Do you know how to use context menus, which open when you right-click (Windows) / Control-click (Mac OS) items?

If you need to review these basic and generic computer skills, see the documentation included with your Microsoft® Windows® or Apple® Mac® OS X software.

Installing Adobe Photoshop Lightroom

Before you begin using *Adobe Photoshop Lightroom 3 Classroom in a Book*, make sure that your system is set up correctly and that you've installed the required software and hardware.

You must purchase the Adobe Photoshop Lightroom 3 software separately. For system requirements and complete instructions on installing the software, see the Adobe Photoshop Lightroom 3 Read Me file on the application CD or the Adobe Photoshop Lightroom Support Center on the web at www.adobe.com/support/photoshoplightroom.

Copying the Classroom in a Book files

● **Note:** The files on the CD are practice files, provided for your personal use in these lessons. You are not authorized to use these files commercially, or to publish or distribute them in any form without written permission from Adobe Systems, Inc. and the individual photographers who took the pictures, or other copyright holders.

The CD attached to the inside back cover of this book includes a Lessons folder containing all the image files you'll need for the lessons. You'll import these images into your Lightroom library and learn to organize them using the catalog that is central to many of the projects in this book. Keep the lesson files on your computer until you have completed all the exercises.

Copying the Lesson files from the CD

1   Create a new folder named **LR3CIB** inside the *username*/My Documents (Windows) or *username*/Documents (Mac OS) folder on your computer.

2   Insert the *Adobe Photoshop Lightroom 3 Classroom in a Book* CD into your CD-ROM drive.

3 Locate the Lessons folder on the CD and copy it into the LR3CIB folder you created in step 1.

4 When your computer finishes copying the Lessons folder, remove the CD from your CD-ROM drive and put it away.

Creating a catalog file for working with this book

The catalog file stores information about all the photos in your library. It includes the location of the master files, any metadata you've added in the process of organizing your images, and a record of every adjustment or edit you've made. Most users will keep all their photos in a single catalog, which can easily manage thousands of files. Some might want to create separate catalogs for different purposes, such as home photos and business photos. Although you can create multiple catalogs, you can only have one catalog open in Lightroom at a time.

For the purposes of working with this book, you'll create a new catalog to manage the image files that you'll use in the lessons. This will allow you to leave the default catalog untouched while working through the lessons, and to keep your lesson files together in one easy-to-remember location.

Creating a library folder

First you'll create a folder to contain your new catalog as well as the files that you'll create as you complete the lessons in this book.

1 Locate the LR3CIB folder you've created on your computer.

2 Within that folder, create a new folder called **LR3CIB Library**. This new folder should be located right next to the Lessons folder that you've just copied from the CD.

Creating a new catalog file

The first time you launch Lightroom, a catalog file named Lightroom Catalog.lrcat is automatically created on your hard disk. This default Lightroom catalog file is created in the *username*/My Documents/My Pictures/Lightroom (Windows) or *username*/Pictures/Lightroom (Mac OS) folder.

You'll create your new catalog file inside your LR3CIB Library folder.

1 Start Adobe Photoshop Lightroom 3.

2 From the Lightroom menu bar, choose File > New Catalog.

3 In the Create Folder With New Catalog dialog box, navigate to the LR3CIB Library folder inside the LR3CIB folder you created on your hard disk.

● **Note:** In this book, the forward arrow character (>) is used to denote submenus and commands found in the menu bar at the top of the workspace or in context menus; for example, Menu > Submenu > Command.

4   Create a new catalog by doing one of the following:

- On Windows, type **LR3CIB Library Catalog** in the File Name text box, and then click Save.

- On Mac OS, type **LR3CIB Library Catalog** in the Save As text box, and then click Create.

Lightroom opens your new library catalog, which is empty as you have not yet imported any photos.

In order to be sure that you're always working with the right catalog as you progress through the lessons in this book, you will now set the preferences so that you will be prompted to specify the LR3CIB catalog each time you launch Lightroom. It is recommended that you keep this preference set as long as you're working through the lessons in this book.

5   Choose Edit > Preferences (Windows) / Lightroom > Preferences (Mac OS).

6   In the Preferences dialog box, click the General tab. From the Default Catalog menu, choose Prompt Me When Starting Lightroom.

Note: In the remainder of this book, instructions that differ for Macintosh users and those working on Windows systems are given in a compact format as follows; the forward slash character (/) is used to separate equivalent terms and commands for Windows / Mac OS, in the order shown here.

7   Click OK (Windows) / the Close button (⬤) (Mac OS) to close the Preferences dialog box.

Next time you start Lightroom the Select Catalog dialog box will appear, giving you the opportunity to make sure that your LR3CIB Library Catalog is selected before Lightroom launches.

▶ **Tip:** You can hold down the Clrl+Alt / Control+Option keys immediately after you launch Lightroom to open the Select Catalog dialog box regardless of your Default Catalog preference settings.

Additional resources

Adobe Photoshop Lightroom 3 Classroom in a Book is not meant to replace documentation that comes with the program or to be a comprehensive reference for every feature. Only the commands and options used in the lessons are explained in this book. For comprehensive information about program features and tutorials, please refer to these resources:

Adobe Community Help Community Help brings together active Adobe product users, Adobe product team members, authors, and experts to give you the most useful, relevant, and up-to-date information about Adobe products. Whether you're looking for a code sample or an answer to a problem, have a question about the software, or want to share a useful tip or recipe, you'll benefit from Community Help. Search results will show you not only content from Adobe, but also from the community. With Adobe Community Help you can:

- Access up-to-date definitive reference content online and offline
- Find the most relevant content contributed by experts from the Adobe community, on and off Adobe.com
- Comment on, rate, and contribute to content in the Adobe community
- Download Help content directly to your desktop for offline use
- Find related content with dynamic search and navigation tools

To access Community Help If you have any Adobe CS5 product, then you already have the Community Help application. To invoke Help, press F1 or choose Help Lightroom help. This companion application lets you search and browse Adobe and community content, and to comment on and rate any article just as you would in the browser.

You can also download Adobe Help and language reference content for use offline, and subscribe to new content updates (which can be downloaded automatically) so that you'll always have the most up-to-date content for your Adobe product. You can download the application from www.adobe.com/support/chc/index.html

Adobe content is updated based on community feedback and contributions. You can contribute in several ways: add comments to content or forums—including links to web content, publish your own content using Community Publishing, or contribute Cookbook Recipes. Find out how to contribute at www.adobe.com/community/publishing/download.html

See http://community.adobe.com/help/profile/faq.html for answers to frequently asked questions about Community Help.

Adobe Photoshop Lightroom 3 Help and Support www.adobe.com/support/photoshoplightroom where you can find and browse Help and Support content on adobe.com.

Adobe TV http://tv.adobe.com is an online video resource for expert instruction and inspiration about Adobe products, including a How To channel to get you started with your product.

Adobe Design Center www.adobe.com/designcenter offers thoughtful articles on design and design issues, a gallery showcasing the work of top-notch designers, tutorials, and more.

Adobe Developer Connection www.adobe.com/devnet is your source for technical articles, code samples, and how-to videos that cover Adobe developer products and technologies.

Resources for educators www.adobe.com/education includes three free curriculums that use an integrated approach to teaching Adobe software and can be used to prepare for the Adobe Certified Associate exams.

Also check out these useful links:

Adobe Forums http://forums.adobe.com lets you tap into peer-to-peer discussions, questions and answers on Adobe products.

Adobe Marketplace & Exchange www.adobe.com/cfusion/exchange is a central resource for finding tools, services, extensions, code samples and more to supplement and extend your Adobe products.

Adobe Photoshop Lightroom 3 product home page
http://www.adobe.com/products/photoshoplightroom.

Adobe Labs http://labs.adobe.com gives you access to early builds of cutting-edge technology, as well as forums where you can interact with both the Adobe development teams building that technology and other like-minded members of the community.

Adobe certification

The Adobe training and certification programs are designed to help Adobe customers improve and promote their product-proficiency skills. There are four levels of certification:

- Adobe Certified Associate (ACA)
- Adobe Certified Expert (ACE)
- Adobe Certified Instructor (ACI)
- Adobe Authorized Training Center (AATC)

The Adobe Certified Associate (ACA) credential certifies that individuals have the entry-level skills to plan, design, build, and maintain effective communications using different forms of digital media.

The Adobe Certified Expert program is a way for expert users to upgrade their credentials. You can use Adobe certification as a catalyst for getting a raise, finding a job, or promoting your expertise.

If you are an ACE-level instructor, the Adobe Certified Instructor program takes your skills to the next level and gives you access to a wide range of Adobe resources.

Adobe Authorized Training Centers offer instructor-led courses and training on Adobe products, employing only Adobe Certified Instructors. A directory of AATCs is available at http://partners.adobe.com.

For information on the Adobe Certified programs, visit www.adobe.com/support/certification/main.html.

1 A QUICK TOUR OF PHOTOSHOP LIGHTROOM

Lesson overview

This lesson will help you understand how Lightroom works and familiarize you with the workspace.

The exercises will guide you through a typical workflow: you'll import, review, organize, and edit images, and then create your own web gallery to present them.

In the process, you'll be introduced to the Lightroom workspace modules:

- The Library Module, where you'll import, review, and organize your images so that you can access them quickly and easily

- The Develop Module, where you can correct, adjust, retouch, and enhance your photos

- The Slideshow Module

- The Print Module

- The Web Module, where you'll create your own web page

Further lessons in this book provide more in-depth exercises and specific details of the workspace modules, tools and features.

 You'll probably need between one and two hours to complete this lesson.

In this lesson, you'll get an overview of how Lightroom works. You'll familiarize yourself with the workspace, tools, and controls, while you explore the Library, Develop, Slideshow, Print and Web Modules.

Understanding how Lightroom works

Working with Lightroom will be easier and more productive if you have an understanding of how Lightroom differs from other image processing applications in the way it handles digital images.

When you bring a photo into your library, Lightroom does not actually import the image file itself but merely creates a new entry in the library catalog to record the location in which the file is stored. When you add a flag, a keyword, or a rating to the image, or group it in collections with other photographs in your library, those changes and groupings are recorded and added to the entry in the catalog file. Even when you edit the image by cropping, correcting color, or applying effects, the modifications are actually recorded only as instructions in the catalog file. This is called non-destructive editing; Lightroom shows you a preview of the effects of your work, but the original image file remains unaltered. The modifications are applied only when you export or output your image. In this respect, Lightroom works very differently from other image processing applications such as Photoshop or Photoshop Elements, which write changes directly to the source file.

Managing photos in a library

To begin working with your photos you must first bring them into the Lightroom library. You can import files from your computer hard disk, from external storage media, or download them directly from a digital camera or card reader.

Even during the import process, Lightroom offers you several options to help you manage your files; you can choose to leave them at their current locations, preserving the folder structure to which you are accustomed, copy them to a new location leaving the originals intact, or move them and delete the originals to avoid having two copies of the files. When you copy or move your files, you can choose to replicate the original folder structure in which they are stored, to consolidate them into a single folder, or to sort them into subfolders based on capture date.

You'll learn more about the import options in Lesson 3, "Importing." For now, the important thing to remember is that the images in your Lightroom library can be located anywhere on your computer hard disk, or even on external storage media, and that references to their locations are stored in the library catalog file.

If you wish to rename or move an image file that you've already imported into your library, you should only do so from within Lightroom; otherwise, Lightroom will report the renamed or moved file as missing and you'll be asked to reestablish the link so that the information in the catalog file can be updated.

Non-destructive editing

When you make adjustments or modifications to an image in your library, such as changing the white balance or removing spots, Lightroom stores this editing information only in the library catalog file; the original image file remains unchanged. The library catalog file also stores embedded metadata, and any keywords, flags, color label or rating you may have assigned to an image, together with information about its place in the collections you create to group your photos. Everything you do with an image in Lightroom is recorded in the catalog.

There are many advantages in storing modifications separately from the image data. Did you ever save a document only to realize that you'd just overwritten an important previous version? Or realize too late that you should have cropped an image differently? If you were lucky you may have had a copy of the original file, but you would still have lost any other edits and modifications you had already made.

In Lightroom, non-destructive editing frees you to experiment with adjusting, cropping, or otherwise modifying your images. Crop an image and later change your mind—no problem! You can undo, redo, or tweak any modification that you've made without ever losing any information from the original file. Changes will be applied to an image only during output—while it is being exported either as a low resolution JPEG image to be used in a web page, as a preview image to be displayed in the Lightroom workspace, or as part of a print layout. The original image data remains unchanged and only copies created as part of the rendering process will be altered according to the editing instructions captured in the catalog.

Should you wish to edit an image using an external image processing application, you should always launch the process from within Lightroom. In this way, you can be sure that Lightroom will keep track of changes made to the file, and the edited copy will automatically be added to your Lightroom library. For a JPEG, TIFF, or PSD image, Lightroom gives you the option to edit the original file, or a copy— either with or without the adjustments that you've already applied in Lightroom. For files in any other file format, you can edit a copy to which your Lightroom adjustments have already been applied.

The Lightroom workspace

The Lightroom workspace is divided into six main panels. At the center of the workspace is the work area, flanked by the left and right panel groups. Above the work area and the left and right panel groups is the top panel, with an identity plate at the left and the Module Picker to the right. Immediately below the work area is the Toolbar, and below that, across the bottom of the workspace, the Filmstrip.

Although Lightroom has five distinct workspace *modules*, the basic arrangement of the panels in each module is identical. Only the contents of the panels change from module to module, to address the specific requirements of each working mode.

▶ **Tip:** You can specify your favorite external editor in the External Editing preferences. If you have not nominated an external editor, Lightroom will preselect Photoshop or Photoshop Elements by default, if either application is installed on your computer.

● **Note:** The illustration at the right shows the Windows version of Lightroom. On Mac OS, the arrangement of the workspace is the same except for minor differences in style between the two operating systems. On Windows, for example, the menu bar is located under the title bar of the application window, whereas on Mac OS the menu bar is anchored at the top of the screen, above the title bar of the application window.

The top panel

The top panel displays an identity plate on the left and the Module Picker on the right. The identity plate can be customized to feature your own company name or logo and will be temporarily replaced by a progress bar whenever Lightroom is performing a background process. You'll use the Module Picker to move between the different workspace modules by clicking their names. The name of the currently active module is always highlighted in the Module Picker.

The work area

At center-stage is the main preview and working area. This is where you select, review, sort, compare, and apply adjustments to your images, and where you pre-view the work in progress. You can increase the size of the work area by hiding any or all of the surrounding panels. The work area is the only element of the Lightroom workspace that can't be hidden from view. From module to module, the work area offers different viewing options, allowing you to see either one photo or multiple images at a range of magnification levels, and to preview your slideshows, web galleries, and print layouts.

The left and right panel groups

The content of the side panel groups changes as you switch between the workspace modules. As a general rule, you'll use panels in the left group to find and select items, and panels in the right group to edit or customize settings for your selection.

In the Library Module for example, you'll use the panels below the Navigator panel in the left group (Catalog, Folders, Collections, and Publish Services) to locate, select, and group the images you want to work with, and the panels below the Histogram panel in the right panel group (Quick Develop, Keywording, Keyword List, Metadata, and Comments) to apply changes to them. In the Develop Module, you can choose from develop presets on the left, and fine-tune their settings on the right. In the Slideshow, Print and Web Modules, you can select templates on the left, and customize their appearance on the right.

The Toolbar

The tools available in the Toolbar also vary as you move from module to module. You can customize the Toolbar for each module independently to suit your working habits, choosing from a variety of tools and controls for switching viewing modes, setting ratings, flags, or labels, adding text, and navigating through preview pages. You can show or hide individual controls, or hide the Toolbar altogether until you need it. There are also menu commands or keyboard shortcuts for most of the options available in the Toolbar.

The Filmstrip

The Filmstrip always displays the same set of images as the Grid view in the Library module; it can show every image in the library, the contents of a selected folder or collection, or a selection filtered by subject, date, keyword, or a range of other criteria. You can work directly with the thumbnails in the Filmstrip—or the Grid view in the Library module—to assign ratings, flags and color labels, apply metadata and developing presets, and rotate, move, or delete photos.

The Filmstrip keeps the images you're working with accessible when you're using a view other than the Grid view in the Library Module, and while you're working in one of the other modules. Whichever module you're working in, you can use the Filmstrip to quickly navigate through a selection of images, or to move between different sets of images.

Customizing the workspace

All of the workspace panels are highly customizable. You can expand, collapse, resize, hide, and show panels and groups of panels, either manually or automatically. You can add or remove control elements, change the font size, background color, and more. All of these options will be covered in more detail in Lesson 2, "Introducing the Workspace."

The Lightroom modules

Lightroom has five workspace modules: Library, Develop, Slideshow, Print, and Web. Each module offers a specialized set of tools and features tailored to the different phases of your workflow: importing, organizing and publishing, adjusting and enhancing, producing presentations, and generating output for print or web.

You can move effortlessly between modules to suit the task at hand. Some operations, such as creating backup copies or exporting images in various file formats, are not tied to any specific module and are always accessible via menu commands.

The Library module

In the Library module you can review and organize the images in your library. The work area offers several different viewing modes so you can browse, inspect, compare, or select images with ease.

You can move between the different viewing modes either using menu commands or the View Mode buttons at the left of the Toolbar.
From left to right, the buttons invoke the Grid, Loupe, Compare, and Survey views.

You can customize the Toolbar for each of the viewing modes independently, choosing features, tools, and controls from the menu at the far right of the Toolbar.

View Modes
- ✓ Sorting
- ✓ Flagging
- ✓ Rating
- ✓ Color Label
- ✓ Rotate
- ✓ Navigate
- ✓ Slideshow
- ✓ Zoom

Tools and controls that are currently visible in the Toolbar have a check mark beside their names in the menu. The order of the tools and controls from left to right in the Toolbar corresponds to their order from top to bottom in the menu.

In the Library module, the left panel group consists of the Navigator panel and any combination of the Catalog, Folders, Collections, and Publish Services panels, which help you to find, organize, and share the images in your library. At the top of the group, the Navigator panel is always available but you can show or hide any of the other four panels as you create additional folders and collections and move your photos between them. The right panel group contains the Histogram panel, which can be collapsed but not hidden, and any combination of the Quick Develop, Keywording, Keyword List, Metadata, and Comments panels. Use these five panels to quickly apply developing presets, make color corrections and tonal adjustments, and review or edit any keyword tags, metadata, or published comments that are attached to an image.

To choose which panels are expanded, collapsed, displayed, or hidden in a panel group, right-click (Windows) / Control-click (Mac OS) on any panel header in the group, and choose from the options in the context menu. To choose from options that affect the behaviour of the panel group as a whole, Right-click / Control-click the outside edge of the panel group (beyond the scrollbar).

The buttons below the panel groups give quick access to the Import, Export, Synchronize Settings, and Synchronize Metadata dialog boxes.

The Develop module

Although the Quick Develop panel in the Library module offers some basic image editing options, you'll work in the Develop module when you wish to make more detailed adjustments and modifications to your photos. You can correct the color balance or tonal range, crop or straighten an image, remove red eye, and apply selective local adjustments—all non-destructively.

In the Develop module, the work area offers two viewing modes: the Loupe view, which enables you to view an image at different levels of magnification, and the Before/After view (with a variety of layout options), which makes it easy to compare the original and edited versions of the photo. You can move between these viewing modes using the controls at the left of the Toolbar.

The Toolbar can be customized for each viewing mode independently by choosing from a range of controls—Flagging, Rating, Color Label, Navigate, Slideshow, and Zoom—available in the menu at the right of the Toolbar. Some tools are available only in one module, such as the Painter tool, which can be used to apply attributes and settings directly to your images in the Library module. Others appear only in a particular viewing mode, such as the Before & After controls, which let you swap or copy develop settings between the original and edited versions of a photo in the Before/After view of the Develop module.

 Tip: You can make more space available for your working view by hiding any panels that you're not currently using, as has been done with the Filmstrip in the illustration at the right.

The left panel group contains the Navigator panel, which can be collapsed but not hidden, and any combination of the Presets, Snapshots, History, and Collections panels, which can be shown or hidden to suit the way you prefer to work.

Develop presets are used to apply a series of develop settings with a single click. Lightroom ships with a set of default presets, and also allows you to add your own. Snapshots are development stages that you have chosen to save during the editing process. The History panel enables you to selectively undo or redo changes.

The right panel group always contains the Histogram panel and an array of editing tools—the Crop Overlay, Remove Spots, Remove Red Eye, Graduated Filter, and Adjustment Brush tools—but you can select any combination of the Basic, Tone Curve, Adjustments (HSL / Color / B&W), Split Toning, Detail, Lens Corrections, Effects, and Camera Calibration panels. You can use these panels to fine-tune many aspects of your photos: adjust the tonal balance, create special dual tone effects, correct lens vignetting, or add film grain. The buttons below the panel groups simplify the process of copying and pasting settings between photos, applying previously used settings to an image, and resetting an edited photo to its original state.

The Slideshow module

In the Slideshow module you can easily create stylish presentations from any image collection in your library. The images in your collection are displayed in the Filmstrip, where you can choose which photos you wish to include in your slideshow, and drag their thumbnails to change the order in which they will appear. The work area shows one image at a time in the Slide Editor view, where you can work on the slides individually, or preview your slideshow as a whole.

The left panel group contains the Preview, Template Browser, and Collections panels. The Collections panel allows you to navigate between your collections or create new ones and the Template Browser offers a list of customizable slide layouts. The right panel group can contain any combination of the Options, Layout, Overlays, Backdrop, Titles, and Playback panels. Use the Options, Layout, Overlays, and Backdrop controls to customize your slides. You can specify the way text or ratings appear, choose a background, or change the layout, and then save your customized settings as a new template. The Titles panel lets you add intro and ending screens, and the Playback panel offers options for adding a soundtrack, and controls for fades and timing. In the Toolbar below the Slide Editor view you'll find playback controls for the slideshow preview and tools for rotating images and adding text to your slides. Buttons below the left panel group make it simple to export a single slide or the whole presentation in either PDF or video formats.

The Print module

The Print module offers a range of preset templates and all the layout tools you'll need to quickly prepare any selection of images from your library for printing.

The photos in your collection are displayed in the Filmstrip, where you can select the images you want to print. You can drag the thumbnails in the filmstrip to change the placement of your photos in the layout. The work area—the Print Editor view—shows your print layout, which may include only one image, a single image repeated at a variety of sizes, or multiple images.

The left panel group contains the Preview panel, the Template Browser, and the Collections panel. You can use the Collections panel to navigate between your collections or to create new ones, and the Template Browser to choose from a list of customizable print layout templates. The right panel group contains the Layout Style panel and a suite of other panels that varies slightly with your choice of layout style. Use the Image Settings, Layout, Rulers, Grid & Guides, Cells, and Page panels to customize your print layout. If you wish, you can save your settings as a custom template. The Print Job panel has settings for print resolution, color management and other output options. The Toolbar below the Print Editor view contains controls for navigating through multiple-page print previews and buttons below the panel groups provide easy access to page setup and print settings.

The Web module

In the Web module you can build, preview, and export or upload your own website to showcase your photos. As in the Slideshow and Print modules, you can select and arrange images from your collections using the Filmstrip. The panels in the left panel group are similar to those in the Slideshow and Print modules, providing access to your image collections and a wide range of Web Gallery templates. The work area—the Gallery Editor view—shows a working preview of your web gallery. The panels in the right panel group offer settings and controls that enable you to customize the gallery templates, add text, and manage output. The Toolbar below the Gallery Editor view offers controls for navigating through multiple-page galleries and buttons below the panel groups make it easy to preview your work in a web browser and export or upload your presentation.

A typical workflow

These are the basics of the Lightroom workflow:

- Import digital images into your library.

- Organize and sort your photos using keywords, flags, and ratings, and group them in image collections.

- Adjust, correct, retouch, and apply effects to your images. Optionally, launch an external image editor from within Lightroom for additional pixel-based editing.

- Present your photos in a slide show or web gallery, share them via the Publish Services feature, or output them for print.

- Export pictures and presentations as e-mail attachments, or create backups on CD or DVD-ROM.

Importing photos

You can import photos into your Lightroom library from your hard disk, your camera, a memory card reader, or from external storage media. During the import process you can choose from many options to help you manage and organize your files. For the purposes of this Quick Tour we will ignore most of these advanced options; Lesson 3, "Importing," will go into more details.

Before you begin, make sure that you have correctly copied the Lessons folder from the CD in the back of this book onto your computer's hard disk and created the LR3CIB Library Catalog file as detailed in "Copying the Classroom in a Book files" on page 2 and "Creating a catalog file for working with this book" on page 3.

1 Start Lightroom. In the Adobe Photoshop Lightroom - Select Catalog dialog box, make sure the file LR3CIB Library Catalog.lrcat is selected under Select A Recent Catalog To Open, and then click Open.

2 Lightroom will open in the screen mode and workspace module that were active when you last quit. If necessary, click Library in the Module Picker to switch to the Library module.

▶ **Tip:** If you can't see the Module Picker, choose Window > Panels > Show Module Picker, or press the F5 key. Note that on Mac OS the function keys are assigned to specific operating system functions by default and may not work as expected in Lightroom. If you find this to be the case, either press the fn key (not available on all keyboard layouts) together with the F5 key, or change the keyboard behavior in the system preferences.

3 Choose File > Import Photos.
   If the Import dialog box appears in compact mode, click the Show More Options button at the lower left of the dialog box to see all the options in the expanded Import dialog box.

4 Under Source at the left of the expanded Import dialog box, navigate to the Lessons folder that you copied into the LR3CIB folder on your hard disk.

5 Select the Lesson 1 folder. Ensure that all nine images in the Lesson 1 folder are checked for import.

6 In the import options above the thumbnail previews, click Add to add the imported photos to your catalog without moving or copying them. Under File Handling at the right of the expanded Import dialog box, choose Minimal from the Render Previews menu and ensure that the Don't Import Selected Duplicates option is activated. Under Apply During Import, choose None from both the Develop Settings menu and the Metadata menu and type **Lesson 1** in the Keywords text box. Make sure your settings are exactly as shown in the illustration below, and then click Import.

Congratulations! You've just imported the first photos into your library. You can see thumbnails of the nine Lesson 1 images in the Grid view of the Library module and in the Filmstrip. You're now ready to start the exercises in this lesson.

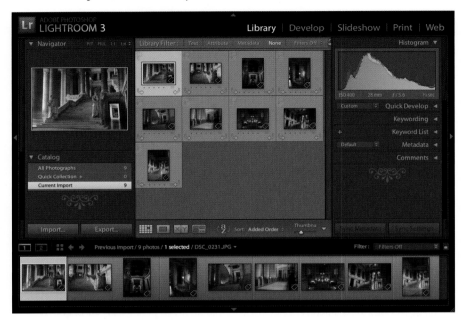

▶ **Tip:** If you don't see the Filmstrip across the bottom of the Lightroom workspace, press the F6 key or choose Window > Panels > Show Filmstrip.

Reviewing and organizing

When you work with a library containing many images, you need to be able to find exactly what you're looking for quickly. Lightroom delivers numerous tools to make finding and organizing your files intuitive and enjoyable. You've already begun to structure your catalog by applying the keyword tag "Lesson 1" to the images that you imported. Keyword tags enable you to find or group image files based on any description you associate with them, independent of how they are named or where they are stored. You should make it a working habit to go through a few cycles of reviewing and organizing your files each time you import new images. This makes it much easier to retrieve the photos you want when you need to work with them.

Working while watching a slideshow

As a convenient way to review the images you've just imported, you can now sit back and enjoy an impromptu slideshow:

1 In the Library module, make sure the Grid view is displaying the thumbnails from the previous import, and then choose Window > Impromptu Slideshow, or press Ctrl+Enter / Command+Return. This will play a slideshow in full-screen

mode using the settings current in the Slideshow module. The slideshow will repeat until you return to the Library module by pressing the Esc key.

2   While the slideshow is playing, press the spacebar to pause and resume playback. Press the left arrow key to return to the previous image or the right arrow key to advance to the next image.

Even as the slideshow plays, you can assign star ratings to rank your photos. You can then use a search filter to sort your images on this basis.

3   To quickly assign a rating to the image currently displayed in your slideshow, press a number between 1 (for 1 star) and 5 (for 5 stars) on your keyboard. To remove the rating, press 0. You can attach only one rating to each photo; assigning a new rating will replace the old one.

Rating stars are displayed under the thumbnail images in all of the Library module views and in the Filmstrip, as shown in the illustration at the right.

About keyword tags

Keyword tags are labels (such as "Sculpture" or "New York") that you attach to your images to make them easy to find and organize. There's no need to painstakingly sort your photos into subject-specific folders or rename files according to their content; simply assign one or more keyword tags to each image and you can easily retrieve it by searching the images in your library with the Metadata and Text filters located in the Filter bar across the top of the work area. You can create keyword tags for photographic categories, people, places, events, colors, or even moods.

Attach multiple keyword tags to a photo to make retrieving it even easier; you could quickly find all the images that you've tagged with the keyword Sculpture, and then narrow the search to return only those that are also tagged New York—regardless of how the photos are named or where they are stored.

For more detail on using keyword tags, see Lesson 5, "Organizing and Selecting."

Another way to mark your images for searching and sorting is to flag them.

4   Press the P key on your keyboard to flag the image currently displayed in your slideshow as a pick (🏳), press the X key to flag it as a reject (🏴), or press the U key to remove any flags.

You have the option to display flags—along with other information—in the thumbnail image cells in the Library views and in the Filmstrip. Images that are flagged as rejects are grayed out.

Use color labels to mark photos for specific purposes or projects. You might use a red label for images you intend to crop, green for those that need color correction, or blue to identify photos you wish to use in a particular presentation.

▶ **Tip:** To help you remember the meaning you've attached to each color, you can assign your own names to the color labels by choosing Metadata > Color Label Set > Edit. In fact, you can create several presets, each with a different set of names for the color labels, and switch between them as needed. For example, you could customize one set for working in the Library module and another to suit your workflow in the Develop module.

5   To assign a color label to the image currently displayed in your slideshow, use the number keys. Press 6 on your keyboard to assign a red color label, 7 for yellow, 8 for green, or 9 for blue. There's no keyboard shortcut to assign a purple color label. To remove a color label simply press the same number again.

In the Grid View of the Library module and in the Filmstrip, a photo with a color label will be framed in that color when it's selected, and will be surrounded by a tinted image cell background when it's not, as shown in the illustration at the right. If you prefer, you can change the view options so that the color label will appear only under the thumbnail image in the Grid view. You'll learn about customizing view options and more about assigning ratings, flags, and color labels, using both menu commands and the controls in the Toolbar, in Lesson 5, "Organizing and Selecting."

6   Press the Esc key to stop the slideshow and return to the Grid view in the Library module.

In the Library module, you can user the Filter bar above the thumbnail grid to search your images by text or metadata content, and then refine your search by specifying one or more common attributes—star rating, flag status, color label, and file type—so that only those photos you wish to work with are displayed in the Grid view and the Filmstrip.

7 If the Filter bar is not already visible above the work area, open it by choosing View > Show Filter Bar. Click the Attribute filter. Click the third star, and choose Rating Is Greater Than Or Equal To from the Rating menu. Lightroom will now display only those photos with at least a 3 star rating.

When you're working with only a few images, as you are in this lesson, rating, flagging, and filtering seems unnecessary, but as your photo library grows to contain hundreds or even thousands of photos you'll find these tools invaluable. The objective of this step in your workflow is to organize your images, ready for processing in the Develop, Slideshow, Print, and Web modules.

Creating a collection

Once you've reviewed and sorted your library, searched your photos by keywords or text, and filtered out unwanted images using the attributes filters, you can group the remaining photos as a *collection*, so that you can easily retrieve the same selection at any time without repeating your search. To group your photos in a collection you can choose between several options:

- The Quick Collection: a temporary holding collection in the Catalog panel, where you can assemble a selection of images.

- A "standard" Collection: a permanent grouping of photos that will be listed in the Collections panel.

- A Smart Collection: a selection of images automatically filtered from your library according to whatever criteria you specify.

- A Publish Collection: a selection of images intended for publishing that will be listed in the Publish Services panel. A Publish Collection will keep track of images you've published, enabling you to check at a glance whether the versions you're sharing are up-to-date.

1 If the star rating filter is still active in the Grid view, clear this setting by choosing Library > Filter by Rating > Reset This Filter, or simply click None in the Filter bar above the Grid view to disable all active filters.

2 Ensure that Previous Import is selected in the Catalog panel; the Grid view and the Filmstrip should display all nine images.

● **Note:** A selected image is highlighted in the Grid view and the Filmstrip by a thin white border (or a colored border if the image has a color label) and a lighter background color. If more than one photo is selected, the active photo is indicated by an even lighter background. Some commands affect only the active photo while others affect all selected photos.

When you select a folder in one of the panels in the left group, the Grid view and the Filmstrip display the images in that folder. Right now, you have the Previous Import folder in the Catalog panel selected. The next time you import photos, the Previous Import folder will contain those new images. In this case, you would still be able to retrieve the current selection of images by choosing the Lesson 1 folder in the Folders panel, but what if you need to retrieve a group of photos that are not all located in the same folder, or if you want only a selection of all the images in one folder? Simply create a collection. You'll now save the group of 9 images from the Previous Import folder as a new collection. Your new collection will be listed in the Collections panel, so you'll be able to retrieve your images at any time.

▶ **Tip:** Folders in the Collections panel can be nested. For example, you could create a Portfolio folder, and then create subfolders named Portraits, Landscape, Product shots, Black &White, etc. Each time you import an outstanding image, add it to one of these collections to slowly build up your portfolio.

3 Choose Edit > Select All; then choose Library > New Collection. In the Create Collection dialog box, type **My First Collection** as the collection name. Select None from the Set menu, activate Include Selected Photos, disable Make New Virtual Copies; then click Create.

Your new collection is now listed in the Collections panel. The listing includes an image count showing that the collection My First Collection contains nine photos.

Rearranging and deleting images in a collection

Once you've grouped a selection of images as a collection you can do things with them in the Grid view and the Filmstrip that you couldn't do before, such as rearranging their order and removing them from the working view without deleting them from the catalog.

1   If your new collection is not already selected in the Collections panel, click to select it now.

Although nothing has changed in the Grid view or the Filmstrip—because for the moment the My First Collection folder contains the same set of images as the Previous Import folder—you're now working with a collection, where you are free to rearrange the order of your images.

2   Choose Edit > Select None. If necessary, scroll down in the Grid view and Ctrl-click / Command-click to select the last two images. Drag the selected images towards the top of the view. As you drag, the view will automatically scroll up as necessary. Drag your selection between the second and third photos and release the mouse button when the vertical black insertion line appears.

▶ **Tip:** You need to drag the thumbnail of one of your selected images, rather than the image cell frame.

The selected photos snap to their new position in the Grid view and the Filmstrip.

3   Choose Edit > Select None. Right-click / Control-click the fourth image in the Grid view and choose Remove From Collection from the context menu.

In the Collections panel (and in the header bar of the Filmstrip) the image count shows that My First Collection now contains only 8 images.

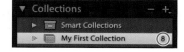

Although you've removed a photo from the collection, it hasn't been deleted from your catalog. The Previous Import folder and the All Photographs folder in the Catalog panel still contain all nine images. A collection contains only references to the files in your catalog; deleting the reference does not affect the file in the catalog.

Tip: Should you wish to edit the same image differently in two collections, you'll first need to make a virtual copy—an additional catalog entry for the image—for inclusion in the second collection. You'll learn about this in Lesson 6, "Developing and Editing."

You can include a single image in any number of collections—each collection will then contain its own reference to the same file. If you apply a modification to a photo in a collection, the modification will be visible in each folder and collection that references the same photo. This is because Lightroom stores only one entry for each image file in its library catalog, and a record of modifications is associated with that entry; any collection including that image links to the same catalog entry, and therefore displays the modified photo. Although the original image file itself remains untouched, its catalog entry has changed to include your modifications. For more information on collections, please refer to "Using collections to organize images" in Lesson 5.

Comparing photos side by side

Often you'll have two or more similar photos that you'd like to compare side by side. The Library module features a Compare view for exactly this purpose.

Tip: If you see only part of each image in the Compare view in the work area, choose Fit from the zoom options in the header of the Navigator panel.

1   If you have any images selected in the Grid view, choose Edit > Select None.

2   Click the Compare View (×Y) button in the Toolbar to switch to the Compare view. Alternately, choose View > Compare, or press C on your keyboard.

By default, Lightroom selects the first two images in the collection for comparison.

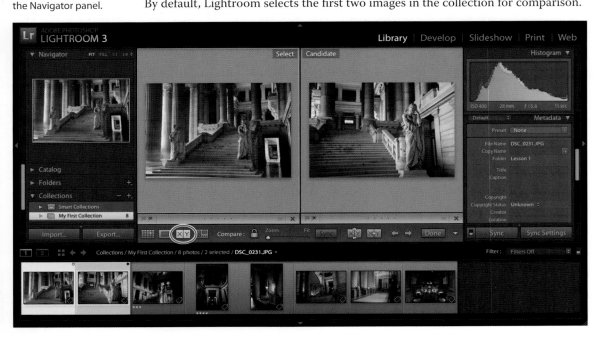

3 Press the Tab key on your keyboard to quickly hide the side panel groups so that your photos can be displayed at a larger size in the Compare view.

4 Click the Candidate pane at the right to select it, and then press the right arrow key on your keyboard to select the next candidate photo from the Filmstrip.

5 Click the Make Select button (![XY]) in the Toolbar to choose the Candidate photo as the new Select image; then continue to use the arrow keys to compare the new Select photo with other candidates from the collection.

6 When you've made your choice, click the Done button at the right end of the Toolbar. The Select image will appear in the Loupe view.

7 Press the Tab key on your keyboard to show the hidden side panel groups.

Comparing several photos

The Survey view lets you compare and select from several photos at the same time; you can narrow your selection one by one, until only the best photo remains.

1 Choose Edit > Select None. In the Filmstrip, Ctrl-click / Command-click three or four images that you'd like to compare, and then click Survey view (![survey]) in the Toolbar. Alternatively, choose View > Survey, or press N on your keyboard.

The Survey view will display all the selected images; the more images you select the smaller the individual preview images in the Survey view. You can make more room for the images you're reviewing by hiding the Filmstrip and side panel groups as necessary, though the right panel group can be useful for viewing additional information about the active photo—from a histogram to information in the Metadata

▶ **Tip:** Even while you're working in the Compare view or the Survey view, you can use menu commands and the controls in the Toolbar to assign star ratings, flags, and color labels to your photos. If necessary, use the Toolbar Content menu to show the controls you need.

panel about what camera, lens, and ISO settings were used. The active image is indicated by a thin white border; to activate a different photo, you can either click its thumbnail in the Filmstrip or click the image directly in the work area.

2 Drag any of the images to reposition it in the Survey view. The other images will automatically be shuffled to accommodate your action.

► **Tip:** If you have eliminated a photo accidentally, choose Edit > Undo to return it to the selection, or simply Ctrl-click / Command-click its thumbnail in the Filmstrip. You can easily add a photo to the selection in the Survey view in the same way.

3 As you move the pointer over each of the images, a Deselect Photo icon (☒) appears in the lower right corner. Click this icon to remove a photo from the selection in the Survey view.

4 Continue to eliminate photos from the Survey view until you've narrowed your selection to a single image, and then press E on your keyboard to switch to the Loupe view.

As you eliminate candidates the remaining photos are progressively resized and shuffled to fill the space available in the work area. Eliminating a photo from the Survey view does not remove it from the collection.

Developing and editing

Once you've selected the photos you wish to work with, you can make use of the comprehensive set of tools and features in Lightroom to correct and enhance your images. The Quick Develop panel in the right panel group enables you to do some quick, but effective, adjustments without even having to leave the Library module. Additional adjustment tools as well as a more convenient editing environment are available in the Develop module.

Using Quick Develop in the Library module

The Quick Develop panel offers simple controls for making basic adjustments to color and tone, and a choice of develop settings presets. In the following example you'll quickly brighten up an underexposed image using the Auto Tone button.

1   If you are not already in the Loupe view from the previous exercise, press E on your keyboard to switch to it now.

2   If the Filmstrip is not visible, choose Window > Panels > Show Filmstrip. In the Filmstrip, select the file DSC_0244.JPG. You can see the name of the file in the tooltip that appears when you hold the pointer over its thumbnail, and also in the status bar above the Filmstrip when the image is selected.

As you can see from both the image preview in the Loupe view, and the Histogram panel (in the right panel group) this photo is much too dark. You'll fix that in the next few steps.

3   To make more space available for a larger preview of this photo in portrait format, you can hide the Filmstrip by pressing the F6 key or by disabling the menu option Window > Panels > Show Filmstrip.

4 In the Quick Develop panel, click the Auto Tone button and you'll notice an immediate and substantial improvement in the image.

5 Click the triangle to the right of the Auto Tone button to reveal more controls for fine-tuning the tonal balance. Experiment with the settings for Exposure, Recovery, Fill Light, Blacks, Brightness, and Contrast.

6 Click the Reset All button in the lower right corner of the Quick Develop panel to return the image to its original, un-edited state.

Working in the Develop module

The controls in the Quick Develop panel let you change settings but don't indicate absolute values for the adjustments you make to your images. In our example there is no way to tell which parameters were changed by Auto Tone to improve the photo, or how much they were changed. For that level of control, and a far more comprehensive editing environment, you need to move to the Develop module.

1   Switch to the Develop module now by doing one of the following:

-   Click Develop in the Module Picker.

-   Choose Window > Develop.

-   Press Ctrl+Alt+2 / Command+Option+2.

2   In the Basic panel in the right panel group, click the Auto button in the Tone settings—the equivalent of clicking Auto Tone in the Quick Develop panel.

Notice that for this image clicking Auto Tone increases Brightness significantly, decreases Contrast slightly, and nudges Blacks up by 1 unit. Applying Auto Tone to another photo will produce different adjustment values. Note that once you've clicked the Auto button it becomes disabled for this image; the automatic adjustments needed in this photo have already been made.

3   In the Toolbar (View > Show Toolbar), make sure the View Modes controls are selected in the Toolbar Content menu. From the menu beside the Before/After button select Before/After Left/Right.

4   Press the F7 key to hide the left panel group and make more space in the work area for the two images side by side.

Auto Tone did a great job of lightening the image, but you can improve it even more by making further adjustments manually.

5   Drag the Brightness slider to about +100, or click the number beside the slider, type **100**, and then press Enter on your keyboard. Increase the Contrast to +7.

Your adjustments have improved the image considerably but in some places the white marble of the portal has become too bright and detail has been lost. Using the Recovery slider you can tone down these clipped highlights while only slightly changing the brightness of the image as a whole.

6   Drag the Recovery slider to the right until you see the detail reappear in the marble above the portal. We used a value of 88.

Rather than experimenting with every slider in the right panel group, you can try some of the Develop module presets to quickly apply different combinations of settings and achieve a wide range of effects. You can use the Lightroom develop presets as a starting point, and then create your own.

▶ **Tip:** If the left panel group doesn't appear and disappear automatically, press the F7 key to manually show and hide it; you'll learn how to set the behavior of the panel groups in Lesson 2, "Introducing the Workspace."

7   Move your pointer close to the left edge of the Lightroom window. The left panel group should appear and remain visible until you move the pointer away.

8   If necessary, expand the Presets panel and the Lightroom Presets folder within that panel. Move the pointer slowly down the list of presets in the Lightroom Presets folder. The Navigator panel displays a preview of how each preset would affect your image. Scroll further down the list using the scroll bar at the left. Click General - Punch. The General - Punch preset adds depth and improves the perceived sharpness of the photo by increasing the Clarity and Vibrance values, whilst leaving your Tone settings unchanged.

By comparing the Before and After images, you can see how dramatically you've improved the picture with just a few clicks.

There's much more to learn about the tools and features in the Develop module, but we'll leave that for later. For now you'll straighten this slightly tilted photo, and then crop it.

Note: For the purposes of this illustration, the Lightroom Presets menu has been abridged. You'll actually find many more varied and versatile develop presets listed.

Using the Crop Overlay tool

1   Press D on your keyboard to activate the Loupe view in the Develop module, and then press the F7 key to show the left panel group again.

2   Click the Crop Overlay Tool button (▦), located below the Histogram in the right panel group. The Crop Overlay Tool enables you to both crop and straighten your image.

3   Additional controls are now available below the Crop Overlay Tool button. Click to select the Straighten tool (⬬). The pointer changes to a cross-hair, and the spirit level icon of the Straighten tool follows your movement across the preview.

4 Look for a line in the image that should be either true horizontal or vertical. For this image we can use the vertical axis that runs through the center of the portal and the hanging lights.

Starting at the apex of the portal, drag downward with the Straighten tool, aligning the white plumb line with the lights.

Release the mouse button; the image is rotated so that your plumb line becomes vertical, and the Straighten tool returns to its tool well in the Crop Overlay Tool controls.

The image is now straight, but it needs to be cropped slightly so that the round opening above the portal is centered in the frame. To crop an image you can either use the Crop Frame tool—located above the Straighten tool—or simply drag the handles of the cropping rectangle already overlaid on your image, as you'll do next.

▶ **Tip:** You can crop the image either by dragging any of the six handles on the cropping rectangle, or by dragging the image itself to change its position within the cropping rectangle. To maintain the original aspect ratio of the image when you crop it, make sure that Original is selected from the cropping Aspect menu.

5 Drag the left handle of the cropping rectangle slightly to the right so that the oval opening in the image sits centered in the picture frame.

6 (Optional) While you're in the process of cropping your image, press the L key on your keyboard (Window > Lights Out > Lights Dim) to dim everything around the cropping rectangle. Press L again to darken the workspace altogether (Lights Off). Now press L a third time to return to normal Light Mode (Lights On). Choose a different grid overlay from the Tools > Crop Guide Overlay menu, or turn the grid off altogether by choosing Tools > Tool Overlay > Never Show.

7 When you're done, exit the Crop Overlay mode by clicking the Close button in the lower right corner of the panel with the crop tool controls.

Correcting lens distortion

The combination of perspective and the characteristics of the lens you use to capture a photograph may result in any of several types of distortion in an image.

First we'll look at *keystone distortion*, which occurs when an object is photographed from an angle rather than from a straight-on view. You can see keystone distortion in a picture of a tall building taken from ground level—the edges of the building appear closer to each other at the top than they do at the bottom.

1   Expand the Lens Corrections panel and click Manual at the top of the panel.

2   Drag the Vertical slider to the left to set a value of -80.

This image is a particularly extreme example, but the adjustment we made might be acceptable if you intended to crop the shot to feature the central portal. You can see that the change has given the image a very different feel; all of the distortion sliders can be used not only to "correct" an image, but also to create effects.

3   Undo the last step

This image also shows *barrel distortion*—a lens distortion effect that causes straight lines to bow out toward the edges of the image. The opposite of this effect is known as *pincushion distortion*—where straight lines bend inward.

4   In the Lens Corrections panel, drag the Distortion slider to the extreme left, and then to the right to see the effect on the image. To effectively correct the barrel distortion making the pillars in our image curve outwards, set the value to 40.

The edges of the image are drawn inwards, leaving curved gray areas showing on all four sides. These artifacts can be cropped automatically.

5   Click the checkbox just below the five Transform sliders to activate the Constrain Crop option.

6   Undo the last two steps and experiment with the other four Transform sliders, with and without the Constrain Crop option. Try combinations of settings.

Using Fill Light

In a previous exercise you adjusted the Recovery control to darken highlights. For this exercise you will use the Fill Light feature to lighten areas that are too dark without affecting the rest of the tonal range.

1 If You are still in Before /After view, click the Loupe view button in the Toolbar. Press F6 to show the Filmstrip; then click to select the photo DSC_0265.JPG.

The statue at the right of the image is much too dark—but you may be surprised how much detail is still available in the image data and how easily it can be retrieved and enhanced by yet another powerful Lightroom feature.

2 Collapse the Lens Corrections panel or scroll upwards in the right panel group to see the Basic panel. In the Basic panel, drag the Fill Light slider to the right until you see the lost detail reappear in the marble on the side of the plinth; we set a value of 70.

Adjusting the Exposure and Blacks settings

Although there is much more detail visible, the photo now appears a little dull overall. In this exercise you'll improve the tonal range—the spread between dark and light tones—without losing the gains you made in the last exercise.

A glance at the histogram at the top of the right panel group make the reason for the "flat" look of the photo quite clear: there is a lack of image data at both ends of the curve.

1   In the Basic panel, drag the Exposure slider to the right, or type in the text box, to set a value of 0.5. Note the change in the histogram. Now watch the histogram as you set the Blacks value to 10.

2   In the History panel in the left panel group, right-click / Control-click the entry for the Fill Light adjustment you made in the previous exercise and choose Copy History Step Settings To Before from the context menu. This sets the Fill Light step as the Before image for the Before & After view.

3   From the menu beside the Before/After button in the Toolbar, choose Before/After Top/Bottom to assess the results of the adjustments you have made in this exercise.

● **Note:** You'll get even better results with the tools in the Develop module when working with Raw images.

This short exercise completes the section of this lesson that deals with the Develop module. Lesson 6, "Developing and Editing," will cover the Develop module in much more detail.

Sharing your work

Now that you've edited and enhanced your photos, the next step is to present them to your client, share them with your friends and family, or display them for the world to see on a photo-sharing website or in your own web gallery. In Lightroom, it takes only seconds to create a sophisticated slideshow, customize a print layout, publish your photos online, or generate a stylish interactive gallery ready to be uploaded directly to your web server from within Lightroom.

In the next exercise, you'll use the images from your collection to create a web gallery, with just a few clicks. Lesson 7, "Creating Slideshows," Lesson 8, "Printing Images," and Lesson 9, "Publishing your Photos" will provide much more detail on the many Lightroom tools and features that make it simple to create stylish presentations, layouts, and galleries to showcase your photos.

Whether you're working on a slideshow, a print layout, or a web presentation, the workflow follows the same basic steps. You start by creating an image collection; then choose a preset template, customize the settings, preview your work, and generate the appropriate output—whether that's a printed page, a slideshow in PDF or video format, or an interactive web gallery ready to upload to a server.

Exploring the Web module

You should create a new collection for each presentation. Your layouts and settings will be saved with the collection so you can return at any time to refine or add to your work or to tweak the output settings. For this exercise you'll use the collection you created earlier in this lesson.

Tip: As you create more collections, you can manage them in the Collections panel. Group related collections—all those assembled for presentations made to a particular client, for example—as nested subfolders.

1 Click Web in the Module Picker to switch to the Web module.

2 In the left panel group, collapse the Template Browser panel, or scroll down, if necessary, to see the Collections panel. Ensure that the collection My First Collection is selected in the list.

3 From the Use menu in the Toolbar, choose All Filmstrip Photos.

4 Press the F6 key to hide the Filmstrip.

The Gallery Editor view shows a preview of how your images will look in a web gallery. You can now choose a new gallery template, and quickly customize the design and layout.

5 In the left panel group, scroll up, if necessary, so that you can see the Template Browser panel. Move the pointer slowly down the list of gallery templates in the Lightroom Templates folder; the Navigator panel displays a preview of each layout. Click a template in the browser to see your photos previewed in that layout in the Gallery Editor view. Choose the template named "HTML gallery (default)." The Layout Style panel in the right panel group reflects your choice.

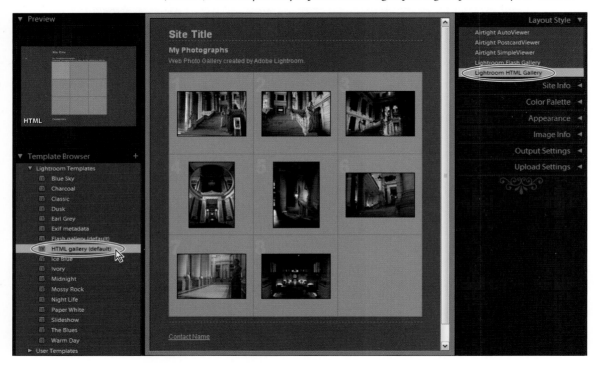

Note: For the purposes of this illustration, the Lightroom Templates menu has been abridged. You'll actually find many more varied and versatile web gallery designs listed.

6 The preview in the Gallery Editor view functions exactly as your published web gallery will. Click a thumbnail to see a larger version of the image. Click the Previous and Next buttons to navigate through the collection. Click the Index button to return to the first page.

You can customize the text that appears on the HTML pages, and the design of your gallery, using the various panels in the right panel group. You'll examine these in more detail in Lesson 9, "Publishing your Photos."

As well as the templates available in the Template Browser, you can also select from website templates developed by Airtight Interactive. These templates are not located in the Template Browser; you'll find them in the Layout Style panel at the top of the right panel group.

7 In the Layout Style panel, choose the Airtight PostcardViewer template. An animated intro scatters your images across the screen as if they were postcards.

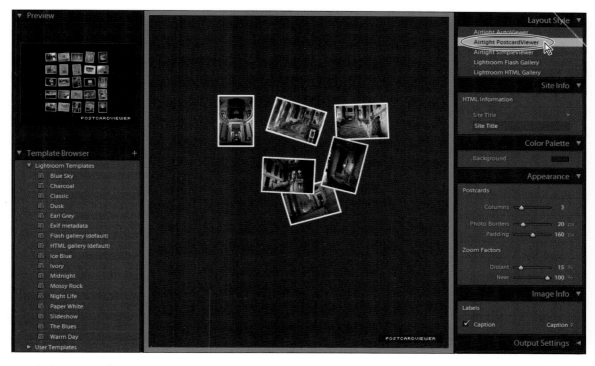

8 Click a postcard for a closer look. Click again to return to the index page.

Previewing in a browser

Of course, the Airtight galleries work not only in Lightroom but also in your regular web browser.

1 Choose Web > Preview In Browser or click the Preview In Browser button below the left panel group.

Lightroom will generate the necessary files in a temporary location on your hard disk and then launch your default web browser to display the website. While the files are being generated, a progress bar is displayed at the top left of the workspace.

2 The Airtight PostcardViewer requires that Adobe Flash is installed on your system. If your web browser displays a notification as shown in the illustration at the top of the facing page, do the following:

- If you don't yet have Adobe Flash, click Get Adobe Flash and follow the installation instructions.

- Click the link Click To View Gallery.

3   Depending on the security settings on your computer, you might also see a notification concerning running scripts or ActiveX controls. Click that notification, and a menu will appear—choose Allow Blocked Content.

4   Finally, click Yes in the Security Warning dialog box.

5   Your browser will play the scattering postcards animation, and present your gallery just as you saw it previewed in Lightroom. Click a thumbnail to see an enlarged view. Use the arrow keys on your keyboard to navigate to the previous, or next postcard, or to the picture above or below the current view.

6   Click the zoomed image or press the spacebar on your keyboard to return to the index page. When you're done previewing your website, close the page in your web browser and return to Lightroom.

7   (Optional) Experiment with customizing the settings for this website using the panels in the right group. In the Site Info panel you can change the title displayed in your browser's title bar; choose a different background color in the Color Palette panel, change the number of columns for the index page in the Appearance panel, or adjust the size of the large images in the Output Settings panel. Be sure to review your changes not only in the Lightroom preview, but also in your web browser.

The final step is to upload the site to a web server. You can enter the necessary information in the Upload Settings panel, and then upload the site from within Lightroom. For more details, see Lesson 9, "Publishing your Photos on the Web."

Getting help

Help is available from several sources, each one useful to you in different circumstances:

Help in the application: The complete user documentation for Adobe Photoshop Lightroom is available from the Help menu, in the form of HTML content that displays in the Adobe Community Help application. Even without the Community Help application, this content will display in your default browser. This documentation provides quick access to summarized information on common tasks and concepts, and can be especially useful if you are new to Lightroom or if you are not connected to the Internet.

Note: You don't need to be connected to the Internet to view Help in Lightroom. However, with an active Internet connection, you can access the most up-to-date information.

Help on the Web: You can also access the most comprehensive and up-to-date documentation on Lightroom via your default browser, whether Lightroom is currently running or not.

Help PDF: Help is also available as a PDF document, optimized for printing; you can download the document at: www.adobe.com/go/learn_lightroom_helppdf_en.

Navigating Help in the application

1   Choose Help > Lightroom Help, or press the F1 key. Even if you are not currently connected to the Internet, the Adobe Community Help application (or, if the Community Help application is not installed, your default web browser) will open to the front page of Adobe Photoshop Lightroom Help documentation that was installed on your computer with the Lightroom application. To quickly access Help documentation specific to the Lightroom module in which you are currently working, press Ctrl+Alt+/ (Windows) / Command+Option+/ (Mac OS).

2 Choose a topic from the table of contents. Click the plus sign (+) to the left of any topic heading to see a list of sub-topics.

3 Click a sub-topic to see its content displayed on the right.

If you do have an active Internet connection, the Community Help application gives you access to the most up-to-date information about Lightroom and other Adobe products. You can search and browse Adobe and community content, and comment on or rate any article just as you would in your default browser. Search results will show you not only content from Adobe, but also from the community.

You can also download reference content for use offline, and subscribe to new content updates (which can be downloaded automatically) so that you'll always have the most up-to-date information.

Adobe content is updated based on community feedback and contributions. You can contribute in several ways: add comments to content or forums—including links to web content, publish your own content using Community Publishing, or contribute Cookbook Recipes. Find out how to contribute at www.adobe.com/community/publishing/download.html.

See http://community.adobe.com/help/profile/faq.html for answers to frequently asked questions about Community Help.

Accessing Help and Support on the Web

You can access Lightroom Help, Support and other useful resources on the Web, even if Lightroom is not currently running.

1 Do one of the following::

- If Lightroom is currently running, choose Help > Lightroom Online.

- If Lightroom is not currently running, point your default web browser to www.adobe.com/support/photoshoplightroom where you can find and browse Lightroom Help and Support content on adobe.com.

2 To search for a particular topic in the Help documentation, enter a search term in the Search text box at the top of the page, and then click Search.

3 If necessary, narrow your search by selecting either Show All Community Content or Show Only Adobe Content on the results page.

Search tips

Adobe Help Search searches the entire Help text for topics that contain all the words typed in the Search box. To improve your search results in Help:

- Make sure that the search terms are spelled correctly.

- If a search term doesn't yield results, try using a synonym, such as "photo" instead of "picture."

More resources

On adobe.com, you can also check out these useful links:

Adobe Photoshop Lightroom 3 product home page
http://www.adobe.com/products/photoshoplightroom.

Adobe Forums http://forums.adobe.com lets you tap into peer-to-peer discussions, questions and answers on Adobe products.

Adobe TV http://tv.adobe.com is an online video resource for expert instruction and inspiration about Adobe products, including a How To channel to get you started with your product.

Adobe Design Center www.adobe.com/designcenter offers thoughtful articles on design and design issues, a gallery showcasing the work of top-notch designers, tutorials, and more.

Adobe Developer Connection www.adobe.com/devnet is your source for technical articles, code samples, and how-to videos that cover Adobe developer products and technologies.

Resources for educators www.adobe.com/education includes three free curriculums that use an integrated approach to teaching Adobe software and can be used to prepare for the Adobe Certified Associate exams.

Adobe Marketplace & Exchange www.adobe.com/cfusion/exchange is a central resource for finding tools, services, extensions, code samples and more to supplement and extend your Adobe products.

Adobe Labs http://labs.adobe.com gives you access to early builds of cutting-edge technology, as well as forums where you can interact with both the Adobe development teams building that technology and other like-minded members of the community.

Congratulations! You've reached the end of the first lesson. You've imported images, reviewed and organized your library, edited and enhanced photos, and created a web gallery. The following lessons will cover each of these subjects in far greater detail.

Before you move on to the next lesson, take a minute or two to review the what you've learned by working through the questions and answers on the next page.

Review questions

1 What is non-destructive editing?

2 What are the five Lightroom workspace modules and how do they relate to your workflow?

3 How can you increase the viewing area without resizing the application window?

4 What advantage is there to grouping images in a collection, rather than grouping them by a shared keyword tag?

5 Why is it recommended to create a special collection for each slideshow, print, or web project?

Review answers

1 Whatever modifications you make to an image in your library—cropping, rotation, corrections, retouching, or effects—Lightroom records the editing information only in the catalog file. The original image data remains unchanged.

2 The Lightroom workflow begins in the Library module: a hub where you'll import, organize, sort, and search your photos, manage your growing catalog, and keep track of the images you publish. Move to the Develop module for a comprehensive editing environment with all the tools you need to correct, retouch, and enhance digital images and ready them for output. The Slideshow, Print and Web modules each provide a range of stylish preset templates together with a suite of powerful, intuitive controls to help you customize them so that you can quickly create sophisticated layouts and presentations to share and showcase your work in its best light.

3 You can hide any of the panels and panel groups surrounding the work area. The working view automatically expands into the space available. The work area is the only part of the Lightroom workspace that you cannot hide from view.

4 The difference between grouping images in a collection and applying keyword tags is that, in a collection, you can change the order of the photos displayed in the Grid view and the Filmstrip, and you can remove an image from the group.

5 Layouts and settings applied to your presentation are saved with the collection. You can return to the collection to refine your work, to add to it, or to tweak output settings.

2 INTRODUCING THE WORKSPACE

Lesson overview

Whether you prefer to use menu commands, keyboard shortcuts, or buttons and sliders—whether you use a small screen or a large one, one monitor or two—you can customize the flexible Lightroom workspace to suit the way *you* work. Customize each of the modules individually so that you always have your favorite tools and controls at hand, arranged just the way you like them.

To help familiarize you with the Lightroom workspace, this lesson will focus on the interface elements and skills that are common to all the workspace modules:

- Toggling between screen modes
- Adjusting the workspace layout
- Showing and hiding panels and panel groups
- Collapsing or expanding panels
- Changing and customizing view modes
- Working with a second display
- Personalizing the workspace
- Choosing interface options
- Using keyboard shortcuts

 You'll probably need between one and two hours to complete this lesson.

Make working with Lightroom even more pleasurable, and ultimately more productive, by personalizing the workspace so that you always have your favorite tools at hand. Lightroom streamlines your workflow, allowing you to move effortlessly between the different modules and viewing modes and freeing you up to spend less time in front of the computer and more time behind the lens!

Getting started

Before you begin, make sure that you have correctly copied the Lessons folder from the CD in the back of this book onto your computer's hard disk and created the LR3CIB Library Catalog file as detailed in "Copying the Classroom in a Book files" on page 2 and "Creating a catalog file for working with this book" on page 3.

1 Start Lightroom.

2 In the Adobe Photoshop Lightroom - Select Catalog dialog box, make sure the file LR3CIB Library Catalog.lrcat is selected under Select A Recent Catalog To Open, and then click Open.

3 Lightroom will open in the screen mode and workspace module that were active when you last quit. If necessary, click Library in the Module Picker to switch to the Library module.

Importing images into the library

The first step is to import the images for this lesson into the Lightroom library.

1 Choose File > Import Photos.

2 If the Import dialog box appears in compact mode, click the Show More Options button at the lower left of the dialog box to see all the options in the expanded Import dialog box.

3   Under Source at the left of the expanded Import dialog box, navigate to the Lessons folder that you copied into the LR3CIB folder on your hard disk. Select the Lesson 2 folder. Ensure that all seven images in the Lesson 2 folder are checked for import.

4   In the import options above the thumbnail previews, click Add to add the imported photos to your catalog without moving or copying them.

5   Under File Handling at the right of the expanded Import dialog box, choose Minimal from the Render Previews menu and ensure that the Don't Import Selected Duplicates option is activated.

6   Under Apply During Import, choose None from both the Develop Settings menu and the Metadata menu and type **Lesson 2** in the Keywords text box. Make sure your settings are exactly as shown in the illustration below, and then click Import.

7   If necessary, press the F6 key to show the Filmstrip across the bottom of the Lightroom workspace.

Thumbnails of the seven Lesson 2 images appear in the Grid view of the Library module and in the Filmstrip. You're now ready to start the exercises in this lesson.

Toggling screen modes

Note: Whether you are running Lightroom on Windows or Mac OS, the workspace looks almost identical—any variations are simply due to the different user interface conventions on each platform.

Lightroom can operate in any of three *screen modes*. In the default mode the work-space appears inside a regular document window that you can resize and position as you like on your screen. In the other two modes, the workspace expands to fill the entire screen—either with or without a menu bar—maximizing the space avail-able for working with images. You can switch between screen modes at any time.

1   Choose Window > Screen Mode > Normal to ensure that you are in the default screen mode.

In Normal screen mode on Windows, the Lightroom workspace appears inside an application window with the menu bar just below the window's title bar.

Normal screen mode on Windows.

In Normal screen mode on Mac OS, the Lightroom workspace appears inside a docu-ment window with the menu bar across the top of the screen.

Normal screen mode on Mac OS.

2 Choose Window > Screen Mode > Full Screen With Menubar.

Full Screen With Menubar screen mode on Windows.

In Full Screen With Menubar screen mode on Windows, the Lightroom workspace expands to fill the screen with the menu bar across the top of the screen and the Windows task bar across the bottom.

Full Screen With Menubar screen mode on Mac OS.

In Full Screen With Menubar screen mode on Mac OS, Lightroom expands to fill the screen with the menu bar across the top of the screen and the Dock—if not currently hidden— at the bottom.

3 Choose Window > Screen Mode > Full Screen.

In Full Screen mode on Windows, the Lightroom workspace fills the entire screen with both the menu bar and the Windows task bar hidden.

In Full Screen mode on Mac OS, the Lightroom workspace fills the entire screen with both the menu bar and the Dock hidden.

4 Press Alt+Ctrl+F / Option+Command+F to return to Normal screen mode.

▶ **Tip:** In Full Screen mode, the menu bar appears when you move the pointer to the top edge of the screen, allowing access to menu commands.

5   Choose Window > Screen Mode > Full Screen And Hide Panels, or use the keyboard shortcut Shift+Ctrl+F / Shift+Command+F.

6   In Grid view, double-click any of the thumbnails to enter Loupe view.

A variant of the Full Screen mode, Full Screen And Hide Panels is ideal for viewing an image as large as possible in Loupe view. By pressing T on your keyboard you can even hide the Toolbar below the work area, so that you see nothing but your photo. You'll learn more about showing and hiding panels later in this lesson.

7   Press F on your keyboard. This is the keyboard shortcut for Window > Screen Mode > Next Screen Mode. Press F repeatedly to cycle through the three screen modes. As you switch between the screen modes, you'll notice that the panels around the work area remain hidden.

8   To reveal all hidden panels, press Shift+Tab once or twice. If the Toolbar is hidden, press T to show it.

9   Press Alt+Ctrl+F / Option+Command+F to return to Normal screen mode.

Adjusting the workspace layout

Working with the application window on Windows

In Normal screen mode on Windows, you can resize and reposition the application window just as you are used to doing with other applications.

1 Move the pointer to any edge of the window. When the pointer changes to a horizontal or vertical double-arrow icon, you can drag the window's edge.

2 Move the pointer to any corner of the application window. When the pointer changes to a diagonal double-arrow (↗), you can drag the corner.

3 Click the Maximize button (▣), located beside the Close button (x) at the right of the title bar; the application window expands to fill the entire screen, though you are still in Normal screen mode with both the title bar and the menu visible. While the window is maximized, it's no longer possible to resize it as you did in steps 1 and 2, or reposition it by dragging the title bar.

4 Click the Restore Down button (▣) to return to the previous window size.

Working with the application window on Mac OS

1 In Normal screen mode on Mac OS, resize the application window by dragging its lower right corner.

2 Click the green Zoom button (⬤), located beside the Close and Minimize buttons at the left of the title bar. The application window expands to fill the screen. Click the Zoom button again to return to the previous window size.

3 Reposition the application window on your screen by dragging the title bar.

Using a secondary display

If you have a second monitor connected to your computer, you can use it to display an additional view that is independent of the module and view mode currently active on your main monitor. Choose between Grid, Loupe, Compare, and Survey views for your secondary display. You also have the option to display a secondary view in a window that can be resized and repositioned rather than filling the second screen.

If you have only one monitor connected to your computer, you can open the additional display in a separate window that you can resize and reposition as you work.

1   To open a separate window—whether you're using one or two monitors—click the Use Second Monitor / Show Second Window button (■2■), located at the upper left of the Filmstrip.

▶ **Tip:** You can use keyboard shortcuts to change the view in the secondary display— Shift+G for Grid, Shift+E for Loupe, Shift+C for Compare, and Shift+N for Survey. If the second window is not already open, you can use these keyboard shortcuts to quickly open it in the desired viewing mode.

2   In the top panel of the secondary display, click Grid or press Shift+G.

3   Use the Thumbnails slider in the lower right corner of the secondary display to change the size of the thumbnail images. Use the scrollbar on the right side, if necessary, to scroll to the end of the Grid view.

The Grid view in the secondary display shows the same images as the Grid view and the Filmstrip in the main application window. The source indicator and menu on the left side of the lower panel work the same way as they do in the Filmstrip, and the top and bottom panels can be hidden and shown, just as they can in the main window. You'll learn more about working with panels later in this lesson.

4 In the secondary display, select an image from the grid, and then click Loupe in the top panel. Make sure that Normal is selected in the view mode picker at the right of the top panel.

When the secondary display is in Normal mode, the Loupe view displays the active image from the Grid view and Filmstrip in the main display.

● **Note:** If your secondary display is open in a window rather than on a second screen, you may need to click inside the main window or on its title bar to change the focus of any keyboard input.

5 Use the left and right arrow keys on your keyboard to select either the previous or next photo in the Filmstrip. The new selection becomes the active image and the secondary display is updated accordingly.

6 In the secondary display, click Live in the view mode picker at the right of the top panel.

In Live mode, the secondary display shows the image that is currently under your pointer in either the Filmstrip, Grid, Loupe, Compare, or Survey view in the main window. You can set a different zoom level for the secondary display by choosing from the menu at the lower right of the secondary window.

7 Select an image in the Filmstrip, and then click Locked in the view mode picker in the top panel of the secondary window. The current image will now remain fixed in the secondary display until you switch back to Normal or Live mode—regardless of the image displayed in the main window.

8 Change the zoom level for the secondary display by choosing from the options at the right of the lower panel: click Fit, Fill, or 1:1, or choose a zoom ratio from the menu at the far right.

9 Drag the zoomed image to reposition it in the secondary window, and then click the image to return to the previous zoom level.

10 (Optional) Right-click / Control-click the image to choose a different background color or texture from the context menu. These settings will apply to the secondary display independently of the options chosen for the main window.

11 Choose Compare from the view picker in the top panel of the secondary window. In the main window, select two or more images—either in the Grid view or in the Filmstrip.

The image in the left pane of the Compare view is the *Select* image; the image in the right pane is the *Candidate*. You can change the candidate image by clicking the Select Previous Photo button (⬅) or the Select Next Photo button (➡). If you selected more than two images, only images from the selection are considered as candidates. To replace the Select image with the current Candidate, click the Make Select button (▨).

12 In the main window, select three or more images—either in the Grid view or in the Filmstrip, and then click Survey in the top panel of the second window. Use the Survey view to compare more than two images at the same time. *(See illustration on next page.)* To remove an image from the Survey view, move the pointer over the unwanted image and click the Close button (x) that appears in

the lower right corner of the image. You'll learn more about the Compare and Survey views later in this book.

13 Close the secondary display by disabling the menu option Window > Secondary Display > Show, or by clicking the Close button (x) (Windows) / (⬤) (Mac OS).

Resizing panels

You can customize the layout of the Lightroom workspace to suit the way you work or make more space for the task at hand by adjusting the width of the side panel groups and the height of the Filmstrip panel, or by hiding any of these elements.

1 Move the pointer over the right edge of the left panel group; the pointer changes to a horizontal double-arrow cursor. Drag to the right and release the mouse button when the panel group has reached its maximum width. The central work area contracts to accommodate the expanded panel group. You might use this arrangement to maximize the Navigator preview.

2 Click Develop in the Module Picker to switch to the Develop module. You'll notice that the left panel group returns to the width it was when you last used the Develop module.

Lightroom remembers your customized workspace layout for each module independently, so that the workspace is automatically rearranged to suit the way you like to work for each stage in your workflow as you move between modules.

3 Press Alt+Ctrl+Up Arrow / Option+Command+Up Arrow to return quickly to the previous module.

4 In the Library module, drag the right edge of the left panel group to return the group to its minimum width.

5 Move the pointer over the top edge of the Filmstrip panel; the pointer changes to a vertical double-arrow cursor. Drag the top edge down until the Filmstrip reaches its minimum height.

The work area expands to fill the available space. This arrangement increases the screen space available for the Grid view when you're selecting photos, or for reviewing images in the Loupe, Compare and Survey views.

Note: For the side panel groups, double-clicking the border will produce a different result. This is discussed in the next section, "Showing and hiding panels or panel groups."

6 Switch to the Develop module. The Filmstrip remains unchanged as you move between modules. Whichever module you switch to, the Filmstrip will remain at its current height until you resize it.

7 Move the pointer over the top edge of the Filmstrip panel; the pointer changes to a vertical double-arrow cursor. Double-click the top edge of the Filmstrip to reset the panel to its previous height; then switch back to the Library module.

8   Drag the top border of the Filmstrip to its maximum height. The thumbnails are enlarged and, if necessary, a scrollbar appears along the bottom of the Filmstrip. Scroll to view all the thumbnails.

9   Double-click the top edge of the Filmstrip with the vertical double-arrow cursor to reset the panel to its previous height.

Showing and hiding panels or panel groups

As you've seen, one way of making more space for your work area is to resize the side panel groups and the Filmstrip. Another way is to completely hide panels from view. You can hide any of the panels surrounding the work area in the workspace. In some screen modes Lightroom even hides the title bar, the menu bar, and the Windows task bar or the Mac OS Dock.

1   To hide the left panel group, click the Show / Hide Panel Group icon (◀) in the left margin of the workspace window. The panel group disappears and the arrow icon is reversed.

2   Click the reversed Show / Hide Panel Group icon to reveal the left panel group.

You can use the arrows in the top, right, and bottom margins of the workspace to show and hide the top panel, the right panel group, and the Filmstrip.

3   Disable the menu option Window > Panels > Show Left Module Panels or press the F7 key to hide the left panel group. To show the group again, press F7 or choose Window > Panels > Show Left Module Panels. Disable the menu option Window > Panels > Show Right Module Panels or press the F8 key to hide the right panel group. To show the group again, press F8 or choose Window > Panels > Show Right Module Panels.

4   Disable the menu option Window > Panels > Show Module Picker or press the F5 key to hide the top panel. To show it again, press F5 or choose Window > Panels > Show Module Picker. To hide the Filmstrip, press the F6 key or disable the menu option Window > Panels > Show Fimstrip. To show it again, press F6 or choose Window > Panels > Show Filmstrip.

5   To hide or show both side panel groups together, press the Tab key or choose Window > Panels > Toggle Side Panels. To hide or show the side panel groups, the top panel, and the Filmstrip together, press Shift+Tab, or choose Window > Panels > Toggle All Panels.

● **Note:** You can't change the height of the top panel, but you can hide or reveal it as you wish.

▶ **Tip:** You don't need to be accurate when you click the Show / Hide Panel Group icons. In fact, you can click anywhere in the workspace margins to hide and show panels.

▶ **Tip:** On Mac OS, some function keys are assigned to specific operating system functions by default. If pressing a function key in Lightroom does not work as expected, either press the fn key (not available on all keyboard layouts) together with the respective function key, or change the keyboard behavior in the system preferences.

Lightroom offers even more options for showing and hiding panels or panel groups; you can have them show and hide automatically in response to the movements of the pointer.

6 Right-click / Control-click the Show / Hide Panel Group icon (◀) in the left margin of the workspace window. Choose Auto Hide & Show from the context menu.

7 Hide the left panel group by clicking the Show / Hide Panel Group icon (◀). Move the pointer over the icon, or anywhere in the left margin of the work-space. The left panel group automatically slides into view, partly covering the work area. You can click to select catalogs, folders, and collections; the left panel group will remain visible as long as the pointer remains over it. Move the pointer outside the left panel group and it will disappear again. To show or hide the left panel group regardless of the current panel settings, press the F7 key.

8 Right-click / Control-click the Show / Hide Panel Group icon (◀) in the left margin of the workspace window and choose Auto Hide from the context menu. Now the panel group disappears when you are done with it and does not reappear when you move the pointer into the workspace margin. To show the left panel group again, click in the workspace margin, or press the F7 key.

9 To turn off automatic show and hide, right-click / Control-click the Show / Hide Panel Group icon (◀) in the left margin of the workspace and choose Manual from the context menu.

10 To reset the left panel group to its default settings, activate Auto Hide & Show in the context menu. If necessary, press the F7 key or the F8 key to show the left and right panel groups.

Keep it in mind that Lightroom remembers your customized panel layout for each module independently, including your preferred show and hide options, so you can set these options differently to suit the way you like to work in each module. The options you choose for the Filmstrip and the top panel, however, remain unchanged as you move between modules.

Working with the left and right panel groups

Up to this point in our lesson, we've dealt with the left and right panels only as groups. Now you'll learn to work with the individual panels within the groups.

Expanding and collapsing panels

1   If you are not already in the Library module, switch to it now. Create more space to work with the side panel groups by hiding both the top panel and the Filmstrip. *(See step 4 in the previous exercise.)*

In the Library module, the left panel group contains the Navigator, Catalog, Folders, Collections, and Publish Services panels. Each panel within a group can be *expanded* to show its content or *collapsed* so that only the panel header is visible. A triangle next to the panel name indicates whether a panel is expanded or collapsed.

2   To expand a collapsed panel, click the triangle next to its name; the triangle turns downward and the panel expands to show its content. Click the triangle again to collapse the panel.

▶ Tip: You don't need to be accurate when you click the triangle. Clicking anywhere in the panel header will do, as long as you don't click any other control that might be located in the header, such as the Plus icon (+) in the header of the Collections panel.

Folders within a panel—such as the Smart Collections folder in the Collections panel—can be expanded and collapsed by clicking the triangle next to the folder name, or by double-clicking the folder header.

3   Panels that are currently expanded and fully visible in the panel group show a check mark in front of their names in the Window > Panels menu. Choose a panel from that menu and toggle its display status.

4   In the Window > Panels menu, look at the keyboard shortcuts for expanding and collapsing the individual panels. For the panels in the left group, the keyboard shortcuts begin with Ctrl+Shift / Control+Command followed by a number. The panels are numbered from the top down, so you press Ctrl+Shift+0 / Control+Command+0 for the Navigator panel, Ctrl+Shift+1 / Control+Command+1 for the Catalog panel, and so on. For the panels in the right group, the keyboard shortcuts begin with Ctrl / Command followed by a number. Press Ctrl+0 / Command+0 to collapse the Histogram panel. Press the same keyboard shortcut again to expand it. These keyboard shortcuts may be assigned to different panels in another workspace module, but this should not be too confusing if you remember that the panels are always numbered from the top of the group, starting at 0.

You can expand and collapse all panels (except the topmost in each group) with one command, or have all the panels other than the one you're working with (and the top panel in the group) close automatically. The top panel in each group has a special role and is not affected by these commands.

Tip: You can also right-click / Control-click the empty area below the last panel to bring up this context menu.

5   To collapse all panels in either of the side groups, right-click / Control-click the header of any panel other than the top panel in the group, and then choose Collapse All from the context menu. The top panel remains unaffected.

6   To expand all panels in either side group, right-click / Control-click the header of any panel—other than the top panel in each group—and choose Expand All from the context menu. Once again, the top panel remains unaffected.

Tip: To quickly activate or disable Solo mode Alt-click / Option-click the header of any panel.

7   To close all the panels in a group other than the one you're working with, right-click / Control-click the header of any panel—other than the top panel in the group—and choose Solo mode from the context menu. Only one panel will remain open. The triangles next to the panel names change in appearance, from solid to dotted, when Solo mode is activated. Click the header of a collapsed panel to expand it. The previously expanded panel collapses automatically.

Hiding and showing panels

If you use some panels in a group less often than others, you can hide them from view to create more space to expand the remaining panels in the group.

1   To hide all the panels in a group other than the topmost, right-click / Control-click the header of any panel and choose Hide All from the context menu. All the panels in the group are now hidden, except the Navigator panel at the top.

2 To show all panels, right-click / Control-click inside the empty space below the visible panels and choose Show All from the context menu.

3 To show or hide an individual panel, choose it from the same context menu. Panels that are currently visible have a checkmark in front of their names.

Customizing the appearance of the panel groups

By default, Lightroom displays an ornament—the panel end mark—below the bottom panel in each group. You can select any of the designs that come preinstalled in Lightroom, change the panel end mark to one of your own design, or choose not to display a panel end mark at all.

1 Right-click / Control-click inside the empty space below the panels. Choose an ornament from the Panel End Mark submenu in the context menu, or select None.

The same panel end mark is used for both side panel groups in all the modules. To use your own PDF, JPEG, GIF, PNG, TIFF, or PSD image, place it in the Panel End Marks Folder. To find the Panel End Marks Folder, choose Go To Panel End Marks Folder from the Panel End Mark submenu. The names of any images you place in the Panel End Marks folder will appear grouped below the pre-installed end marks in the menu. The panel end marks that come pre-installed in Lightroom are no more than 56 pixels high, but you can use a taller image if you wish. If you image is too wide, Lightroom will automatically scale it to the width of the panel. Your end mark design may contain transparent pixels.

You can also change the panel end mark—and the size of the font used in the panels—in the Preferences dialog box.

2 Choose Edit > Preferences / Lightroom > Preferences. In the Preferences dialog box, click the Interface tab.

You'll find the End Mark and Font Size menus in the Panels options. The End Marks menu offers the same options you saw in step 1. From the Panel Font Size menu you can choose either Small (the default) or Large, although the difference is subtle. Changes to the font size will take effect next time you launch Lightroom.

3 Without making any changes, click Cancel / the Close button (⊝) to close the Preferences dialog box.

Working with the main display area

The main display area—the work area—in the center of the application window is where you select, sort, and compare the images in your library, and preview the work in process as you make adjustments and create presentations. The work area serves different purposes in each of the Lightroom workspace modules. The Library and Develop modules offer a choice of view modes to suit a range of tasks, from organizing and sharing your collections to editing the individual photos. In the Slideshow, Print, and Web modules, the work area presents a working preview of your projects and presentations.

View modes

In the Library module, you may see the Filter bar across the top of the work area, as shown in the illustration below. You can use filters to limit the photos that are displayed in the Grid view and the Filmstrip to those that have been assigned a specified star rating or flag status, or contain particular metadata content. You'll learn more about the using the Filter bar controls in Lesson 5, "Organizing and Selecting."

Across the bottom of the work area is the Toolbar. The Toolbar is common to all the workspace modules but contains different tools and controls for each.

1   If you're not already in the Library module, switch to it now.

2   If the Filter bar is not already visible at the top of the work area, show it by pressing the backslash character (\) on your keyboard or by activating the menu option View > Show Filter Bar. Press backslash again or disable the menu option View > Show Filter Bar to hide it.

3   If the Toolbar is not already visible, press T to show it. Press T again to hide it.

4 Switch to the Develop module. If the Toolbar is not already visible, press T to show it. Switch back to the Library Module. In the Library module the Toolbar is still hidden from step 3; Lightroom remembers your Toolbar setting for each module independently. Press T to show the Toolbar in the Library module.

5 Double-click an image in Grid view to switch to Loupe view. The Loupe view is available in both the Library and Develop modules, but the controls available in the Loupe view Toolbar differ for each of these modules.

6 You can hide or show individual tools by choosing their names from the menu at the right end of the Toolbar. Tools that are currently visible in the Toolbar have a checkmark in front of their names.

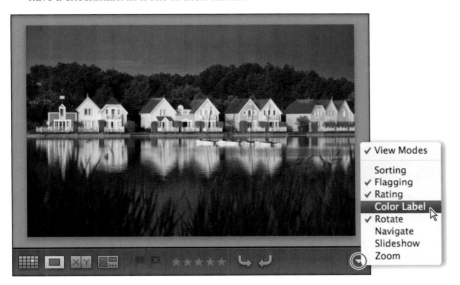

Tip: If you have selected more tools than can be displayed in the width of the Toolbar, you can hide either of the side panel groups to increase the Toolbar's width, or disable tools that you don't need at the moment.

In Loupe view, you can view your images at different levels of magnification. The zoom controls in the top right corner of the Navigator panel in the left panel group enable you to switch quickly between preset magnification levels. You can choose from Fit, Fill, 1:1, or choose another option from a menu of 8 zoom ratios.

You can toggle between zoom levels by choosing View > Toggle Zoom View, or pressing Z on your keyboard. To better understand the Toggle Zoom View command, you should be aware that the magnification controls in the Navigator panel are organized into two groups: Fit and Fill are in one group, and the zoom ratio settings are in the other. The Toggle Zoom View command toggles between the magnification levels last used in each group.

7   Click Fit in the zoom controls in the top right corner of the Navigator panel. Now click the 1:1 control. Choose View > Toggle Zoom View, or press Z. The zoom setting reverts to Fit. Press the Z key; the zoom setting reverts to 1:1.

8   Click Fill in the zoom controls in the top right corner of the Navigator panel. Now choose a zoom ratio from the menu at the far right of the Navigator panel header; we used 2:1. Click the image in the Loupe view. The zoom setting reverts to Fill. In Loupe view, clicking the image is equivalent to pressing the Z key, or choosing View > Toggle Zoom View, except that the zoomed view of the image will be centered on the area you clicked.

9   While the view is magnified, drag the zoom rectangle in the Navigator preview, or drag in the Loupe view to change the image area currently visible in the work area. At higher zoom levels you may find using the Navigator panel more convenient, while dragging the image in the Loupe view is better suited to working at lower zoom levels.

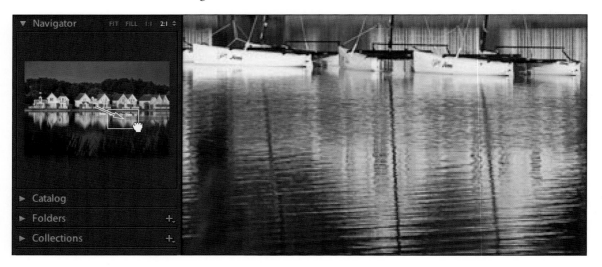

10 Press the Home key to position the zoom rectangle in the top left corner of the image; then press the Page Down key repeatedly to scroll through the magnified image one section at a time. When you reach the bottom of the image the zoom rectangle jumps to the top of the next column. To start in the lower right corner of the image, press the End key; then use the Page Up key. This feature can be very helpful when you wish to inspect the entire image in close detail.

The zoom controls and the Navigator panel work the same way for the Loupe view in both the Library and Develop modules.

The other two view modes, Compare view and Survey view, will be covered in Lesson 4, "Reviewing," and Lesson 6, "Developing and Editing."

Grid and Loupe view options

You can customize the information Lightroom displays for each image in the Grid and Loupe views. Choose your preferences from the many options in the Library View Options dialog box. For Loupe view and the thumbnail tooltips you can activate two sets of options, and then use a keyboard shortcut to switch between them.

1 Press G to switch to Grid view in the Library module.

2 Choose View > View Options. The Library View Options dialog box will appear with the Grid View tab already selected. Position the Library View Options dialog box so you can see some of the images in the Grid view.

3 Disable the Show Grid Extras option in the top left corner of the Grid View tab. This will disable most of the other options.

4 The only options still available are Tint Grid Cells With Label Colors and Show Image Info Tooltips. If they are not already activated, click the checkboxes for both of these options. As the images have not yet been assigned color labels, activating the first option has no visible effect in the Grid view. Right-click / Control-click any thumbnail in the Grid view—you can do this while the Library View Options dialog box is open—and choose a color from the Set Color Label

menu. A color-labeled image that is currently selected will show a thin colored frame around the thumbnail; a color-labeled image that is not selected has a tinted cell background.

5 Position the pointer over a thumbnail in the Grid view or the Filmstrip; a tooltip appears. In Mac OS you'll need to click anywhere in the Lightroom workspace window to bring it to the front before you can see the tooltips. By default, the tooltip will display the file name, capture date and time, and the cropped dimensions. You can specify the information to be displayed in the tooltip by choosing from the Loupe View options.

6 On Mac OS, if the Library View Options dialog box is now hidden behind the main application window, press Command+J to bring it back to the front.

7 Activate the Show Grid Extras option and choose Compact Cells from the menu beside it. Experiment with each setting to see its effect in the Grid view display. Activate and disable the settings for Options, Cell Icons, and Compact Cell Extras. Position the pointer over the various icons in the image cells to see tooltips with additional information.

8   Under Compact Cell Extras, click the Top Label menu to see the long list of choices available. For some choices, such as Title or Caption, nothing will be displayed until you add the relevant information to the image's metadata.

9   Now choose Expanded Cells from the Show Grid Extras menu. Experiment with the options under Expanded Cell Extras to see the effects in the Grid view. Click any of the Show Header With Labels menus to see the many choices available to customize the information that is displayed in the cell headers.

10 Click the Loupe View tab. The work area switches from Grid to Loupe view so you can preview the effects of the changes you'll make in the Library View Options dialog box.

For the Loupe view, you can activate the Show Info Overlay option to display image information in the top left corner of the view. Choose items from the menus in Loupe Info 1 and Loupe Info 2 to create two different sets of information, and then choose either set from the Show Info Overlay menu. When you choose an information item such as Capture Date And Time, Lightroom extracts those details from the image metadata. If the image's metadata does not contain the specified information, nothing will be displayed for that item. For both the Grid and Loupe view options you can choose the information item Common Attributes, which will display the flagged status, star rating and color label for each image.

You can reset either group to its default state by clicking the Use Defaults button. Activate the Show Briefly When Photo Changes option to show the info overlay for only a few seconds when a new image is displayed in the Loupe view. Activate the Show Message When Loading Or Rendering Photos option to display a notification in the lower part of the view while the image preview is updated. It is recommended that you keep this option activated so that you don't inadvertently make judgments about the quality of an image before the update is complete.

11 Click the Close button (x) / (⊖) to close the Library View Options dialog box.

12 You can choose which of the two information sets will be displayed by choosing an option from the View > Loupe Info menu, or by pressing the I key to cycle the info overlay through Loupe Info 1, Loupe Info 2, and its disabled state.

13 Switch to the Grid view. From the View > Grid View Style menu you can choose whether or not to display additional information, using either the Compact Cells layout or the Expanded Cells layout. Press the J key to cycle through the Compact Cells layout, with and without additional information, and the Expanded Cells layout.

Dimming lights

Lightroom gives you the option to darken the workspace so that you can focus on the image or images with which you're working. In the Library and Develop modules, everything is dimmed or darkened except your selected photos. In the other three modules, everything except the presentation preview in the work area is dimmed or darkened. All tools and controls will still work in the Lights Dim or Lights Off modes—if you can find them! You could pick up the crop tool for example, and then switch to either the Lights Dim or Lights Off mode to help you concentrate on achieving the best result.

1 To dim the lights, press the L key or choose Window > Lights Out > Lights Dim.

2   If you're in the Grid view, double-click an image to switch to Loupe view. Click the image to switch between zoom levels. If you can see the Filmstrip, click to select a different image. Switch to a different module. If you remember the keyboard shortcuts they can really come in handy now.

3   To darken the workspace around the image completely, press the L key again or choose Window > Lights Out > Lights Off—if you can still see the menu bar.

4   To return to the normal display mode, press the L key a third time, or choose Window > Lights Out > Lights On.

Lightroom achieves the dimming and darkening effects by means of a black overlay applied to the interface—at a default opacity of 80% for Lights Dim and 100% for Lights Off. You can choose instead to have the workspace fade to white or a shade of grey. This might be useful, for example, if your images contain a lot of black or dark colors. You can also adjust the level of opacity for the Lights Dim mode so that you can still see the controls if necessary.

5   To change the Lights Out screen color or to adjust the opacity for the Lights Dim mode, choose Edit > Preferences / Lightroom > Preferences. In the Preferences dialog box, click the Interface tab and choose a new opacity value from the Dim Level menu in the Lights Out options. From the Screen Color menu, choose white or a shade of grey.

6   Click OK / the Close button (⊙) to close the Preferences dialog box, and press the L key repeatedly to see your new settings in effect. Return to step 5 to modify your settings or reinstate the defaults.

Personalizing the identity plate

If you're using Lightroom to make presentations to clients on your computer, or if you'd simply like to personalize the workspace, you can change the graphic that is displayed as an identity plate in the top panel.

1   If the top panel is not currently visible, press the F5 key on your keyboard, or choose Window > Panels > Show Module Picker.

2 Choose Edit > Identity Plate Setup / Lightroom > Identity Plate Setup. Position the Identity Plate Editor dialog box so you can see both the dialog box and the identity plate in the top panel.

3 If not already selected, activate the Use A Styled Text Identity Plate option. Then activate the Enable Identity Plate option. You'll notice an immediate change in the appearance of the identity plate.

● Note: If your Identity Plate Editor dialog box differs from the one shown in the illustration—apart from the name used in the text box on the left—click the Show Details button in the lower left corner.

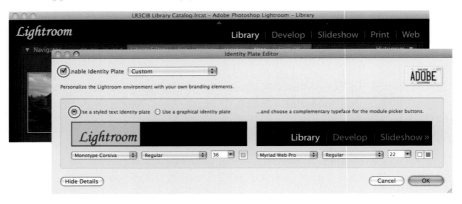

To personalize the identity plate, you can either use styled text or place a graphic of your choice. If you wish, you can also change the typeface and text color used for the Module Picker at the other end of the top panel to better suit your design.

4 Select the text in the text box and replace it with your own.

▶ Tip: You can use more than one typeface, font style, size, or color in your identity plate text. Simply select a portion of your text and make the desired changes.

5 Press Ctrl+A / Command+A to select your new text, and choose a typeface, font style, and font size from the menus beneath the text box. Use your company's corporate typeface or your own favorite—not necessarily mutually exclusive choices. Click the color box beside the font size menu and choose a new color from the Colors palette. Keep an eye on how your choices look in the top panel. Click OK to apply your changes or Cancel to reject them.

▶ Tip: If your text is too long to be fully visible in the text box, either resize the dialog box or reduce the font size until you've finished editing.

6 (Optional) You can also change the typeface, font style, and font size used for the text in the Module Picker to better suit your new identity plate design. There is a second set of controls in the Identity Plate Editor dialog box for this purpose. Click the first color box to change the color used to highlight the name of the active module and the second to change the color used for the others.

7 To use an image as your identity plate, Choose Edit > Identity Plate Setup / Lightroom > Identity Plate Setup. In the Identity Plate Editor dialog box, activate the Use A Graphical Identity Plate option, and then click Locate File. In the Locate File dialog box, navigate to your Lesson 2 folder, select the file Identityplate.png, and click Choose.

● **Note:** On Windows, you can choose a JPEG, PNG, GIF, BMP, or TIFF image for your graphical identity plate. The image can contain transparent pixels and should not be more than 48 pixels in height. On Mac OS, images in PSD or PDF format are also supported and the image height can be up to 57 pixels.

8 (Optional) You can save several identity plate setups as presets that can be easily accessed for different situations. Choose Save As from the Enable Identity Plate menu, enter a name for your identity plate preset and click Save. Your identity plate presets will appear in the Enable Identity Plate menu.

9 Disable the Enable Identity Plate option, and then click OK to close the Identity Plate Editor dialog box.

Keyboard shortcuts

Press Ctrl+/ (Windows) / Command+/ (Mac OS) to see a list of keyboard shortcuts for the currently active module. When you're done reviewing the keyboard shortcuts, click to dismiss the list.

This concludes your introduction to the Lightroom workspace. You've learned how to switch between the different screen and view modes and how to arrange the workspace layout to suit the way you work in each module. You know how to hide, show, collapse, or expand panels and panel groups, how to customize the Toolbar, and how to use a secondary display. Finally, you have personalized the Lightroom workspace with your own identity plate. Before you move on to the next lesson, take a minute or two to read through the review questions and answers on the following pages.

Review questions

1   How would you view an image at the largest size possible on your screen?

2   How do you adjust the size of the thumbnail images in the Grid view, the Navigator panel, and the Filmstrip?

3   What are the keyboard shorcuts to show or hide the four panels that surround the Lightroom workspace?

4   What do you do if you can't see the tool you're looking for in the Toolbar?

5   How can you personalize the Lightroom interface?

Review answers

1   In the Grid view, double-click the image thumbnail to enter the Loupe view. Choose Window > Screen Mode > Full Screen And Hide Panels, or use the keyboard shortcut Shift+Ctrl+F / Shift+Command+F. A variant of Full Screen mode, Full Screen And Hide Panels is ideal for viewing an image at the largest size possible on your display. Press the T key to hide the Toolbar, leaving nothing on screen but your photo.

2   To change the size of the Grid view thumbnails on your main screen, use the Thumbnails slider in the Toolbar. In Grid view on a secondary display use the slider in the lower right corner of the window. The thumbnail images in the Navigator panel and the Filmstrip are resized automatically as you resize the left panel group or the Filmstrip.

3   The keyboard shortcuts to show or hide the top panel, the Filmstrip, the left panel group, and the right panel group are F5, F6, F7, and F8, respectively.

4   Check what module and view mode you are in. The Toolbar contains different tools for different views and modules. Click the triangle at the right of the Toolbar and activate the missing tool in the tools menu. If the tool is activated and you still can't see it, there may be too many active tools to fit across the Toolbar. Disable tools you are not using in the tools menu and they will be removed from the Toolbar.

5 Lightroom offers several options to personalize the interface:

- You can change the identity plate, the graphic that is displayed at the left corner of the top panel. You can either use styled text or place your own graphic.

- It's also possible to change the typeface and text color used for the Module Picker at the other end of the top panel to better suit your new identity plate.

- You can customize the panel end mark displayed in the left and right panel groups. Choose from the preinstalled designs or use one of your own.

- You can set the color and texture of the background that shows behind the images in many of the working views.

- Set the level of opacity for the Lights Dim modes in the Preferences dialog box.

- Show or hide different workspace panels to suit different tasks. Set panels to show and hide automatically. You can arrange the workspace differently in each of the Lightroom modules so that when you switch between modules, your tools are always set out the way you like them.

3 IMPORTING

Lesson overview

Lightroom allows a great deal of flexibility in importing your photos; you can download images directly from a camera, import them from your hard disk or external storage media, or transfer them between catalogs on different computers. During the import process you can organize your folders, add keywords and metadata to make your photos easy to find, make backup copies, and even apply editing presets.

This lesson will familiarize you with the many options available to you as you add more photos to your Lightroom library:

- Importing images from a camera or card reader
- Importing images from a hard disk or removable media
- Choosing file handling options
- Evaluating images before importing
- Organizing, renaming, and processing images automatically
- Applying keywords and metadata as part of the import process
- Initiating backup strategies
- Creating and saving import presets
- Setting Lightroom to import automatically
- Transferring images between computers and catalogs

 You'll probably need between one and two hours to complete this lesson.

Lightroom starts helping you to organize and manage your growing photo library from the moment you click the Import button; you can make backups, organize folders, inspect images at high magnification, apply editing presets, and add keyword tags and other info that will save you hours of work sorting and searching your image library later—all before your photos even reach your catalog!

Getting started

Before you begin, make sure that you have correctly copied the Lessons folder from the CD in the back of this book onto your computer's hard disk and created the LR3CIB Library Catalog file as detailed in "Copying the Classroom in a Book files" on page 2 and "Creating a catalog file for working with this book" on page 3.

1   Start Lightroom.

2   In the Adobe Photoshop Lightroom - Select Catalog dialog box, make sure the file LR3CIB Library Catalog.lrcat is selected under Select A Recent Catalog To Open, and then click Open.

3   Lightroom will open in the screen mode and workspace module that were active when you last quit. If necessary, click Library in the Module Picker to switch to the Library module.

The import process

Lightroom allows a great deal of flexibility in the import process. You can download images directly from a digital camera or card reader, import them from your hard disk or external storage media, and transfer them from another Lightroom catalog or from other applications.

Import at the click of a button, use a menu command, or simply drag and drop. You can have Lightroom launch the import process when you connect your camera or even import automatically when you move files into a watched folder.

Whether you're downloading photos from a camera or importing them from a hard disk or DVD, you'll be working with the Import dialog box, so we'll begin there.

Lightroom 3 introduces a new Import dialog box that operates in either a compact or expanded mode, providing flexibility in the process from the very beginning. The top panel of the Import dialog box, common to both modes, presents the basic steps in the import process, arranged from left to right: choose an import source, specify how Lightroom is to handle the files you're importing, and set an import destination—whether that's a folder (or folders), or simply your library catalog.

In expanded mode, the Import dialog box works very much like the Lightroom workspace modules. The Source panel at the left provides easy access to your files on any available drive. The Preview pane displays images from the source selection as thumbnails in Grid view or enlarged in Loupe view. Depending on the type of import, the right panel group offers a Destination panel that mirrors the Source panel, and a suite of controls for processing your images as they're imported.

Importing photos from a digital camera

If you have a digital camera or a memory card reader at hand, you can step through this exercise using your own photos. If not, you can simply read through the steps and study the illustrations—most of the information in this exercise is equally applicable to importing from other sources.

To begin with, you'll configure the Lightroom preferences so that the import process is triggered automatically when you connect your camera or a memory card to your computer.

1   Choose Edit > Preferences (Windows) / Lightroom > Preferences (Mac OS). In the Preferences dialog box, click the General tab. Under Import Options, activate the option Show Import Dialog When A Memory Card Is Detected by clicking the checkbox.

Some cameras generate folder names on the memory card. If you don't find these folder names helpful for organizing your images, activate the option Ignore Camera-Generated Folder Names When Naming Folders. You'll learn more about folder naming options later in this lesson.

If your camera records Raw images, it may also generate a JPEG version of each photo. If you wish to import both files, activate the option Treat JPEG Files Next To Raw Files As Separate Photos; otherwise, Lightroom will display only the Raw images in the Import Photos dialog box.

2   Click OK / the Close button () to close the Preferences dialog box.

3   Connect your digital camera or card reader to your computer, following the manufacturer's instructions.

4   This step may vary depending on your operating system and the image management software on your computer:

•   On Windows, if the dialog box shown in the illustration at the right appears, click Cancel.

•   If you have more than one Adobe image management application—such as Adobe Bridge—installed on your computer and the Adobe Downloader dialog box appears, click Cancel.

● **Note:** You'll find more options relating to the creation of DNG files during import on the File Handling preferences tab, but for this exercise, you can ignore those settings. For information on DNG files, see "About file formats" on page 93.

- If the Import dialog box appears, continue to step 5.

- If the Import dialog box does not appear, choose File > Import Photos, or click the Import button below the left panel group.

5   If the Import dialog box appears in compact mode, click the Show More Options button at the lower left of the dialog box to see all the options in the expanded Import dialog box.

The top panel of the Import dialog box—which is visible in both the compact and expanded modes—presents the three basic steps in the import process, arranged from left to right:

- Select the source location of the images you wish to add to your catalog.

- Specify the way you want Lightroom to handle the files you're importing.

- Choose the destination to which the image files will be copied and any develop presets, keywords, or other metadata that you would like applied to your photos as they are added to your catalog.

Your camera or memory card is now shown as the import source in the FROM area at the left of the top panel and under Devices in the Source panel at the left of the Import dialog box.

Depending on your computer setup, it's possible that your camera's memory card will be recognized as a removable storage disk. If this is the case, you may see some differences in the options available in the Import dialog box, but these differences will not affect the actions you'll take in the remainder of this exercise.

6   If your memory card is listed as a removable disk—rather than a device—in the Source panel, click to select it from the Files list and make sure that the Include Subfolders option is activated.

7 From the import type options in the center of the top panel, choose Copy to copy your photos to your hard disk and add them to your catalog, leaving the original files intact on your camera's memory card.

● **Note:** If your memory card has been recognized as a removable disk, the Move and Add options may not be disabled; these options will be discussed later in this lesson.

Lightroom displays a brief description of the action that will be taken for whichever option is currently selected, as shown in the illustration below.

8 Move your pointer over each of the options shown in the bar across the top of the Preview pane to see a tool tip describing the option. For this exercise, leave the default All Photos option selected. Don't click the Import button yet.

● **Tip:** Use the slider below the preview pane to change the size of the thumbnails.

A check mark in the top left corner of an image cell indicates that the photo will be imported. By default, all the photos on your memory card will be check-marked for import; you can exclude an image from the selection to be imported by clicking its checkbox to remove the check mark.

You can select multiple images and then change all their check marks simultaneously. To select a contiguous range of images, select the first image in the range by clicking the thumbnail or the surrounding image cell, then hold down the Shift key and select the last image in the range. Select individual additional photos by Ctrl-clicking / Command-clicking their thumbnails. Click the check mark of any image in a multiple selection to change the import status for the entire selection.

When you import photos from your hard disk or from external storage media, the Import dialog box offers you the option to add them to your catalog without moving them from their current locations. This is possible because Lightroom does not actually import the image files themselves; it only adds entries to the library catalog to record their locations. However, because memory cards are expected to be erased and reused, images on your camera don't have very permanent addresses. For this reason, you're not offered the Add or Move options when you import from a camera—Lightroom expects to copy your photos from your camera to a more permanent location before it adds their addresses to the library catalog.

Therefore, the next step in the process of importing from a camera is to specify a destination folder to which your photos should be copied. This is the time to give some thought to how you are going to organize your photos on your computer hard disk. For now, leave the Import Photos dialog box open; you'll choose a destination folder and deal with the rest of the import options in the following exercises.

Organizing your copied photos in folders

Although there's no technical reason why you can't choose a different destination folder for each import, it will be much easier to keep your hard disk organized if you create a single folder to contain all the images that are associated with a particular catalog. Within this folder you can create a new subfolder for each batch of images downloaded from your camera or copied from other external media.

Before beginning the lessons in this book, you created a folder named LR3CIB inside your *[username]*/My Documents (Windows) or *[username]*/Documents (Mac OS) folder on your computer. This folder already contains subfolders for your LR3CIB Library Catalog file and for the image files used for the lessons in this book. For the purposes of this exercise, you'll create a subfolder inside the LR3CIB folder as the destination for the images that you import from your camera's memory card:

1   In the right panel group of the Import dialog box, collapse the File Handling, File Renaming, and Apply During Import panels; then, expand the Destination panel.

2   In the Destination panel, navigate to your LR3CIB folder. With the LR3CIB folder selected, click the Create New Folder button (✚) at the left of the Destination panel header and choose Create New Folder from the menu.

3   In the Browse For Folder / Create New Folder dialog box, navigate to and select your LR3CIB folder, if it's not already selected. Click the Make New Folder / New Folder button, type **Imported From Camera** as the name for your new folder, and then press Enter (Windows) / click Create (Mac OS).

4   Make sure the new Imported From Camera folder is selected in the Browse For Folder / Create New Folder dialog box, and then click OK / Choose. Note that the new folder is now listed, and already selected, in the Destination panel.

The name of the new destination folder also appears in the TO area at the right of the top panel of the Import dialog box.

The Organize menu, near the top of the Destination panel, offers various options to help you organize your photos into folders as you copy them onto your hard disk:

- **Into One Folder** With the current settings, the images would be copied into the new Imported From Camera folder. You could then use the Into Subfolder option to create a new subfolder for each import.

● **Note:** If your memory card has been recognized as a removable disk, you may also see the Organize option By Original Folders; this option will be discussed later in this lesson.

- **By Date: *[Date Format]*** The remaining options are all variations on organizing your photos by capture date. Your images would be copied into the Imported From Camera folder and placed into one or more subfolders, depending on your choice of date format. Choosing the date format "2010/01/17," for example, would result in one folder per year, containing one folder per month, containing one folder per day for each capture date, as shown in the illustration at the right.

You should think about which system of folder organization best suits your needs before you begin to import photos from your camera for your own purposes and maintain that system for all your camera imports.

5   For the purposes of this exercise, choose the option Into One Folder from the Organize menu.

6   Click the Put In Subfolder checkbox and type **Lesson 3 Import** in the adjacent text box as the name for the new subfolder.

Backup strategies

Your next choice is whether or not to make backup copies of the images from your camera at the same time as Lightroom creates primary copies in the location you've just specified and adds them to the library catalog. It's a good idea to create backup copies on a separate hard disk or on external storage media so you don't lose your images should your hard disk fail or in case you accidently delete them.

1   In the right panel group of the Import Photos dialog box, expand the File Handling panel and activate the option Make A Second Copy To by clicking the checkbox.

2   Click the small triangle to the right and select Choose Folder to specify a destination for your backup copies.

3   In the Browse For Folder / Choose Folder dialog box, navigate to the folder in which you wish to store the backup copies of your images, and then click OK / Choose.

The purpose of this backup is mainly as a precaution against loss of data due to disk failure or human error during the import process; it's not meant to replace the standard backup procedure you have in place—or should have in place—for the files on your hard disk.

It's worthwhile to archive each photo shoot by burning your images to a DVD, which you can store separately. This will also help you organize your image library in Lightroom because you'll feel more secure trimming your collection down to the best images knowing that you have a backup before you press the Delete key.

Renaming files as they are imported

The cryptic file names created by digital cameras are not particularly helpful when it comes to sorting and searching your photo library. Lightroom can help by renaming your images for you as they are imported. You can choose from a list of predefined naming options, or create your own customized naming templates.

1   In the right panel group of the Import Photos dialog box, expand the File Renaming panel and activate Rename Files. Choose Custom Name - Sequence from the Template menu and type a descriptive name in the Custom Text box (we used New York), and then press the Tab key on your keyboard. A sample name at the bottom of the File Renaming panel shows how your settings will be applied for the first image imported.

You can enter a number other than 1 in the Start Number text box; this is useful if you're importing more than one batch of images from the same series.

2   Click the small triangle to the right of the Custom Text box; your new text has been added to a list of recently entered names. You can choose from this list if you import another batch of files that belong in the same series. This not only saves time and effort but helps you ensure that subsequent batches are named identically. Should you wish to clear the list, choose Clear List from the menu.

3   Choose Custom Name (x of y) from the Template menu. Note that the sample name at the bottom of the File Renaming panel is updated to reflect the change.

4   Choose Edit from the Template menu to open the Filename Template Editor.

In the Filename Template Editor dialog box you can set up a filename template that makes use of metadata information stored in your image files—such as file names, capture dates, or ISO settings—adding automatically generated sequence numbers and any custom text you specify. A filename template includes placeholders—or *tokens*—that will be replaced by actual values during the renaming process.

For example, you could rename your photos New York-January 17, 2010-01, New York-January 17, 2010-02, and so on, by setting up a filename template with a custom text token, a date token, and a 2-digit sequence number token, separated by typed hyphens.

After closing the Filename Template Editor you would type **New York** in the Custom Text box; "New York" would replace the custom text token in the filename template. The date token will be replaced by the capture date from the images' metadata and the sequence number will be added automatically.

5   Click Cancel to close the Filename Template Editor without making any changes.

Despite all of the options available for renaming your images during the import process, there's only so much information you can squeeze into a single file name. It might be better to take a minimal approach to renaming your photos and instead take advantage of the other file management capabilities of Lightroom. Metadata and keyword tags are far more powerful and versatile tools for organizing and searching your image library.

You'll learn about using metadata and keyword tags in the following exercises and in Lesson 5, "Organizing and Selecting."

(continued on page 95)

About file formats

Camera raw formats Camera raw file formats contain unprocessed data from a digital camera's sensor. Most camera manufacturers save image data in a proprietary camera format. Lightroom reads the data from most cameras and processes it into a full-color photo. You can use the controls in the Develop module to process and interpret the raw image data for your photo. For a list of supported cameras and camera raw formats, see www.adobe.com/go/learn_ps_cameraraw.

Digital Negative format (DNG) The Digital Negative (DNG) file format is a publicly available archival format for raw files generated by digital cameras. DNG addresses the lack of an open standard for the raw files created by individual camera models, helping ensure that photographers will be able to access their files in the future. You can convert proprietary raw files to DNG from within Lightroom. For more information about the Digital Negative (DNG) file format, visit www.adobe.com/dng.

TIFF format Tagged-Image File Format (TIFF, TIF) is used to exchange files between applications and computer platforms. TIFF is a flexible bitmap image format supported by virtually all paint, image-editing, and page-layout applications. Also, virtually all desktop scanners can produce TIFF images. Lightroom supports large documents saved in TIFF format (up to 65,000 pixels per side). However, most other applications, including older versions of Photoshop (pre-Photoshop CS), do not support documents with file sizes greater than 2 GB. The TIFF format provides greater compression and industry compatibility than Photoshop format (PSD), and is the recommended format for exchanging files between Lightroom and Photoshop. In Lightroom, you can export TIFF image files with a bit depth of 8 bits or 16 bits per channel.

JPEG format Joint Photographic Experts Group (JPEG) format is commonly used to display photographs and other continuous-tone images in web photo galleries, slide shows, presentations, and other online services. JPEG retains all color information in an RGB image but compresses file size by selectively discarding data. A JPEG image is automatically decompressed when opened. In most cases, the Best Quality setting produces a result indistinguishable from the original.

Photoshop format (PSD) Photoshop format (PSD) is the standard Photoshop file format. To import and work with a multi-layered PSD file in Lightroom, the file must be saved in Photoshop with the Maximize PSD and PSB File Compatibility preference turned on. You'll find the option in the Photoshop file handling preferences. Lightroom saves PSD files with a bit depth or 8 bits or 16 bits per channel.

CMYK files Lightroom imports CMYK files but adjustments and output are performed in the RGB color space.

Video files Lightroom 3 will import video files from most digital cameras. You can tag, rate, filter and include video files in collections, but editing is not supported. Click the camera icon on the thumbnail of a video file to launch an external viewer such as QuickTime or Windows Media Player.

File format exceptions Lightroom does not support the following types of files: PNG files; Adobe Illustrator® files; Nikon scanner NEF files; files with dimensions greater than 65,000 pixels per side or larger than 512 megapixels.

Note: To import photos from a scanner, use your scanner's software to scan to TIFF or DNG format, and then import those files into Lightroom.

Creating import presets

When you import photos on a regular basis, you'll probably find that you're setting up the same configurations of options over and over. Lightroom 3 enables you to streamline your import workflow by saving your preferred settings as import presets. To create an import preset, set up your import in the expanded Import dialog box, and then choose Save Current Settings As New Preset from the Import Preset menu below the Preview pane.

Type a descriptive name for your new preset, and then click Create.

Your new preset will include all of your current settings: the source, import type (Copy asDNG, Copy, Move, or Add), file handling and renaming options, develop and metadata presets, keywords, and destination. You might set up one preset to move photos from a single folder on your hard disk into dated subfolders, and another to create a single folder of renamed black-and-white copies. Create separate import presets tailored to the characteristics of different cameras, so you can quickly apply your favorite noise reduction, lens correction and camera calibration settings during the import process, saving yourself time in the Develop module later.

Using the Import dialog box in compact mode

Once you've created the presets you need, you can speed up the process even more by using the Import dialog box in compact mode, where you can use your import preset as a starting point, and then change the source, metadata, keywords, and destination settings as required.

You have now completed this exercise in importing photos from a digital camera or a memory card. You will learn about the remaining options available in the Import dialog box in the exercises to follow.

6   For now, click Import if you wish to bring your photos into the LR3CIB catalog, or Cancel to close the Import dialog box without actually importing any images.

Importing images from a hard disk

When you import photos from your hard disk or from external storage media, Lightroom offers you more options for organizing your image files than are available when importing from a camera.

If you wish, you can still choose to copy your images to a new location during the import process as you did in the previous exercise, but you also have the option to add them to your catalog without moving them from their current locations. You might choose to do this if the images you wish to import are already well organized in a folder hierarchy.

For images that are already located on your hard disk you have an extra option: to *move* them to a new location, removing them from the original location at the same time. This option might appeal if the images on your hard disk are not already organized in a satisfactory manner.

1   To import images from your computer hard disk—or from a CD, DVD, or other external storage media—either choose File > Import Photos, press Ctrl+Shift+I / Command+Shift+I, or simply click the Import button below the left panel group in the Library module.

2   In the Source panel at the left of the Import dialog box, navigate to the Lessons folder you've already copied into the LR3CIB folder on your hard disk. Select the Lesson 3 folder and click the checkbox at the top right of the Source panel to activate the Include Subfolders option.

An image count in the lower left corner of the Import dialog box shows that the Lesson 3 folder and its subfolders contain a total of 28 photos with a combined file size of 27 MB.

3   From the import type options in the center of the top panel, choose Add to add your photos to your catalog without moving them—an option that is not available when importing images from a camera. Do not click Import yet!

4 Use the scrollbar at the right of the Preview pane to view all of the images in the Lesson 3 folder and its subfolders. Drag the Thumbnail slider below the Preview pane to the left to reduce the size of the thumbnails so that you can see as many of the images as possible in the Preview pane.

5 In the Source panel, disable the Include Subfolders option. The Preview pane now displays only the nine images in the Lesson 3 folder and the image count in the lower left corner of the Import dialog box reads: 9 photos / 9 MB.

In the next exercise, you'll apply keywords and other metadata to these images to make them easier to organize once you've added them to your catalog. For now, you can review the import type options above the Preview pane.

6 Click each of the import type options in turn, from left to right:

 • Choose the option Copy As DNG to create copies of your images in DNG (Digital Negative) file format, which will be stored in a new location, and then added to your catalog. Collapse all of the panels in the right panel group. For the Copy As DNG, Copy, and Move options, the right panel group offers the same suite of panels—File Handling, File Renaming, Apply During Import, and Destination.

 • Choose the option Copy to create copies of your images in a new location and add them to your catalog, leaving the originals in their current locations and preserving their original folder hierarchy. As you learned in the previous exercise, you can specify a destination for your copies in the Destination panel. Expand the Destination panel and click the Organize menu. When you import from your hard disk or external storage media using the options

Copy As DNG, Copy, or Move, the Organize menu offers the choice to copy the photos into a single folder, into subfolders based on their capture dates, or into a folder structure that replicates their original arrangement.

- Choose the option Move to move the images to a new location on your hard disk and delete them from their original locations. For this option, you can also select one of the three folder arrangements from the Organize menu.

- Choose the option Add to add the images to your catalog without moving or copying them from their current locations, or altering the folder structure in which they are stored. Note that for the Add option, the right panel group offers only the File Handling and Apply During Import panels; you cannot rename the original source images during import, and there is no need to specify a destination because the files will remain where they are. Expand the File Handling and Apply During Import panels to see the options available.

Applying metadata

Lightroom uses the metadata information attached to image files to enable you to quickly find and organize your photos. You can search your image library and filter the results by keyword, creation date, flag status, color label, shooting settings, or any combination of a wide range of other criteria. You can also choose specific information about your images from this metadata and have Lightroom display it as a text overlay applied to each image in a slideshow, web gallery, or print layout. Some metadata is automatically generated by your camera when you take a photo. You can also add your own information as part of the import process, making it even easier to locate and organize your images on your own terms.

1   In the Apply During Import panel, choose New from the Metadata menu.

2   In the New Metadata Preset dialog box, type a descriptive name for these nine photos in the Preset Name box (we used "New York Trip Aug 2009"); then, enter metadata information that is applicable to the images as a group, such as copyright information. You can customize the metadata for each individual image in Lightroom later, adding information such as titles and captions.

3   Click Create to close the New Metadata Preset dialog box, and then confirm that your new metadata preset is selected in the Metadata menu.

You can edit your metadata presets by choosing Edit Presets from the Metadata menu in the Apply During Import panel. In the Edit Metadata Presets dialog box you can edit, rename, or delete presets, or save modified settings as a new preset.

4 In the Apply During Import panel, choose None from the Develop Settings menu, and then type **Lesson 3, New York** in the Keywords text box.

5 In the File Handling panel, choose Minimal from the Render Previews menu. Check that your settings are the same as those shown in the illustration below, and then click Import.

The nine photos from the Lesson 3 folder are imported into your library catalog and thumbnails of the images appear in the Grid view and the Filmstrip in the Library module.

6 Right-click / Control-click any of the images in the Grid view and choose Go To Folder In Library from the context menu. In the Folders panel in the left panel group, the Lesson 3 folder is highlighted and the image count indicates that it contains 9 photos.

7 Right-click / Control-click the Lesson 3 folder in the Folders panel, and then choose Show In Explorer / Show In Finder from the context menu.

8 The Lessons folder opens in a Windows Explorer / Finder window, with the Lesson 3 folder highlighted. Leave the Windows Explorer / Finder window open for use in the next exercise.

Importing via drag and drop

Perhaps the easiest way to add photos to your image library is to simply drag a selection of files—or even an entire folder—directly into Lightroom.

1   The Windows Explorer / Finder window showing your Lesson 3 folder should still be open from the previous exercise. Position the window so that you can see the Grid view in the Lightroom workspace beside it.

2   Open your Lesson 3 folder, if necessary, and drag the Batch1 folder from the Windows Explorer / Finder window onto the Grid view.

The Import dialog box opens. The Batch1 subfolder is now selected in the folder list in the Source panel and the seven photos stored in that folder are displayed in the Preview pane, but the rest of the settings from your last import remain unchanged.

3   Don't click Import yet; keep the Import dialog box open for the next exercise.

Evaluating photos before importing

Lightroom 3 makes it easier to decide which of your photos you wish to import by providing an enlarged Loupe view in the Import dialog box; you can examine each image in detail so that you can choose between similar images or exclude a photo that is out of focus.

1 Double-click any of the thumbnails to see the photo in Loupe view, or select the thumbnail and click the Loupe view button (▣) below the preview pane; the image is enlarged to fit the preview area and the pointer becomes a magnifying glass cursor (⊕).

2 Click the image again to further magnify the image to a zoom ratio of 1:1. Use the Zoom slider below the preview pane to see even more detail. Drag the enlarged image in the preview pane to inspect portions of the photo that are not currently visible.

While you're examining the photo in Loupe view, you can check mark the image for import or un-check it to exclude it by clicking the Include In Import check box below the preview pane. Alternatively, press the P key to check-mark the photo, the X key to un-check it, or the Tilde key (~) to toggle between the two states.

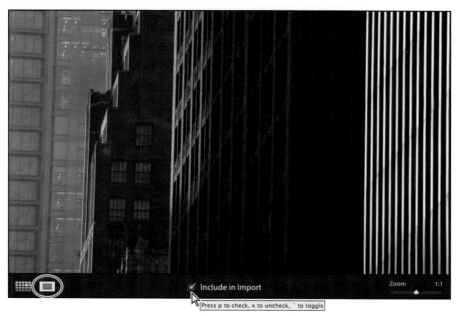

3 Drag the Zoom slider all the way to the left to return to the Fit view where the entire image is visible. Double-click the image, or click either the Loupe view button or the Grid view button beside it to return to the thumbnail display.

4 For the purposes of this exercise, un-check one of the images to exclude it, and then click Import.

5 In the Folders panel, click the triangle beside the Lesson 3 folder, if necessary, to see the listing for the Batch1 subfolder inside it.

Both the Batch1 subfolder and the Previous Import listing in the Catalog panel show an image count of 6 and the six newly imported photos are displayed in the Grid view and the Filmstrip.

6 Switch back to Windows Explorer / the Finder and drag the Batch1 folder onto the Grid view in the Library module again.

In the Import dialog box, the six photos already imported are dimmed and unavailable for import. Clicking New Photos above the Preview pane would remove them from view entirely.

7 Click Import to add the remaining Batch1 photo to your library catalog.

8 In the Folders panel, the Batch1 folder now shows an image count of 7; click the Batch1 folder to see all seven photos in the Grid view and the Filmstrip.

Importing to a specific folder

From within the Library module, you can import photos directly to a folder in the Folders panel without going to the trouble of specifying a destination in the Import dialog box.

1 In the Folders panel, right-click / Control-click the Batch1 folder and choose Import Into This Folder from the context menu.

2 In the Import dialog box, click Select A Source at the left of the top panel, above the Source panel, and choose the path to the Lesson 3 folder from the list of recent sources in the menu.

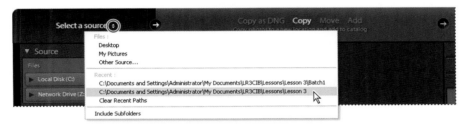

3 Expand the Source panel; then expand the Lesson 3 folder so that you can see the subfolders inside it. Select the folder Extras. In the Preview pane, you can see that the Extras folder contains two photos.

4 In the top panel, choose Move from the import type options to move the photos from the Extras folder to the destination folder and add them to your catalog. Check that your previous settings are still active in the Apply During Import panel. You may need to re-type **Lesson 3, New York** in the Keywords box.

5 Expand the Destination panel, if necessary. You can see that the Batch1 folder has been automatically selected as the destination to which the photos from the Extras folder will be moved. Click Import. Thumbnails of the two images appear in the Grid view and the Filmstrip in the Library module.

6 In the Folders panel, the Batch1 folder now shows an image count of 9. Click the Batch1 folder to see all nine images together in the Grid view and the Filmstrip.

7 In the Folders panel, right-click / Control-click the Lesson 3 folder and choose Show In Explorer / Show In Finder from the context menu. In the Windows Explorer / Finder window, open the Extras folder inside the Lesson 3 folder; the two image files have been removed and the Extras folder is now empty.

Importing from other catalogs

If you work on a laptop while you're on location and need to merge your new photos with the Lightroom library on your desktop computer, or if you work in a situation where more than one person will be using the same images in Lightroom on different computers, you can move photos from one computer to another using the Export As Catalog and Import From Catalog commands. Your images will be transferred with all of your edits, adjustments, and settings in place—including any keywords or other metadata you may have added.

Lesson 10, "Backup and Exporting" will discuss exporting photos as a catalog; for this lesson you'll import photos from a catalog you'll find in the Batch2 folder inside the Lesson 3 folder on your hard disk.

1 Choose File > Import From Catalog.

2 In the Import From Lightroom Catalog dialog box, navigate to the Batch2 folder inside the Lesson 3 folder on your hard disk. Select the file Batch2 Catalog.lrcat in the Batch2 folder and click Choose.

3 In the Import From Catalog dialog box, choose Add New Photos To Catalog Without Moving from the File Handling menu, and then click Import.

▶ **Tip:** The option Don't Import New Photos in the File Handling menu is useful when you've exported images from one computer, modified the files on a different computer, and then wish to re-import them without importing any new images.

4 If you see the Photo Is Missing icon (⊟?) in the top right corner of the image cells in the Grid view, click the icon on the first image, and then click Locate in the Confirm dialog box. Navigate to the Images folder inside the Batch2 folder, select the missing photo, activate the Find Nearby Missing Photos option, and then click Select.

Re-importing existing photos

If you wish to re-import photos that already exist in your library, select from the following options in the Existing Photos area of the Import From Catalog dialog box:

- From the Replace menu, choose Metadata, Develop Settings, And Negative Files to override all the settings in the current catalog. If you choose this option, activate the option Preserve Old Settings As A Virtual Copy to keep a backup. You can also activate the option Replace Non-Raw Files Only to avoid replacing raw negatives. If changes to raw negative files affect only metadata, selecting this option helps save time.

- From the Replace menu, choose Metadata And Develop Settings Only to leave the negative files (the source photos) unchanged. If you choose this option, activate the option Preserve Old Settings As A Virtual Copy to keep a backup.

- From the Replace menu, choose Nothing to import only new photos.

- If photos in the current catalog are missing and can be found in the imported catalog, indicate whether you want to update the metadata and Develop settings for these files. Activate the option Preserve Old Settings As A Virtual Copy to keep a backup. If the photos missing in the current catalog appear in the imported catalog, specify whether the missing files should be copied and where they should be copied to.

—From Lightroom Help

5 The Batch2 subfolder is now listed in the Folders panel and three newly imported photos are displayed in the Grid view and the Filmstrip.

When you import images from a Lightroom catalog, you don't have the option to apply develop settings or to add keywords and other metadata during the import process as you do when you import from your camera or hard disk.

Lightroom preserves the keywords and other metadata that were exported in the catalog with the images; once the photos have been added to your catalog, you can modify the metadata as you wish.

6 Select one of the images in the Grid view. In the Keywording panel in the right panel group, you can see that the keywords "Lesson 3" and "New York" have already been applied. If you wished, you could add more keywords—such as **Sculpture** or **Art Deco**—to the images individually.

7 Expand the Metadata panel in the right panel group. If necessary, collapse the other panels in the group or scroll down so that you can see the contents of the Metadata panel. Note that the New York trip Aug 2009 metadata preset has already been applied to the images. You can edit the metadata to your liking.

The imported images have also been edited. Lightroom records every editing operation performed on an image in the entry for that image in the library catalog file. When images are exported in a catalog their entire edit history is exported with them.

8 Select one of the images in the Grid view, and then switch to the Develop module. If necessary, scroll down in the left panel group so that you can see the contents of the History panel. Click the Import entry at the bottom of the History panel to see how the image looked originally. Then, choose Edit > Undo to return to the edited version.

9 Switch back to the Library module in readiness for the next exercise.

Importing from a watched folder

Designating a folder on your hard disk as a *watched folder* can be a very convenient way to automate the import process. Once you've nominated a folder that is to be watched, Lightroom will detect any photos that are placed or saved into it, then automatically move them to a specified location and add them to the catalog. You can even have Lightroom rename the files and add metadata in the process.

1   Choose File > Auto Import > Auto Import Settings.

2   In the Auto Import Settings dialog box, click the first Choose button to designate a watched folder.

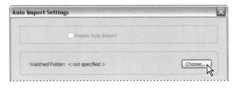

3   In the Browse For Folder / Auto-Import From Folder dialog box, navigate to the Lesson 3 folder. Open the Auto Import folder and select the subfolder named Watched Folder; then, click OK / Choose.

4   Now that you have designated a watched folder, you can click the checkbox at the top of the Auto Import Settings dialog box to enable Auto Import.

5   Click the second Choose button under Destination to specify a folder to which Lightroom will move your photos in the process of adding them to the library catalog.

6   In the Browse For Folder / Choose Folder dialog box, navigate to the Lessons folder. Select the Lesson 3 folder (you'll set up a subfolder inside the Lesson 3 folder in the next step), and then click OK / Choose.

7   Still in the Destination section in the Auto Import Settings dialog box, type **Batch3** in the Subfolder Name text box. Lightroom will create this subfolder inside the Lesson 3 folder.

8   Choose Filename from the File Naming menu.

9   Under Information, choose the metadata preset you created earlier in this lesson from the Metadata menu and type **Lesson 3, New York** in the Keywords text box. Choose None from the Develop Settings menu and Minimal from the Initial Previews menu. Click OK to close the Auto Import Settings dialog box.

10 Switch to Windows Explorer / the Finder and navigate to the Lesson 3 folder. Note that as yet there is no Batch3 folder inside the Lesson 3 folder. Open the folder Auto Import and drag the seven image files inside it to the Watched Folder. When Lightroom has finished importing, you'll see the newly created Batch3 folder inside the Lesson 3 folder. The Watched Folder is empty once more and the seven lesson images have been moved into the Batch3 folder.

▶ **Tip:** Once you've set a watched folder, you can activate or disable Auto Import at any time, without opening the Auto Import Settings dialog box, by choosing File > Auto Import > Enable Auto Import. A check mark beside this menu command indicates that the Auto Import feature is currently enabled.

11 Return to Lightroom; the Batch3 folder is now listed in the Folders panel and the newly imported photos are displayed in the Grid view and the Filmstrip.

You can now import images into your Lightroom library by simply dragging them onto the watched folder. This makes importing photos directly from a camera or memory card reader even easier; there's no need to attend to a dialog box and yet your images can be renamed and have custom metadata added automatically.

Specifying initial previews when importing

As photos are imported, Lightroom can immediately display a photo's embedded preview, or display higher-quality previews as the program renders them. You can choose the rendered size and quality for previews using the Standard Preview Size and Preview Quality menus in File Handling tab of the Catalog Settings (choose Edit > Catalog Settings / Lightroom > Catalog Settings). Please keep in mind that embedded previews are created on-the-fly by cameras and are not color managed therefore they don't match the interpretation of the camera raw files made by Lightroom. Previews rendered by Lightroom are color managed.

In the Import Photos dialog box, do one of the following:

- To immediately display images using the smallest previews embedded in the photos, choose Initial Previews > Minimal. Lightroom renders standard-size previews when needed.

- To display the largest possible preview available from the camera, choose Initial Previews > Embedded & Sidecar. This may take longer to display than a Minimal preview but is still faster than rendering a standard-size preview.

- To display previews as Lightroom renders them, choose Initial Previews > Standard. Standard-size previews use the ProPhoto RGB color space.

- To display previews that are a 1 to 1 view of the actual pixels, as in the Develop module, choose Initial Previews > 1:1.

—From Lightroom Help

Tethered shooting

Many modern digital cameras support tethered shooting, a process where you connect—or tether—your digital camera to your computer and save images to the computer's hard disk rather than to the camera's memory card. With tethered shooting you can view a photo on your computer screen immediately after you shoot it—a vastly different experience from seeing it on your camera's LCD screen.

For a range of DSLR cameras including many models from Canon and Nikon, you can capture photographs directly into Lightroom 3 without the need for any third-party software. If your camera allows tethered shooting, but is not on the list of models supported by Lightroom, you can still capture images into your Lightroom library using either the image capture software associated with the camera or any of a number of third-party software solutions.

▶ **Tip:** To see a list of cameras for which integrated tethered shooting is currently supported, please refer to Lightroom Help.

You can have Lightroom name the photos, add metadata, apply developing settings, and organize them in your library then and there. If necessary, you can adjust your camera settings (white balance, exposure, focus, depth of field, and others), or even change cameras, before taking the next shot. The better the quality of the captured image the less time you'll need to spend adjusting it later.

Tethered shooting with a supported camera

1 Connect your camera to the computer.

2 In the Library module, choose File > Tethered Capture > Start Tethered Capture.

3 In the Tethered Capture Settings dialog box, type a name for your shooting session. Lightroom will create a folder with this name inside the destination folder of your choice; this session folder will appear in the Folders panel.

● **Note:** Depending on your camera model and the operating system your computer uses, you may also need to install the necessary drivers for your camera.

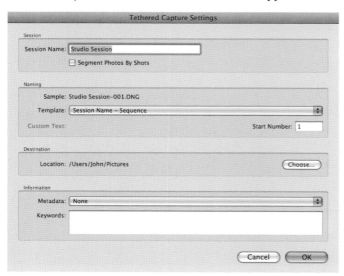

4 Chose a naming scheme for your shots, select a destination folder, and specify any metadata or keywords that you want Lightroom to apply as the newly captured images are imported.

5 Click OK to close the Tethered Capture Settings dialog box. The tethered capture control bar appears.

The control bar displays the model name of the connected camera, the name you entered for the shooting session, and the current camera settings. You can choose from a wide range of Develop presets in the Develop Settings menu at the right. Trigger the shot either with the shutter button on your camera or by clicking the large circular button at the right of the control bar.

As you shoot, the images captured will appear in both the Grid view and the Filmstrip. To see each captured photo as large as possible, use the Loupe view and hide unwanted panels—as shown in the illustration below—or chose Window > Screen Mode > Full Screen And Hide Panels.

Tethered shooting with other cameras

If your camera allows tethered shooting, but is not on the list of models for which the process is integrated in Lightroom, you can still capture images into your Lightroom library by using the image capture software associated with your camera—or a third-party software solution—to save your photos to a watched folder. Lightroom will remove the images from the watched folder and add them to your catalog as soon as it detects them.

▶ **Tip:** To find out about third-party image capture software compatible with your camera, search "tethered shooting" on the Internet or in Adobe Community Help.

1   Choose File > Auto Import > Auto Import Settings. In the Auto Import Settings dialog box, click the first Choose button to choose a watched folder. Once you've designated a folder to be watched, you can click the checkbox at the top of the Auto Import Settings dialog box to enable Auto Import.

2   Click the second Choose button under Destination to specify a folder to which Lightroom will save your photos in the process of adding them to the library catalog. Type a name for your photo shoot in the Subfolder Name text box; Lightroom will create this subfolder inside the designated destination folder.

3   Choose a naming option for your images from the File Naming menu. Under Information, you can choose a metadata preset and enter any keywords that you wish Lightroom to apply as your newly captured images are imported. If you wish, you can also choose a developing preset and specify a preview option. Click OK to close the Auto Import Settings dialog box.

4   Use your camera's image capture software to designate your new watched folder as the destination to which the camera will save your photos.

By way of an example, this illustration shows the download and metadata options from the Camera Control component of Nikon's Capture NX software.

5   Before you begin shooting, make sure that you are in the Library module. In the Folders panel, select the subfolder you created for your tethered shoot in step 2, so that your newly captured photos will be displayed as they are imported.

Review questions

1 When would you choose to copy imported images to a new location on your hard disk and when would you want to add them to your library catalog without moving them?

2 Which file formats are supported by Lightroom?

3 What is DNG?

4 When would you use the Import dialog box in compact mode?

5 How can you transfer photos between Lightroom libraries on separate computers?

Review answers

1 You don't have the option to import photos from a camera at their current location; Lightroom needs to record a location for each file in the library catalog, and as memory cards are expected to be erased and reused the images need first to be copied to a more permanent location. Copying or moving images might also be useful when you want Lightroom to organize the files into a more ordered folder hierarchy during the import process. Images that are already arranged in a useful way on the hard disk or removable media can be added to the library catalog in their current locations.

2 Lightroom supports the following file formats: most camera raw formats, Digital Negative (DNG), TIFF, JPEG, and Photoshop PSD. and CMYK files, Lightroom does not support PNG files, Adobe Illustrator® files, Nikon scanner NEF files, or files with dimensions greater than 65,000 pixels per side or larger than 512 megapixels.

3 The Digital Negative (DNG) file format is a publicly available archival format intended to address the lack of an open standard for raw files generated by cameras. Converting raw files to DNG in Lightroom will help ensure that you'll be able to access your raw files in the future even if the original proprietary format is no longer supported.

4 Once you've created import presets to suit your workflow, you can speed up the import process by using the Import dialog box in compact mode. Use your import preset as a starting point, and then modify the settings as required.

5 On one computer, export the images from Lightroom as a catalog file. On the other computer, choose File > Import From Catalog to import the photos into the Lightroom library together with their develop settings and metadata.

4 REVIEWING

Lesson overview

It's a good policy to spend some time reviewing, sorting, and marking your newly imported images. A little time spent organizing and grouping photos at this stage will make it much easier to find exactly the images you want when you need them.

In this lesson you'll become familiar with using a variety of viewing modes, tools, and techniques for reviewing your images and navigating through your Lightroom catalog:

- Working in the different Library module views
- Navigating through your catalog
- Using the Navigator panel
- Comparing photos
- Flagging rejects and deleting images
- Using the Quick Collection
- Converting and clearing the Quick Collection
- Designating a target collection
- Hiding the Filmstrip and adjusting its size
- Applying the Filmstrip Source Filters
- Rearranging photos in the Grid view or the Filmstrip

 You'll probably need between one and two hours to complete this lesson.

The Lightroom Library module offers you a variety of ways to review, evaluate, mark, and label your photos after you import them, making it easier to organize and manage your growing image library. You can sort and group thumbnails in the Grid view, examine a single photo up close in Loupe view, assess images side by side in Compare view, or refine a multiple selection of shots in Survey view.

Getting started

This lesson assumes that you are already familiar with the Lightroom workspace and with moving between the different modules. If you find that you need more background information as you go, refer to Lightroom Help, or review the previous lessons in this book.

Before you begin, make sure that you have correctly copied the Lessons folder from the CD in the back of this book onto your computer's hard disk and created the LR3CIB Library Catalog file as detailed in "Copying the Classroom in a Book files" on page 2 and "Creating a catalog file for working with this book" on page 3.

1 Start Lightroom.

2 In the Adobe Photoshop Lightroom - Select Catalog dialog box, make sure the file LR3CIB Library Catalog.lrcat is selected under Select A Recent Catalog To Open, and then click Open.

3 Lightroom will open in the screen mode and workspace module that were active when you last quit. If necessary, click Library in the Module Picker to switch to the Library module.

Importing images into the library

The first step is to import the images for this lesson into the Lightroom library.

1 In the Library module, click the Import button below the left panel group.

2 If the Import dialog box appears in compact
   mode, click the Show More Options button at the
   lower left of the dialog box to see all the options in
   the expanded Import dialog box.

3 Under Source at the left of the expanded Import dialog box, navigate to the
   Lessons folder that you copied into the LR3CIB folder on your hard disk. Select
   the Lesson 4 folder. Ensure that all twelve images in the Lesson 4 folder are
   checked for import.

4 In the import options above the thumbnail previews, click Add to add the
   imported photos to your catalog without moving or copying them.

5 Under File Handling at the right of the expanded Import dialog box, choose
   Minimal from the Render Previews menu and ensure that the Don't Import
   Selected Duplicates option is activated.

6 Under Apply During Import, choose None from both the Develop Settings
   menu and the Metadata menu and type **Lesson 4, New York** in the Keywords
   text box. Make sure your settings are exactly as shown in the illustration below,
   and then click Import.

The twelve images are imported from the Lesson 4 folder and now appear in both
the Grid view of the Library module and in the Filmstrip across the bottom of the
Lightroom workspace.

Viewing and managing your images

The Library module offers a range of viewing modes and a variety of tools and controls to help you evaluate, compare, sort, mark, and group your images. During the import process you applied common metadata in the form of keyword tags to the selection of images as a whole. As you review your photos in the Library module you can add another layer of organization to your catalog, flagging images as picks or rejects, assigning ratings, and applying tags and labels. The Library module also provides sophisticated search functions and customizable filters that enable you to leverage the metadata you attach to your photos. You can search and sort the images in your library by category, subject, or any other association, and then create Collections and Smart Collections to group them—making it easy to retrieve exactly the photos you want quickly, no matter how extensive your catalog.

In the left panel group of the Library module are panels where you can access and work with the folders and collections containing your photos. The right panel group contains panels for adjusting your images and working with keywords and metadata. At the top of the work area is the Filter bar, where you can set the criteria for a customized search of your catalog. The Toolbar, immediately below the work area, provides easy access to your choice of tools and controls.

Switching views

In the Library module you can move between four viewing modes to suit different phases of your workflow. Press the G key or click the Grid view button (▦) in the Toolbar to see thumbnails of your images while you search, apply flags, ratings and labels, or create collections. Use the keyboard shortcut E or click the Loupe view button (▢) to inspect a single photo at a range of magnifications. Press C or click the Compare view button (X|Y) to see two images side by side. Click the Survey view button (▣) in the Toolbar or use the keyboard shortcut N to evaluate several images at once. The Toolbar displays a different set of controls for each view mode.

The Grid view

By default your images will be displayed in Grid view after they've been imported.

1   Click the triangle at the right end of the Toolbar and ensure that View Modes is activated in the tools menu. If you're working on a small screen, you can disable all the other options except Thumbnail size for this lesson.

Tools and controls that are currently visible in the Toolbar have a check mark beside their names in the menu. The order of the tools and controls from top to bottom in the menu corresponds to their order from left to right in the Toolbar.

2   If Grid view is not already selected, click the Grid view button (▦). Adjust the size of the thumbnails by dragging the Thumbnails slider so that you can see about two rows of thumbnails in the Grid view without having to scroll down.

3 To specify how your photos will be displayed in the Grid view image cells, choose View > View Options. The Library View Options dialog box appears.

4 Activate the Show Grid Extras option and choose Compact Cells from the menu beside it. Customize the Options, Cell Icons, Compact Cell Extras, and Expanded Cell Extras settings to your liking. As a guide to the options available, please refer to "View Options for the Grid view" on the next page.

5 From the Show Grid Extras menu at the top of the Library View Options dialog box, choose Expanded Cells. Examine the options available and make whatever changes you wish. When you're done, choose Compact Cells from the Show Grid Extras menu and close the Library View Options dialog box.

▶ **Tip:** To conveniently cycle through the different Grid view styles, press the J key on your keyboard repeatedly, or choose View > Grid View Style > Cycle View Style.

To switch quickly between the two groups of options that you just set in the Library View Options dialog box, choose from the Grid View Style options on the View menu.

6 Switch to the Expanded Cell mode by choosing the Expanded Cells option from the View > Grid View Style menu. Make sure that the Show Extras option is activated in the same menu.

View options for the Grid view

Depending on the way you like to work, you can choose from a wide range of options that affect the way your photos are displayed in the Grid view image cells—from simplified cells containing nothing but the image thumbnails to expanded cells that display your choice of image information, status indicators, labels, and clickable (interactive) controls.

Show Grid Extras Displays your choice of labels, markers, and controls in each image cell. If this option is disabled most of the other Grid view options are unavailable.

Compact Cells Shows simple cells with less information so more thumbnails are visible in the Grid.

Expanded Cells Expands the image cells to include more information in cell headers and footers.

Show Clickable Items On Mouse Over Only Displays rotation controls, flags, and labels only when you move the pointer over an image cell. Disable this option to show these controls at all times.

Tint Grid Cells With Color Labels Tints the image cell around a photo to indicate its color label.

Show Image Info Tooltips Displays a brief description of an item when you hold the pointer over it, including image info and the names of the controls, status badges, and indicators in the image cell.

Flags Activates clickable flag status indicators in the upper left corner of the image cells. Click the indictor to change the flag status.

Quick Collection Markers Shows a clickable Quick Collection marker in the upper right corner of each thumbnail. Images with a solid grey dot are part of the Quick Collection. Click the marker to add an image to, or remove it from, the Quick Collection.

Thumbnail Badges Displays indicator badges on the thumbnail images indicating which photos have keywords attached and which have been adjusted or cropped.

Unsaved Metadata An icon with a down arrow in the upper right of a cell indicates that an image has changes in its metadata that have not yet been saved to file. An up arrow icon shows that the image file's metadata has been changed in an external application and an exclamation mark icon indicates that a photo's metadata has unsaved changes made in both Lightroom and an external application.

Index Number Shows image cell numbers indicating the order of the photos in the Grid view.

Rotation Displays Rotation buttons in the lower corners of the image cells.

Top Label and **Bottom Label** Displays your choice of image information and attributes above and below the thumbnail in a compact image cell.

Show Header With Labels Displays up to four labels in the headers of expanded image cells, showing whatever information you specify. For each label, you can choose from a menu of image information and attributes.

Use Defaults Restores the Header Label options to their default settings.

Show Rating Footer Shows the rating stars, and optionally the color label and rotation buttons, below the thumbnail in expanded image cells.

Zooming with the Navigator in Loupe view

In Loupe view you can look closely at one photo at a time at a wide range of zoom levels. Use the Loupe view to help you to evaluate your images as you sort them in the Library module and to inspect and adjust them in the Develop module. In the Navigator panel you can set the level of magnification for the Loupe view and find your way around a zoomed image with ease. Like the Loupe view, the Navigator is common to both the Library and Develop modules.

1   Select the first image NY_Signs_03.jpg in the Grid view or the Filmstrip, and then click the Loupe view button (▣) in the Toolbar. Alternatively, press the E key or double-click the thumbnail in the Grid view or the Filmstrip.

2   If necessary, expand the Navigator panel at the top of the left panel group. The zoom controls for the Loupe view are in upper right corner of the Navigator panel. Click 1:1 to see this photo at 100% (or "actual pixels") magnification.

3 Click the small triangle at the right of the Navigator panel header and choose the zoom ratio 3:1 from the menu.

4 When you're working at such a high level of magnification, the Navigator helps you to move around in the image quickly and easily. Click anywhere in the Navigator preview and the zoomed view will be centered on that point. Drag in the Navigator preview to reposition the view. The white rectangle indicates the area currently displayed in the Loupe view. Click in the Loupe view to move back and forth between the last two zoom levels used; when zooming in, the view will be centered on the point you click. Double-click the image to switch quickly back and forth between the Loupe and Grid views.

▶ **Tip:** The Show Grid Extras option on the Grid View tab of the Library View Options dialog box enables you to display a range of information about your photos in their image cells. In the Loupe View options, activate Show Info Overlay to display the same kind of information overlaid on your enlarged image in the Loupe view. By default, the Loupe view info overlay in disabled.

5 In the header of the Navigator panel, click each of the four zoom levels in turn (Fit, Fill, 1:1, and 3:1—the option you chose from the menu). Press the Ctrl key (Windows) / Command key (Mac OS) together with the Minus key (-) repeatedly to zoom out through the last four zoom levels used and to finally switch to Grid view; press the Ctrl key / Command key together with the Equal key (=) repeatedly to switch back to Loupe view and to progressively zoom in. Finally, set the zoom level to Fit.

Comparing photos

As the name suggests, the Compare view is ideal for examining and evaluating images side by side.

1   In the Filmstrip, click to select the photo ChryslerBuilding_01.jpg, and then Ctrl-click / Command-click its neighbor, ChryslerBuilding_02.jpg. Click the Compare View button (⊠Ⓨ) in the Toolbar.

The first image selected becomes the *Select* image, which is displayed in the left pane of the Compare view; the image displayed in the right pane is the *Candidate*. In the Filmstrip, the Select image is marked with a white diamond in the upper right corner, and the Candidate image with a black diamond.

To use the Compare view to make a choice from a group of more than two photos, select your favored choice first to place it as the Select image, and then add the other photos to the selection. Click the Select Previous Photo and Select Next Photo buttons (⇐ ⇒) in the Toolbar or press the left and right arrow keys on your keyboard to move between the selected candidates. Should you decide that the current Candidate is better than the Select image, you can reverse their positions by clicking the Swap button (⊠↻) in the Toolbar.

2 To compare fine detail in the images, zoom in by dragging the Zoom slider in the Toolbar. You'll notice that the images are zoomed together. Drag either of the images in the Compare view and the images move in unison. The closed lock icon to the left of the Zoom slider indicates that the view focus of the two images is locked.

3 If you wish to zoom and move the Select and Candidate images independently, you need to click the view focus lock icon to unlink them.

A thin white line surrounds whichever of the two images in the Compare view is currently the active image: the image that will be affected by the Zoom slider, the controls in the right panel group, or any menu command you may apply.

4 Click the lock icon to link the view focus for the two images, and then choose Fit from the zoom levels at the top of the Navigator panel.

5 Click the Candidate photo to make it the active image; then expand the Quick Develop panel, if necessary. From the Saved Preset menu, choose the BW Creative - Selenium Tone preset. In the Tone Control area, click the double-arrow at the right of the Recovery control four times.

▶ **Tip:** For the purposes of the illustration above, the Saved Preset menu has been abridged; you'll find the preset BW Creative - Selenium Tone much further down the list.

Using the controls in the Quick Develop panel while you're working in Compare view can be a helpful aid in making a choice between images. Although the candidate image in our example contains more detail and is a less cluttered composition, the Select image is more atmospheric. Applying a develop preset or making other adjustments in the Quick Develop panel can help you to make a judgement on how a candidate image will look once it's edited and adjusted. You can then either undo your Quick Develop operations and move to the Develop module to edit the image with greater precision, or keep the modifications you've made as a starting point.

Using Survey view to narrow a selection

The last of the four viewing modes in the Library module, the Survey View lets you see multiple images together on one screen, and then refine your selection by dropping one photo after another from the view.

1 In the Filmstrip, select the five images of the Flatiron Building. Click the Survey view button (⊞) in the Toolbar, or press the N key on your keyboard.

2 Navigate between the images by pressing the arrow keys on your keyboard or click the Select Previous Photo and Select Next Photo buttons (⟵⟶) in the Toolbar. The active image is surrounded by a thin white border.

3 Position the pointer over the third photo. A Deselect Photo icon (✕) appears in the lower right corner of the image. Click this icon to drop the image from the selection in the Survey view.

▶ **Tip:** If you have eliminated a photo accidentally, choose Edit > Undo to return it to the selection, or simply Ctrl-click / Command-click its thumbnail in the Filmstrip. You can easily add a photo to the selection in the Survey view in the same way.

As you eliminate candidates the remaining photos are progressively resized and shuffled to fill the space available in the work area. To help in comparing the photos, you can drag any of the images to reposition it in the Survey view. The other images will automatically be shuffled to accommodate your action.

4 Continue to eliminate photos from the Survey view. For the purposes of this exercise, deselect all but one favorite (we chose the active photo—marked with a white border—in the illustration below).

Dropping a photo from the Survey view doesn't delete it from its folder or remove it from the catalog; the dropped image is still visible in the Filmstrip—it has simply been deselected. You can see that the images that are still displayed in the Survey view are also the only ones that remain selected in the Filmstrip.

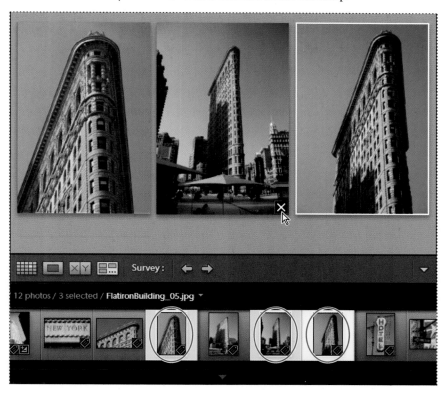

Flagging and deleting images

Now that you have narrowed down a selection of images to one favorite in the Survey view, you can mark your choice with a flag.

Flagging images as either picks or rejects as you review them is an effective way to quickly sort your work; flag status is one of the criteria by which you can filter your photo library. You can also quickly remove images flagged as rejects from your catalog using a menu command or keyboard shortcut.

A white flag denotes a pick (⚑), a black one with an x marks a reject (⚑), and a neutral grey flag indicates that an image has not been flagged (⚑).

▶ **Tip:** Press the P key on your keyboard to flag a selected image as a pick (⚑), the X key to flag it as a reject (⚑), or the U key to remove any flags.

1   Still in the Survey view, move the pointer over the
    remaining photo to see the flag icons just below
    the lower left corner. The grayed icons indicate
    that the image is not yet flagged. Click the flag to
    the left. The flag turns white, which marks this
    image as a pick. In the Filmstrip, you can see that
    the thumbnail now displays a white flag in the
    upper left of the image cell.

2   Select a different image in the Filmstrip, and
    then press the X key. The black reject flag icon
    appears at the lower left corner of the image
    in the Survey view and at the upper left of the
    thumbnail in the Filmstrip. The thumbnail of
    the rejected image is dimmed in the Filmstrip.

3   Choose Photo > Delete Rejected Photos, or simply press the Delete key on your
    keyboard. A confirmation dialog box appears; click Remove to remove the
    photo from your catalog without deleting the master file from your hard disk.

Having been removed from the Lightroom library catalog file, the rejected image is
no longer visible in the Filmstrip.

4   Press the G key or click the Grid view icon in the Toolbar to see all the
    remaining images as thumbnails in the Grid view.

Grouping images in the Quick Collection

A collection is a convenient way to keep a group of photos together in your catalog, even when the image files are actually located in different folders on your hard disk. You can create a new collection for a particular presentation or use collections to group your images by category or any other association. Your collections are always available from the Collections panel where you can access them quickly.

The Quick Collection is a temporary holding collection: a convenient place to group images as you review and sort your new imports, or while you assemble a selection of photos drawn from different folders in your catalog.

In the Grid view or the Filmstrip, you can add images to the Quick Collection with a single click—and remove them just as easily. Your images will stay in the Quick Collection until you're ready to convert it to a more permanent grouping that will be listed in the Collections panel. You can access the Quick Collection from the Catalog panel so that you can return to work with the same selection of images at any time.

Moving images into or out of the Quick Collection

1 Expand the Catalog panel in the left panel group, if necessary, to see the listing for the Quick Collection.

2 Choose View > Sort > File Name, or choose File Name from the Sort menu in the Toolbar; then, select the five NY_Signs images by Ctrl-clicking / Command-clicking their thumbnails in the Grid view or the Filmstrip.

3 To add the selected photos to the Quick Collection, press the B key or choose Photo > Add To Quick Collection.

4   The image count beside the Quick Collection in the Catalog panel indicates that the Quick Collection now contains five images. If you have activated the option Show Quick Collection Markers in the Library View Options dialog box, each image in the Quick Collection is marked with a gray dot in the upper right corner of its thumbnail in the Grid view. The same markers are also shown in the Filmstrip unless the thumbnail size is too small.

▶ **Tip:** If you don't see the Quick Collection marker when you move your pointer over a thumbnail, make sure that Show Extras is activated in the View > Grid View Styles menu. Choose View > View Options and activate Quick Collection Markers under Cell Icons in the Library View Options dialog box.

You can remove all of the selected photos from the Quick Collection by simply clicking the marker on one of the thumbnails or by pressing the B key.

5   For this exercise, you'll remove only the first image, NY_Signs_01.jpg, from the Quick Collection. First, deselect the other four images, and then, with only the image NY_Signs_01.jpg selected, press the B key. Your Quick Collection is reduced to four images.

Converting and clearing the Quick Collection

1   Click the Quick Collection entry in the Catalog panel. The Grid view now displays only four images. Until you clear the Quick Collection, you can easily return to this group of images to review your selection.

Now that you've refined your selection you can move your grouped images to a more permanent Collection.

2 Choose File > Save Quick Collection.

3 In the Save Quick Collection dialog box, type **Signs of the Times** in the Collection Name box. Activate the option Clear Quick Collection After Saving, and then click Save.

4 In the Catalog panel, you can see that the Quick Collection has been cleared; it now has an image count of 0. If necessary, expand the Collections panel so that you can see the listing for your new collection, which displays an image count of 4.

5 In the Folders panel, click the Lesson 4 folder. The grid view once more shows all the photos of New York including those in the signs collection.

Designating a target collection

By default, the Quick Collection is designated as the *target collection;* this status is indicated by the plus sign (+) that follows the Quick Collection's name in the Catalog panel. The target collection is that collection to which a selected image is moved when you press the B key or click the circular marker in the upper right corner of the thumbnail, as you did in the previous exercise.

You can designate a collection of your own as the target collection so that you can use the same convenient techniques to add and remove photos quickly and easily.

1 Right-click / Control-click the entry for your new Signs of the Times collection in the Collections panel, and then choose Set As Target Collection from the context menu. The name of your collection is now followed by a plus sign (+).

2 Click the Previous Import folder in the Catalog panel, and then select the image NY_Signs_01.jpg in the Grid view or the Filmstrip.

3 Watch the Collections panel as you press the B key on your keyboard; the image count for the Signs of the Times collection increases to 5 as the selected image is added to the collection.

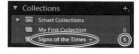

4 Right-click / Control-click the Quick Collection in the Catalog panel and choose Set As Target Collection from the context menu. The Quick Collection once again displays the plus sign (+).

Working with the Filmstrip

No matter which module or view you're working in, the Filmstrip across the bottom of the Lightroom workspace provides constant access to the images in your selected folder or collection.

As with the Grid view, you can quickly navigate through your images in the Filmstrip using the arrow keys on your keyboard. If there are more images than will fit in the Filmstrip you can either use the scroll bar below the thumbnails, drag the Filmstrip by the top edge of the thumbnail frame, or click the shaded thumbnails at either end to access photos that are currently out of view.

Across the top of the Filmstrip, Lightroom provides a convenient set of controls to help streamline your workflow.

At the far left you'll find buttons for working with two displays, with pop-up menus that offer a choice of viewing mode for each.

To the right of these buttons is the Grid view button, and arrow buttons for navigating between the different folders and collections you've recently been viewing.

Next is the Filmstrip Source Indicator, where you can see at a glance which folder or collection you're viewing, how many photos it contains, which images are currently selected, and the name of the image currently under your pointer. Click the Source Indicator to see a menu with all the image sources you've recently accessed.

At the far right of the Filmstrip header are the Filter controls, which we'll look at later in this lesson.

Hiding the Filmstrip and adjusting its size

You can show and hide the Filmstrip and adjust its size, as you can with the side panel groups, to make more screen space available for the image you're working on.

1   Click the triangle in the lower border of the workspace window to hide and show the Filmstrip. Right-click / Control-click the triangle to set the automatic show and hide options.

2   Position the pointer over the top edge of the Filmstrip; the cursor becomes a double arrow. Drag the top edge of the Filmstrip up or down to enlarge or reduce the thumbnails. The narrower you make the Filmstrip the more thumbnails it can display.

Using filters in the Filmstrip

With so few photos in the Lesson 4 folder it's not difficult to see all the images at once in the Filmstrip. However, when you're working with a folder containing many images it can be inconvenient to scroll the Filmstrip looking for the photos you want to work with. You can use the Filmstrip filters to narrow down the images displayed in the Filmstrip to only those that share a specified flag status, rating, color label, or any combination of these attributes.

1   In the Filmstrip you can see that one of the images in the Lesson 4 folder displays the white Pick flag that you assigned in a previous exercise. If you don't see the flag, right-click / Control-click anywhere in the Filmstrip and activate the menu option View Options > Show Ratings And Picks in the context menu. Examine the other options available in the Filmstrip context menu. Many of the commands apply to the image or images currently selected in the Filmstrip; others affect the Filmstrip itself.

2   From the Filter menu at the top right of the Filmstrip, choose Flagged. Only the image with the white flag is displayed in the Filmstrip.

3   The white flag icon is now highlighted among the Filter controls in the top
    bar of the Filmstrip. Click the word Filter at the left of the flag icons to see the
    attribute filter options displayed as buttons in the Filmstrip header.

You can activate or disable any of the filters you saw in the Filter menu by clicking
the respective Filter buttons. You can set up a combination of filters and save it as a
custom preset by choosing Save Current Settings As New Preset from the menu.

4   Click the white flag button to deactivate the active filter or choose Filters Off
    from the menu to disable all filters. The Filmstrip once more displays all the
    images in the folder. Click the word Filter again to hide the filter buttons.

You'll learn more about using filters in Lesson 5, "Organizing and Selecting."

Changing the sorting order of the thumbnails

Use the Sort Direction control and the Sort Criteria menu in the Toolbar to change
the display order of the thumbnails images in the Grid view and the Filmstrip.

1   If the sorting controls are not currently visible in the Toolbar, choose Sorting
    from the tools menu at the right of the Toolbar.

2   Choose Pick from the Sort Criteria menu.

The thumbnails are rearranged in both the Grid view and the Filmstrip to display
the image with the white Pick flag first.

3   Click the Sort Direction control ( ) to reverse the sorting direction of the
    thumbnails. The image with the white Pick flag now appears last in the order.

When you've grouped images in a Collection, you can manually rearrange their
order however you wish. This can be particularly useful when you're creating a
presentation such as a slideshow or web gallery, or putting together a print layout,
as the images will be placed in the template according to their sort order.

4 Expand the Collections panel and click the Signs of the Times collection that you created earlier. Choose File Name from the Sort Criteria menu.

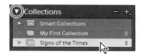

5 In the Filmstrip, drag the second thumbnail (NY_Signs_02.jpg) to the right and release the mouse button when you see a black insertion bar appear between the third and fourth images.

▶ **Tip:** You can also change the order of the photos in a collection by dragging the thumbnail images in the Grid view.

The image snaps to its new location in both the Filmstrip and the Grid view. The new sorting order is also apparent in the Toolbar; your manual sorting order has been saved and is now listed as User Order in the Sort Criteria menu.

6 Choose File Name from the Sort menu; then return to your manual sorting by choosing User Order.

Congratulations; you've finished another lesson. You've gained confidence navigating through your library and learned techniques for reviewing, sorting, filtering, and grouping your images as collections. You'll learn more about structuring and organizing your photo library in the next lesson.

Review questions

1 How would you use each of the views in the Library module?

2 What is the Navigator?

3 How do you use the Quick Collection?

4 What is the target collection?

Review answers

1 Press the G key or click the Grid view button (▦) in the Toolbar to see thumbnails of your images while you search, apply flags, ratings and labels, or create collections. Use the keyboard shortcut E or click the Loupe view button (▪) to inspect a single photo at a range of magnifications. Press C or click the Compare view button (☒Y) to see two images side by side. Click the Survey view button (▦) in the Toolbar or use the keyboard shortcut N to evaluate several images at once or refine a selection.

2 The Navigator is an interactive full image preview that helps you move around easily within a zoomed image in Loupe view. Click or drag in the Navigator preview to reposition the view while a white rectangle indicates the portion of the magnified image that is currently visible in the workspace. The Navigator panel also contains controls for setting the zoom levels for the Loupe view. Click the image in Loupe view to switch between the last two zoom levels set in the Navigator panel.

3 To create a Quick Collection, select one or more images and then press the B key or choose Photo > Add To Quick Collection. The Quick Collection is a temporary holding area; you can continue to add—or remove—images until you are ready to save the grouping as a more permanent Collection. You'll find the Quick Collection listed in the Catalog panel.

4 The target collection that collection to which a selected image will be moved when you press the B key or click the circular marker in the upper right corner of the thumbnail. By default, the Quick Collection is designated as the target collection; this status is indicated by the plus sign (+) that follows the Quick Collection's name in the Catalog panel. You can designate a collection of your own as the target collection so that you can use the same convenient techniques to add and remove photos quickly and easily.

5 ORGANIZING AND SELECTING

Lesson overview

As your photo library grows larger it will become increasingly important that you're able to locate your images quickly. Lightroom offers a range of options for organizing your image files before you even click the Import button—and even more once you've added them to your catalog. You can manage and synchronize your folders or move files between them without leaving the Library module; then apply keyword tags, flags, ratings, and labels, and group your photos in easy-to-access collections, regardless of where they're stored.

This lesson will familiarize you with the tools and techniques you'll use to organize, manage, and search your photo library:

- Creating a folder structure
- Moving files and synchronizing folders
- Understanding Collections
- Working with keywords and keyword sets
- Using Flags, Ratings, and Color Labels
- Adding and editing Metadata
- Using the Painter tool
- Finding and filtering files
- Reconnecting renamed and missing files

 You'll probably need between one and two hours to complete this lesson.

Lightroom delivers powerful, versatile tools to help you organize your image library. Use keywords, flags, labels, and ratings to sort your images, and group them into virtual collections by any association you choose. You can easily configure fast, sophisticated searches, based on practically limitless combinations of criteria, that will put exactly the photos you want at your fingertips, right when you need them.

Getting started

This lesson assumes that you are already familiar with the Lightroom workspace and with moving between the different modules. If you find that you need more background information as you go, refer to Lightroom Help, or review the previous lessons in this book.

Before you begin, make sure that you have correctly copied the Lessons folder from the CD in the back of this book onto your computer's hard disk and created the LR3CIB Library Catalog file as detailed in "Copying the Classroom in a Book files" on page 2 and "Creating a catalog file for working with this book" on page 3.

1   Start Lightroom.

2   In the Adobe Photoshop Lightroom - Select Catalog dialog box, make sure the file LR3CIB Library Catalog.lrcat is selected under Select A Recent Catalog To Open, and then click Open.

3   Lightroom will open in the screen mode and workspace module that were active when you last quit. If necessary, click Library in the Module Picker to switch to the Library module.

Importing images into the library

The first step is to import the images for this lesson into the Lightroom library.

1   In the Library module, click the Import button below the left panel group.

2 If the Import dialog box appears in compact mode, click the Show More Options button at the lower left of the dialog box to see all the options in the expanded Import dialog box.

3 Under Source at the left of the expanded Import dialog box, navigate to the Lessons folder you copied into the LR3CIB folder on your hard disk, and then select the Lesson 5 folder. Ensure that all twelve images in the Lesson 5 folder are checked for import.

4 In the import options above the thumbnail previews, click Add to add the imported photos to your catalog without moving or copying them.

5 Under File Handling at the right of the expanded Import dialog box, choose Minimal from the Render Previews menu and ensure that the Don't Import Selected Duplicates option is activated.

6 Under Apply During Import, choose None from both the Develop Settings menu and the Metadata menu and type **Lesson 5, Europe** in the Keywords text box. Make sure your settings are exactly as shown in the illustration below, and then click Import.

The twelve images are imported from the Lesson 5 folder and now appear in both the Grid view of the Library module and in the Filmstrip across the bottom of the Lightroom workspace.

Organizing folders

Each time you import an image, Lightroom creates a new catalog entry to record the file's address and lists the folder in which it is stored—and the volume that contains that folder—in the Folders panel in the left panel group.

In the Folders panel, you can organize your photo library at the most basic level by rearranging files and folders on your hard disk without ever leaving the Lightroom workspace; you can create or delete folders at the click of a button and move files and folders by simply dragging them. When you use the Folders panel to move a photo between folders, Lightroom will delete the image file from its original location and update the library catalog with the file's new address. Lightroom maintains a single catalog entry for each photo you import, so a master image cannot be duplicated in separate folders or added to the catalog twice.

Creating subfolders

In this exercise you'll use the Folders panel to begin organizing the photos in the Lesson 5 folder into categories by separating them into subfolders. You'll use two methods of creating a subfolder.

1   Click the Lesson 5 folder in the Folders panel; then, Ctrl-click / Command-click to select the four images of coastal landscapes in the Grid view.

2   In the Folders panel header, click the Create New Folder button () and choose Add Subfolder from the menu. Make sure the Show Photos In Subfolders option is activated.

3   In the Create Folder dialog box, type **Landscapes** as the folder name, activate the Include Selected Photos option, and then click Create.

4 In the Folders panel, expand the Lesson 5 folder to see the Landscapes folder nested inside it. The image count for the new subfolder shows that it contains the four images you selected in step 1.

5 With the Lesson 5 folder still selected in the Folders panel, select the four photos featuring architectural details.

6 Right-click / Control-click the Lesson 5 folder and choose Create Folder Inside "Lesson 5" from the context menu. Type **Architecture** as the folder name, activate the Include Selected Photos option, and then click Create.

7 Click the Architecture subfolder inside the Lesson 5 folder to see the four images you selected in step 5.

Making changes to a folder's content

When you rearrange files and folders in the Folders panel the changes are also made on your hard disk. Inversely, the Folders panel needs to be updated to reflect any changes you make to the location, name, or contents of a folder from outside the Lightroom workspace. In this exercise you'll experience this first hand by deleting an image in Windows Explorer / the Finder.

1 Click the Lesson 5 folder in the Folders panel.

2 Right-click / Ctrl-click one of the images of chairs in the Grid view and choose Show In Explorer / Show In Finder from the context menu.

▶ **Tip:** To rename a folder in the Folders panel, right-click / Control-click its name and choose Rename from the context menu. Be aware that when you rename a folder in the Folders panel, the change affects the folder on the hard disk.

3 The Explorer / Finder window opens. Note the Architecture and Landscapes subfolders inside the Lesson 5 folder. Right-click / Ctrl-click the image file DSC_1560.jpg inside the Lesson 5 folder and choose Delete / Move To Trash from the context menu.

4 Switch back to Lightroom. In the Grid view, note that the image that you just deleted in the Explorer / Finder window now has a question mark icon in the upper right corner of its grid cell. This indicates that Lightroom still has an entry for the image in its library catalog but the link to the original file has been broken.

5 Click the question mark icon. A dialog box opens offering you the option to locate the missing file and reestablish its link to the catalog. Click Cancel.

As you deleted the file intentionally you should now remove it from the library catalog. You can remove a missing photo from your catalog by selecting its thumbnail in the Grid view or the Filmstrip and pressing Alt+Backspace / Option+Delete or by choosing Photo > Remove Photos From Catalog. Don't remove the photo from the catalog yet—if you've done so already, choose Edit > Undo Remove Images. In the next exercise you'll learn a different technique for updating the catalog by synchronizing folders.

Synchronizing folders

When you synchronize the folders in the Lightroom catalog with the folders on your hard disk you have the option to remove catalog entries for files that have been deleted, import photos that have been added to your folders, or scan for files with updated metadata.

You can specify which folders and subfolders will be synchronized and which new images you want added to your library.

1   Make sure that the Lesson 5 folder is still selected in the Folders panel.

2   Choose Library > Synchronize Folder.

3   In the Synchronize Folder "Lesson 5" dialog box, the import options are unavailable, indicating that there have been no new photos added to the Lesson 5 folder. Activate the option Remove Missing Photos From Catalog (1), disable Scan For Metadata Updates, and then click Synchronize.

▶ **Tip:** The Import New Photos option in the Synchronize Folders dialog box automatically imports any files that have been added to a folder without yet having been added to your image library. Optionally, activate Show Import Dialog Before Importing to choose which of those files you wish to import. Activate the Scan For Metadata Updates option to check for files with metadata that has been modified in another application.

The missing image is removed from your catalog and its thumbnail is no longer displayed in the Grid view; all the links between your library catalog and the Lesson 5 folder on your hard disk have been restored.

Using collections to organize images

Although a well organized system of folders provides a good foundation for your photo library, grouping images into collections in Lightroom is a far more efficient and flexible way to classify your images—and offers many more options when you need to access them.

A collection is like a virtual folder: a grouping of photos from your library based on your own associations rather than on the actual location of the files. A collection may contain images drawn from any number of separate folders on your hard disk. Although a single master image is located in only one folder it can be included in any number of collections. The same photo might appear in a collection of images with architectural content and also in a compilation of shots suggesting an Autumn theme; it may be listed in a collection you've assembled for a client presentation and in another created for a family vacation slideshow. Grouping your images as collections in your library doesn't affect the arrangement of the files and folders on your hard disk, and removing a photo from a collection won't remove it from the library catalog or delete it from the hard disk.

● **Note:** Once you've grouped a selection of photos as a collection you can rearrange them in the Grid view or the Filmstrip, changing the order in which they will appear in a presentation or a print layout. Your customized sorting order will be saved with the collection.

There are three basic types of collection: Collections, Smart Collections and the Quick Collection. Any collection can also be part of an Output Collection, which links a collection (or a selection of images from that collection) to a particular print template and specific output settings. Any collection or selection of images can become a Publish collection, which keeps track of images that you've shared online.

▶ **Tip:** Output and Publish collections are discussed further in Lesson 8, "Printing Images" and in Lesson 9, "Publishing Your Photos" respectively.

The Quick Collection

Note: If the Thumbnail Badges option is activated in the Library View Options, a photo that is included in a collection of any kind displays the collection badge (▣) in the lower right of its thumbnail.

Photo is in collection

Click the badge to see a menu listing the collections in which the image is included. Select a collection from the list to switch to that collection as the image source folder.

The Quick Collection is a temporary holding collection; a convenient place to group images while you gather photos from different folders. You can access the Quick Collection from the Catalog panel so that you can easily return to work with the same selection of images at any time. Your images will stay in the Quick Collection until you are ready to convert your selection to a permanent collection that will then be listed in the Collections panel.

You can create as many collections and smart collections as you wish, but there is only one Quick Collection; if there is already a selection of images in the Quick Collection, you'll need to convert it to a standard collection, and then clear the Quick Collection before you can use it to assemble a new a new grouping. To create a new collection for images that are currently in the Quick Collection, right-click / Control-click the Quick Collection folder in the Catalog panel and choose Save Quick Collection from the context menu.

If the Quick Collection Markers option is enabled in the View Options for the Grid view, a circular marker appears in the top right corner of a thumbnail in the Grid view or the Filmstrip when you move your pointer over the image cell. You can add the image to the Quick Collection by clicking this marker.

Once the photo is added to the Quick Collection the marker becomes a solid grey circle. Click the solid marker to remove the image from the Quick Collection. You can perform the same operations for a multiple selection of images by clicking the Quick Collection marker on any of the selected thumbnails.

You can also add a selected image or group of images to the Quick Collection by pressing the B key or choosing Photo > Add To Quick Collection, or remove a selected image or group of images from the Quick Collection by pressing the B key again or choosing Photo > Remove From Quick Collection.

Collections

You can create as many permanent collections as you wish. Use a collection to collate the images you need for a particular project or to group photos by subject or any other another association.

When you create a collection of images for a slideshow or a web page, all the work you do on your presentation will be saved with the collection in the catalog file. In fact, the catalog entry for a single collection can incorporate your settings from the Develop module, a slide layout and playback options applied in the Slideshow module, a gallery design you set up in the Web module, and a page layout modified in the Print module. You can also create an output collection for a print job that will include your color management and printer settings.

To create a collection, choose Library > New Collection. Alternatively, click the New Collection button () in the header of the Collections panel and choose Create Collection from the menu. Enter a name in the Create Collection dialog box and click Create. Your new collection will be added to the list in the Collections panel. You can then simply drag photos onto the listing in the Collections panel to add them to the collection.

● **Note:** Remember that a single photo can be included in any number of collections, although the master image file is located in only one folder in your library. For this reason, grouping your images in collections is a far more versatile organizational method than sorting them into categorized folders.

Smart collections

A smart collection searches the metadata attached to your photos and gathers together all those images in your library that meet a specified set of criteria. Any newly imported photo that matches the criteria you've set up for a smart collection will be added to that collection automatically.

You can create a Smart Collection by choosing Library > New Smart Collection, and then specify the search criteria for your smart collection by choosing options from the menus in the Create Smart Collection dialog box.

You can add more search criteria by clicking the + button to the right of any of the rules. Hold down the Alt / Option key and click the Plus button (+) to refine a rule. In the illustration below a second rule has been added to search for images containing "Europe" in any searchable text, and then a refined rule has been added to search for images which were either captured or edited this year.

Stacking images

Another effective way of organizing images within a folder or collection is by creating stacks.

Stacks are ideal for reducing clutter in the Grid view—and the number of thumbnails you need to scroll through in the Filmstrip—by grouping similar or related photos so that only the top image in each stack is displayed. You can stack a selection of images of the same subject, a series of photos shot to test different camera settings, or action shots taken using burst mode or auto-bracketing.

A stack can be identified in the Grid view and the Filmstrip by an icon representing a stack of photos, together with an image count, in the upper left corner of the thumbnail.

You can collapse expand or collapse the stack by clicking the stack icon; rearrange the order of the photos within the stack or specify which image appears at the top either by choosing commands from the Photo > Stacking menu or by using keyboard shortcuts.

When you're working with a folder containing hundreds of photos from the same shoot, you can have Lightroom stack the images automatically based on capture time; you can specify the time interval between stacks so that your shots are grouped in a way that reflects the flow of the shoot.

To create a stack, select two or more images in the Grid view or the Filmstrip, and then choose Photo > Stacking > Group Into Stack.

To learn more about Stacks, please refer to Lightroom Help.

Applying keyword tags

Perhaps the most direct way to mark your photos so that they're easier to find later is by tagging them with keywords—text metadata attached to the image files to categorize them by subject or association.

For example, the image in the illustration at the right could be tagged with the keywords Architecture and Germany, and could therefore be located by searching for either or both of those tags. If the Thumbnail Badges option is activated in the Library View Options dialog box, photos with keyword tags are identified by a keywords badge () in the lower right corner of the thumbnail.

Photo has keywords

You can apply keywords to your photos individually or tag an entire series of images with shared metadata in one operation, thereby linking them by association and making them easier to access amongst all the photos that make up your library. Keywords added to images in Lightroom can be read by Adobe applications such as Bridge, Photoshop, and Photoshop Elements, and by other applications that support XMP metadata.

Viewing keyword tags

Because you applied keyword tags to the images for this lesson during the import process, the thumbnails in the Grid view and the Filmstrip are all marked with the keywords badge. Let's review the keywords you already attached to these photos.

1 Make sure that you are still in the Grid view, and then select the Lesson 5 folder in the Folders panel.

2 In the right panel group, expand the Keywording panel. If necessary, expand the Keyword Tags pane at the top of the Keywording panel. By selecting each thumbnail in the Grid view in turn you can confirm that all the images in the Lesson 5 folder share the keywords "Lesson 5" and "Europe."

Tip: Clicking the thumbnail badge of an image in Grid view will automatically expand the Keywording panel.

3 Select any one of the photos in the Lesson 5 folder. In the Keyword Tags pane at the top of the Keywording pane, select the text "Lesson 5" and press the Backspace key on your keyboard to delete it.

4 Click anywhere in the Grid view, and then choose Edit > Select All or press Ctrl+A / Command+A to select all the Lesson 5 photos. In the Keyword Tags pane, the keyword "Lesson 5" is now marked with an asterisk to indicate that this tag is not shared by every image in the selection.

5 Expand the Keyword List panel.

Tip: You can apply an existing keyword tag to selected images by clicking the tag in the Keyword Suggestions pane in the Keywording panel. To remove a tag from a selected photo or photos, either delete the word from the Keyword Tags pane in the Keywording panel, or click the checkbox to disable that keyword in the Keyword List panel.

In the Keyword List, a check mark in front of the keyword "Europe" indicates that this tag is shared by every image in the selection, while the tag "Lesson 5" is marked with a dash—indicating that it attached to some, but not all, of the selected images. The image count to the right of the Lesson 5 tag shows that it is shared by only ten of the eleven images.

6 With all eleven images still selected, click the dash mark in front of the Lesson 5 tag to reinstate the deleted tag; a check mark replaces the dash and the image count for the Lesson 5 keyword increases to 11.

Adding keyword tags

You already added keywords to your images during the process of importing them into your Lightroom library. Once the images have been added to your Lightroom library, you can add more keywords by using the Keywording panel.

1 In the Folders panel, select the Architecture subfolder inside the Lesson 5 folder, and then choose Edit > Select All or press Ctrl+A / Command+A.

2 In the Keywording panel, click the grey text "Click Here To Add Keywords" in the text box below the Keyword Tags pane and type **Nordingen, Germany**, being sure to add the comma as shown in the illustration at the right, below.

Always use a comma to separate keywords. Using a space or period will not work; Lightroom would treat both "Nordingen Germany" and "Nordingen. Germany" as a single keyword.

3 Press Enter / Return. The new keywords are listed in alphabetical order in the Keyword Tags panel and in the Keyword List panel.

4 In the Folders panel, select the Lesson 5 folder, and then choose Edit > Invert Selection to select all the images other than the four in the Architecture folder.

5 In the Keywording panel, click in the text box below the Keyword Tags pane and type **France**. Press Enter / Return.

6 Choose Edit > Select None or press Ctrl+D / Command+D on your keyboard.

Working with keyword sets and nesting keywords

You can use the Keyword Set pane of the Keywording panel to work with *keyword sets*; groups of keyword tags compiled for a particular purpose. You could create a set of keywords for a specific project, another set for a special occasion, and one for your friends and family. Lightroom provides three basic keyword set presets. You can use these sets as they are or as starting points for creating sets of your own.

▶ **Tip:** Keyword sets are a convenient way to have the keywords you need at hand as you work on different collections in your library. A single keyword tag may be included in any number of keyword sets. If you don't see the Lightroom presets in the Keyword Set menu, open the Lightroom Preferences and click the Presets tab. In the Lightroom Defaults options, click Restore Keyword Set Presets.

1. Expand the Keyword Set pane in the Keywording panel, if necessary, and then choose Wedding Photography from the Keyword Set menu. You can see that the keywords in the set would indeed be helpful in organizing the shots from a big event. Look at the categories covered by the other Lightroom keyword sets. You can use these as templates for your own keyword sets by editing them to suit your needs and saving your changes as a new preset.

Grouping your keywords in Keyword Sets is one way to keep your keywords organized; another handy technique is to nest related tags in a keywords hierarchy.

2. In the Keyword List panel, Ctrl-click / Command-click to select the keywords "France" and "Germany" and drag the selected tags onto the keyword "Europe."

3. Click the triangle at the left of the Europe tag in the keyword list to see the France and Germany tags nested inside it.

4. In the keyword list, drag the Nordingen tag from the bottom of the keyword list onto the keyword "Germany," and then expand the Germany tag.

5. Right-click / Control-click the keyword "France" and choose Create Keyword Tag Inside "France" from the context menu.

6. In the Keyword Tag text box, type **Normandy**. In the Synonyms text box just below, type **Normandie**. Make sure all the Keyword Tag Options are activated as shown in the illustration below, and then click Create.

Include On Export Includes the keyword tag when your photos are exported.

Export Containing Keywords Includes the parent tag when your photos are exported.

Export Synonyms Includes any synonyms associated with the keyword tag when your photos are exported.

7. Expand the keyword "France," and then right-click / Control-click the keyword "Normandy" and choose Create Keyword Tag Inside "Normandy" from the

context menu. In the Keyword Tag text box, type **Etretat**. Make sure all the Keyword Tag Options are activated as in step 6, and then click Create. Expand the keyword "Normandy," so you can see all the tags in your nested hierarchy.

8 In the Folders panel, select the Landscapes subfolder inside the Europe folder, and then choose Edit > Select All or press Ctrl+A / Command+A. Drag the Normandy tag from the Keyword List panel onto any of the selected images in the Grid view.

Both the check mark in front of the Normandy tag in the keyword list, and the image count to the right show that this keyword has been applied to all four selected photos.

9 In the Grid view or the Filmstrip, Ctrl-click / Command click the two flat landscape images to deselect them, leaving only the two photos featuring stone cliffs selected.

10 Drag the keyword "Etretat" from the Keyword List panel onto either of the selected images in the Grid view. The check mark in front of the Etretat tag in the keyword list, and the image count to the right show that this keyword has been applied to both of the selected photos.

Searching by keywords

Once you have taken the time to organize your images by adding keywords and other metadata such as ratings, flags, and labels, it will be very easy to set up sophisticated and detailed filters to find exactly the photo you're looking for.

For now, we'll look at some techniques for searching the photos in your library by keywords alone.

▶ **Tip:** If you find that you cannot open two panels in one of the side panel groups at the same time, right-click / Control-click the header of any panel in the group and disable the Solo Mode option in the context menu

1 In the left panel group, collapse the Navigator, Collections, and Publish Services panels if necessary, so that you can clearly see the contents of the Catalog and Folders Panels. In the Folders panel, select the Lesson 5 folder, and then choose Edit > Select None or press Ctrl+D / Command+D.

2 Use the Thumbnails slider in the Toolbar to reduce the size of the thumbnails until you can see all eleven images in the Grid view. If the Filter Bar is not already visible above the Grid view, choose View > Show Filter Bar, or press the Backslash key (\).

3 In the right panel group, collapse the Histogram, Quick Develop, and Keywording panels, if necessary, so that you can clearly see the whole of the expanded Keyword List panel.

4 In the Keyword list panel, move your pointer over the entry for the keyword "France," and then click the white arrow that appears to the right of the image count.

▶ **Tip:** To transfer lists of keywords between computers or share them with colleagues who are also working in Lightroom, use the Export Keywords and Import Keywords commands, which you'll find in the Metadata menu.

In the left panel group, All Photographs is now selected in the Catalog panel, indicating that your entire catalog has been searched for photos with the France tag. The Metadata filter has been activated in the Filter bar at the top of the work area, and the Grid view now displays only those seven images in your library that are tagged with the keyword "France."

5 In the Keyword column at the left of the Metadata filter pane, click the triangle to expand the France entry, and then click Normandy.

In the Grid view, only the four photos with the Normandy tag are still visible.

6   In the Filter bar at the top of the work area, click None to disable the Metadata filter, then choose Text from the Library Filter options.

7   In the Text filter bar, choose Keywords from the first menu and Contain from the second menu, noting the options available in each menu; then type **Etretat** in the text box at the right and press Enter.

Now, only the two photos of the stone cliffs at Etretat, in Normandy, France are still displayed in the Grid view. Of course, the true power of the Library filters only comes into play when you take advantage of the various search features to set up more complex filters based on a combination of criteria—but this exercise should have given you at least a glimpse of the possibilities.

8   Disable the Text filter by clicking None in the Library Filter options in the center of the Filter bar. In the Folders panel, select the Lesson 5 folder, and then choose Edit > Select None or press Ctrl+D / Command+D.

Using flags and ratings

The Attribute filters in the Filter bar allow you to search and sort your images according to attributes such as flags and ratings.

When you choose Attribute from the Library Filter options in the Filter bar, the Filter bar expands to display controls for sorting your images by flag status, star rating, color label, copy status, or any combination of these attributes.

Flagging images

Assigning flags to sort the good images from the rejects can be a good way to begin organizing a group of photos. An image can be flagged as a pick (⚐), a reject (⚑), or left unflagged (⚐).

1   Choose Attribute from the Library filter options in the Filter bar. The Filter bar expands to show the Attribute filter controls.

2 If the Toolbar is not already visible below the Grid view, press the T key. Click the triangle at the right side of the Toolbar and activate the Flagging tool in the menu to show the Flag As Pick and Flag As Reject buttons in the Toolbar.

▶ **Tip:** In the Grid and Loupe views, you'll find tools for adding ratings, flags, and color labels in the Toolbar. In the Compare and Survey views you can change these attributes using the controls beneath the images. You can also flag, rate, or color label a selected image by using the Set Flag, Set Rating, or Set Color Label commands in the Photo menu.

3 In the Folders panel, select the Architecture subfolder inside the Lesson 5 folder.

4 In the Grid view, select the photo of the staircase: DSC_3647.jpg. If the Flags option is activated in the Library View Options dialog box, a grey flag icon in the upper left corner of the image cell indicates that this photo is unflagged. If necessary, hold the pointer over the image cell to see the flag, or disable Show Clickable Items On Mouse Over Only in the Library View Options dialog box.

5 To change the flag status to Flagged, click the Flag As Pick button (⚑) in the Toolbar. Note that the photo is now marked with a white flag icon in the upper left corner of the image cell.

6 Click the white flag button in the Attribute Filter bar. The Grid view displays only the image that you just flagged. The view is now filtered to display only flagged images from the Architecture folder.

Tip: You can use the Library > Refine Photos command to sort your photos quickly on the basis of their flagging status. Choose Library > Refine Photos, and then click Refine in the Refine Photos dialog box; any unflagged photos are flagged as rejects and the picks are reset to unflagged status.

Lightroom offers a variety of ways to flag a photo. To flag a photo as a pick, choose Photo > Set Flag > Flagged or press the P key on your keyboard. Click the flag icon at the top left corner of the image cell to toggle between Unflagged and Pick status. To flag an image as a reject, choose Photo > Set Flag > Rejected, press the X key, or Alt-click / Option-click the flag icon in the corner of the image cell. To remove a flag from an image, choose Photo > Set Flag > Unflagged or press the U key. To set any flag status for an image, right-click / Control-click the flag icon in the corner of the image cell and choose Flagged, Unflagged, or Rejected from the context menu.

7   Click the grey flag button—the flag in the center—in the Attribute Filter bar. The Grid view now displays any photos flagged as Picks and all unflagged photos, so once again we see all of the images in the Architecture folder.

8   In the Filter bar, click None to disable the Attribute filters.

Assigning ratings

A quick and easy way to sort your images as you review and evaluate them is to assign each photo a rating on a scale from one to five stars.

1   In the Grid view, select the image with the green street lamp: DSC_3637.jpg.

2   Press the 3 key on your keyboard. The message "Set Rating to 3" appears briefly and the photo is now marked with three stars in the lower left of its image cell.

Tip: If you don't see the star rating in the image cell, choose View > View Options and make sure Rating And Label is activated in the image cell display options.

It's easy to change the rating for a selected image; simply press another key between 1 and 5 to apply a new rating or press the 0 key to remove the rating altogether.

3   If necessary, click the triangle at the right of the Toolbar and make sure that the Rating controls are activated in the menu. The stars in the Toolbar reflect the rating you just applied to the selected image.

4   Click the stars in the Toolbar to change the rating. Click the current star rating to remove it.

You can also assign ratings in the Metadata panel, by choosing from the Photo > Set Rating menu, or by right-clicking / Control-clicking a thumbnail and choosing from the Set Rating submenu in the context menu.

Working with color labels

Color labeling can be a very versatile tool for organizing your workflow. Unlike flags and ratings, color labels have no predefined meanings; you can attach your own meaning to each color and customize separate label sets for specific tasks.

While setting up a print job you might assign the red label to images you wish to proof, a blue label to those that need retouching, or a green label to mark images as approved. For another project, you might use the different colors to indicate levels of urgency.

Applying Color Labels

You can use the colored buttons in the Toolbar to assign color labels to your images. If you don't see the color label buttons, click the triangle at the right of the Toolbar and choose Color Label from the menu. You can also click the color label icon displayed in a photo's image cell (a small grey rectangle, for an unlabeled image) and choose from the menu. Alternatively, choose Photo > Set Color Label and choose from the menu; you'll notice that four of the five color labels have keyboard shortcuts.

To see—and set—color labels in the Grid view image cells, choose View > View Options or right-click / Control-click any of the thumbnails and choose View Options from the context menu to open the Library View Options dialog box. On the Grid View tab in The Library View Options dialog box, activate Show Grid Extras. In the Compact Cell Extras options, you can choose Label or Rating And Label from either the Bottom Label or Top Label menus. In the Expanded Cell Extras options, activate the Include Color Label checkbox.

Editing Color Labels and using Color Label Sets

You can rename the color labels to suit your own purposes and create separate label sets tailored to different parts of your workflow. The Lightroom default options in the Photo > Set Color Label menu are Red, Yellow, Green, Blue, Purple, and None. You can change the color label set by choosing Metadata > Color Label Set, and then choosing either the Bridge or Lightroom default sets, or the Review Status set.

The Review Status label set gives you an idea of how you might assign your own label names to help you keep organized. The options in the Review Status set are To Delete, Color Correction Needed, Good To Use, Retouching Needed, To Print, and None.

You can use this label set as it is or as a starting point for creating your own sets. To open the Edit Color Label Set dialog box, choose Metadata > Color Label Set > Edit. You can enter your own name for each color, and then choose Save Current Settings As New Preset from the Presets menu.

Searching by color label

In the Filter bar, click Attribute to see the Attribute filter controls. You can limit your search to a single color label by clicking just one button, or activate more than one button at once. To disable an active color label button, simply click it again. You can use the color label search buttons together with other Attribute filters, or to refine a Text or Metadata search.

The Attribute filters, including the Color Label filters, are also available in the bar above the thumbnails in the Filmstrip.

Adding metadata

You can leverage the metadata information attached to the image files to help you organize and manage your photo library. Much of the metadata, such as capture date, exposure time, focal length and other camera settings, is generated by your camera, but you can also add your own metadata to make it easier search and sort your catalog. In fact, you did just that when you applied keywords, ratings, and color labels to your images. In addition, Lightroom supports the information standards evolved by the International Press Telecommunications Council (IPTC). This standard includes metadata entries for descriptions, keywords, categories, credits, and origins.

You can use the Metadata panel in the right panel group to inspect or edit the metadata attached to a selected image.

1   Select the image DSC_3655.jpg: the photo featuring a medieval city wall with a domed tower.

2   Expand the Metadata panel. If necessary, hide the Filmstrip or collapse the other panels in the right panel group so that you can see as much of the Metadata panel as possible. Choose Default from the Metadata Set menu in the header of the Metadata panel.

Even the default metadata set exposes a great deal of information about the image. Although most of this metadata has been generated by the camera, some of it can still be very useful in sorting your photos; you could filter images by capture date, search for shots taken with a particular lens, or easily separate photos taken on different cameras. However, the default set displays only a subset an image's metadata.

3   Choose EXIF And IPTC from the Metadata Set menu in header of the Metadata panel. Scroll down in the Metadata panel to get an idea of the kinds of information that can be applied to an image.

4   For the purposes of this exercise, you can choose Quick Describe from the Metadata Set menu.

In the Quick Describe metadata set, the Metadata panel shows the File-name, Copy Name (if the image is a virtual copy), Folder, Rating, and some EXIF and IPTC metadata. You can use the Metadata panel to add a title and caption to a photo, attach a copyright notice, provide details about the photographer and the location where the photo was shot, and also change the star rating.

5 Click in the Metadata panel to assign the image a rating, and type **Domed Tower** in the Title text box.

6 Control-click / Command-click the image DSC_3661 (the photo with the arched door) to add it to the selection. In the Metadata panel you can see that the folder name and the camera model are shared by both files; items not shared by both images now show the entry <mixed>. Changes made to any of the items in the metadata panel, even those with mixed values, will affect both of the selected images. This is a convenient way to edit items such as copyright details for a whole batch of images at the same time.

Storage of metadata

File information is stored using the Extensible Metadata Platform (XMP) standard. XMP is built on XML. In the case of camera raw files that have a proprietary file format, XMP isn't written into the original files. To avoid file corruption, XMP metadata is stored in a separate file called a sidecar file. For all other file formats supported by Lightroom (JPEG, TIFF, PSD, and DNG), XMP metadata is written into the files in the location specified for that data.

XMP facilitates the exchange of metadata between Adobe applications and across publishing workflows. For example, you can save metadata from one file as a template, and then import the metadata into other files. Metadata that is stored in other formats, such as EXIF, IPTC (IIM), and TIFF, is synchronized and described with XMP so that it can be more easily viewed and managed. To find out more about Metadata, please refer to Lightroom Help.

—From Lightroom Help

Using the Painter tool

Of all the features Lightroom provides to help you organize your growing image library, the Painter tool () is the most flexible. By simply dragging the Painter tool across your images in the Grid view you can add metadata, assign keywords, labels, ratings, and flags—and even apply developing settings, rotate your photos, or add them to the Quick Collection.

When you pick the Painter tool up from its well in the Toolbar, the Paint menu appears beside the empty tool well. From the Paint menu you can choose which settings or attributes you wish to apply to your images.

The appearance of the Painter tool's spray can icon changes slightly, depending on which option you choose. The illustration below shows the different spray can icons that correspond to the Paint menu options. Reading from left to right, they are: Keywords, Labels, Flag, Rating, Metadata, Settings, Rotation, and Target Collection.

In this exercise you'll use the Painter tool to mark images with a color label.

1   Make sure that the Architecture folder is still selected in the Folders panel and that none of the images are selected in the Grid view. If you don't see the Painter tool in the Toolbar, click the triangle at the right side of the Toolbar and choose Painter from the tools menu.

2   Click the Painter tool to pock it up from its well in the Toolbar; then choose Label from the Paint menu, and click the red color label button.

3   The Painter tool is now "loaded." Move the pointer over any of the thumbnails in the Grid view and a red spray can icon appears.

4   Click the thumbnail in the Grid view and the Painter tool applies the red label. Whether you see the color as a tint in the image cell depends on your settings in the Library View Options dialog box. If you don't see the red color label marker (circled in the illustration at the right), choose View > Grid View Style > Show Extras.

5 Move the pointer back over the same thumbnail, and then hold down the Alt / Option key and; the cursor changes from the Painter tool spray can to an eraser. Click the thumbnail with the eraser cursor and the red color label is removed.

6 Release the Alt / Option key and click the image once more—but this time drag the spray can across all four images. You've applied the red color tag to all the images with one stroke. Hold down the Alt / Option key again, and then remove the label from all the one of the photos with a star rating.

7 Click Done at the right side of the Toolbar, or click the Painter tool's empty well, to drop the Painter tool and return the Toolbar to its normal state.

Finding and filtering files

Now that you're familiar with the different techniques for categorizing and marking your photos, it's time to see some results. Next you'll look at how easy it is to search and sort your images once they've been prepared in this way. You can now filter your images by rating or label or search for specific keywords and other metadata. There are a numerous ways to find the images you need but one of the most convenient is to use the Filter bar across the top of the Grid view.

Using the Filter bar to find photos

1 If you don't see the Filter bar above the Grid view, press the backslash key (\) or choose View > Show Filter Bar. In the Folders panel, select the Lesson 5 folder. If you don't see all eleven photos, choose Library > Show Photos In Subfolders.

The Filter bar contains three filter groups: Text, Attribute, and Metadata filters. Click any of these options and the Filter bar will expand to display the settings and controls you'll use to set up a filtered search. You can use these filters separately or combine them for a more sophisticated search.

Use the Text filter to search any text attached to your images, including filenames, keywords, captions, and the EXIF and IPTC metadata. The Attribute filter searches your photos by flag status, star rating, color label, or copy status. The Metadata filter enables you to set up to eight columns of criteria to refine your search. Choose from the menu at the right end of a column header to add or remove a column.

2 If the Text or Metadata filters are active, click None to disable them. Click Attribute to activate the Attribute filters. If any of the flag filters is still active from the previous exercise, click the highlighted flag to disable it, or choose Library > Filter By Flag > Reset This Filter.

3 In the Rating controls, click the first star to search for any image with a rating of one star or higher.

The grid view displays only the two images to which you've applied a star rating.

4 There are many options for refining your search. Click Text in the header of the Filter bar to add an additional filter. In the Text filter bar, open the first menu to see the search target options. You can narrow the search to Filename, Copy Name, Title, Caption, Keywords, or searchable IPTC and EXIF metadata, but for this exercise you can choose the search target Any Searchable Field. Click the second menu and choose Contains All.

5 In the search text box, type **tower**. Your narrowed search returns only one image in the Grid view.

6 In the Rating controls, click the first star to disable the current Rating filter or choose Library > Filter By Rating > Reset This Filter. Click Attribute in the header of the Filter bar to close the Attribute filter controls.

▶ **Tip:** In the search text box, add an exclamation mark (!) before any word to exclude it from the results. Add a plus sign (+) before any word to apply the "Starting With" rule only to that word. Add a plus sign (+) after a word to apply the "Ending With" rule only to that word.

7 In the Text filter bar, clear the search term "tower" by clicking the x icon at the right of the text box, and then type **France**.

The Grid view now displays only seven of the photos in the Lesson 5 folder.

8 Type a space after the word France, and then type **!Normandy** (note the exclamation mark). The search is narrowed to find those images with searchable text that contains the word France, but doesn't contain the word Normandy. The Grid view now displays only three photos. Leave the Text filters set as it is for the next exercise.

Using the Metadata filter

1 Click Metadata in the header of the Filter bar to open the Metadata filter pane. Choose Default Columns from the menu at the far right of the Filter bar header.

2 Click Date in the header of the first column to see the wide range of search criteria from which you can choose for each of up to eight columns. Choose Aspect Ratio from the menu as the criteria for this column, and then choose Portrait from the Aspect Ratio options in the column. The selection in the Grid view is narrowed to two images.

3 Click Text in the header of the Filter bar to disable the Text filter. This search returns four photos from the Lesson 5 folder.

4 Click the lock icon at the right of the Filter bar header. This will lock the current filter so that it remains active when you change the image source for the search.

5 In the Catalog panel, click All Photographs. The Grid view now displays every portrait format image in your catalog.

As you can see, there are endless possibilities for combining filters to find just the image you're looking for.

6 Click None in the Filter bar to disable all filters. Click the Lesson 5 folder in the Folders panel

Using the filters in the Filmstrip

The Attribute filter controls are also available in the header the Filmstrip. As in the Filter bar the Filter Presets menu lists filter presets and offers the option to save your filter settings as a custom preset, which will then be added to the menu.

The Default Columns preset opens the four default columns of the Metadata search options: Date, Camera, Lens, and Label. Choose Filters Off to turn off all filters and collapse the Filter bar. Select the Flagged filter preset to display photos with a Pick flag. Use the Location Columns preset to filter photos by their Country, State/ Province, City, and Location metadata. The Rated filter preset displays any photos that match the current star rating criteria. Choose Unrated to see all the photos without a star rating.

▶ **Tip:** If you don't see any filter presets in the presets menu, open Lightroom Preferences and click Restore Library Filter Presets under Lightroom Defaults on the Presets tab.

1   Choose Flagged from the Filter Presets menu at the top right of the Filmstrip. The Attribute filter bar opens above the Grid view. The Grid view and the Filmstrip show only one photo that you flagged as a pick in a previous exercise.

2   Click the white flag icon in the header of the Filmstrip to disable the current filter, and then click the red color label button. The Attribute filter settings change in the Filter bar above the Grid view and both the Grid view and the filmstrip display only the image that you labeled with the Painter tool.

▶ **Tip:** To save time and effort setting up searches, save your filter settings as a new preset. Specify criteria for any combination of Text, Attribute, and Metadata filters. Then choose Save Current Settings As New Preset from the Custom Filter menu in the Filter bar or the Filmstrip.

3   To disable all filters and display all the images in the Lesson 5 folder, choose Filters Off from the Filter Presets menu or click the switch at the far right of the Filmstrip's header.

Reconnecting missing files and folders

Remember that when you import a photo into your library, Lightroom adds the image file's name and address to the library catalog file, and displays an entry for the folder in which the photo is stored in the Folders panel.

If you rename or move a photo—or a folder—while you're outside the Lightroom workspace the link to the catalog will be broken and Lightroom may no longer be able to locate the image file.

Lightroom will alert you to the problem by marking the thumbnail of the missing photo—or the entry for the missing folder in the Folders panel—with a question mark icon.

1 Right-click / Control-click one of the photos of yellow chairs and choose Show In Explorer / Show In Finder from the context menu.

2 In the Explorer / Finder window, change the name of the selected file to **cafe_chairs.jpg**. Change the name of the Landscapes folder inside the Lesson 5 folder to **French Coast**.

3 Back in the Grid view in Lightroom, you'll notice the missing file icon in the upper right corner of the image cell. Click the icon, and then click Locate in the dialog box.

4 In the Locate file dialog box, select the renamed file and then click Select.

When you have merely moved, rather than renamed files, you can activate the Find Nearby Missing Photos option in the Locate file dialog box and Lightroom will find any other missing photos in the same folder automatically.

5 Click Confirm to verify that cafe_chairs.jpg is the correct file despite the changed name. You have now reestablished the link to your renamed file; the missing file icon no longer appears in its image cell.

6 In the Folders panel, the Landscapes folder is now dimmed and marked with a question mark icon. Right-click Control-click the Landscapes folder; you *could* choose Find Missing Folder from the context menu, and then locate the renamed folder as you did for the missing file, but we'll take this opportunity to look at a different method instead.

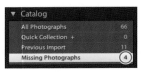

7 Choose Library > Find Missing Photos. A new temporary collection named Missing Photographs is created in the Catalog panel. The new collection is automatically selected and the four photos from the Landscapes folder appear in the Grid view.

Select each image in turn; the missing photo icon appears on each image cell.

8 Click the missing photo icon on any of the images in the Grid view and follow the same steps you used previously. Navigating to the renamed folder and locate the selected file. This time, activate the Find Nearby Missing Photos option in the Locate file dialog box and Lightroom will find the other three missing photos in the renamed folder automatically. Click Select.

9 The renamed folder is now listed in the Folders panel. Although the missing Landscapes folder is still listed in the Folders panel, it now shows an image count of 0. Right-click / Control-click the empty Landscapes folder and choose Remove from the context menu.

10 Right-click / Control-click the Missing Photographs folder in the Catalog panel and choose Remove This Temporary Collection from the context menu.

This concludes the lesson on organizing your image library. You've learned about structuring your folders, sorting and grouping images into collections, and a variety of methods for tagging and marking your photos to make them easier to find by applying a range of search filters.

However, it's worth discussing a final step that is invaluable in managing your growing library of photos: perform regular catalog backups. The library catalog contains not only your entire image database but also all the preview images and metadata, together with records of your collections and all your settings from the Develop, Slideshow, Web and Print modules. It is as important to make backups of your catalog as it is to keep copies of your image files. You'll learn more about backing-up your library in Lesson 10, "Creating Backups and Exporting Photos."

Before you move on to the next lesson, take a moment to refresh some of what you've learned by reading through the review on the next page.

Review questions

1 Can you keep multiple copies of the same master image in different folders?

2 What is a Smart Collection?

3 Why would you create a Stack?

4 What are keyword tags?

5 What are the three modes in the Filter bar?

Review answers

1 You can't keep copies of a master image in separate folders because the same image cannot be added to the Lightroom catalog twice. Although the image must reside in a single folder, it can be included in any number of Collections.

2 A Smart collection can be configured to search the library for images that meet specified criteria. Smart collections stay up-to-date by automatically adding any newly imported photos that meet the criteria you've specified.

3 Stacks can be used to group similar photos and thereby reduce the number of thumbnails displayed at one time in the Grid view and the Filmstrip. Only the top image in a stack appears in the thumbnail display but the stack can be expanded and contracted by clicking the thumbnail.

4 Keyword tags are text added to the metadata of an image to describe its content or classify it in one way or another. Shared keywords link images by subject, date, or some other association. Keywords help to locate, identify, and sort photos in the catalog. Like other metadata, keyword tags are stored either in the photo file or (in the case of proprietary camera raw files) in XMP sidecar files. Keywords applied in Lightroom can be read by Adobe applications such as Bridge, Photoshop, or Photoshop Elements, and by other applications that support XMP metadata.

5 The Filter bar offers three filter groups: Text, Attribute, and Metadata filters. Using combinations of these filters you can search the image library for metadata text, filter searches by flag, copy status, rating, or label, and specify a broad range of customizable metadata search criteria.

6 DEVELOPING AND EDITING

Lesson overview

Artificial light sources, unusual shooting conditions, and incorrect camera exposure settings can all cause faults in an image. In the Develop module Lightroom delivers a suite of powerful developing tools to quickly rectify these problems in your photos.

This lesson introduces you to editing options from easy-to-use presets and retouching tools to an array of specialized settings. Along the way you'll pick up a little computer graphics background knowledge as you become familiar with some basic techniques:

- Applying Develop presets
- Cropping, rotating, and flipping images
- Using the History and Snapshots panels
- Removing blemishes
- Correcting color problems and adjusting the tonal range
- Sharpening images and removing noise
- Making discrete color adjustments
- Working with black and white and split tone effects
- Adjusting specific areas of an image
- Working with an external image editor

 You'll probably need between one and two hours to complete this lesson.

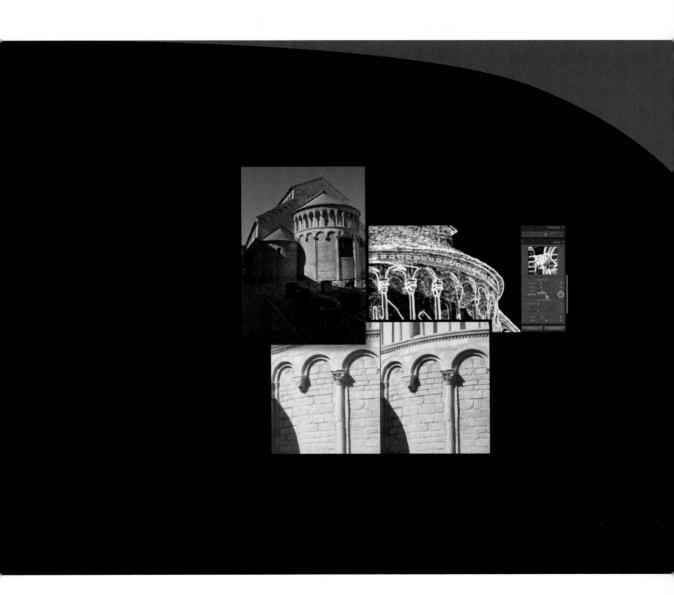

Fine-tune and polish your photographs with precise,
easy-to-use tools—secure in the knowledge that the
modifications you make in Lightroom won't alter your
master image. Take your developing a step beyond
just correcting your images; use the Develop module
controls creatively to customize your own special
effects, and then save them as develop presets.

Getting started

This lesson assumes that you are already familiar with the Lightroom workspace and with moving between the different modules. If you find that you need more background information as you go, refer to Lightroom Help, or review the previous lessons in this book.

Before you begin, make sure that you have correctly copied the Lessons folder from the CD in the back of this book onto your computer's hard disk and created the LR3CIB Library Catalog file as detailed in "Copying the Classroom in a Book files" on page 2 and "Creating a catalog file for working with this book" on page 3.

1   Start Lightroom.

2   In the Adobe Photoshop Lightroom - Select Catalog dialog box, make sure the file LR3CIB Library Catalog.lrcat is selected under Select A Recent Catalog To Open, and then click Open.

3   Lightroom will open in the screen mode and workspace module that were active when you last quit. If necessary, click Library in the Module Picker to switch to the Library module.

Importing images into the library

The first step is to import the images for this lesson into the Lightroom library.

1   In the Library module, click the Import button below the left panel group.

2 If the Import dialog box appears in compact mode, click the Show More Options button at the lower left of the dialog box to see all the options in the expanded Import dialog box.

3 Under Source at the left of the expanded Import dialog box, navigate to the Lessons folder that you copied into the LR3CIB folder on your hard disk. Select the Lesson 6 folder. Ensure that all three images in the Lesson 6 folder are checked for import.

4 In the import options above the thumbnail previews, click Add to add the imported photos to your catalog without moving or copying them.

5 Under File Handling at the right of the expanded Import dialog box, choose Minimal from the Render Previews menu and ensure that the Don't Import Selected Duplicates option is activated.

6 Under Apply During Import, choose None from both the Develop Settings menu and the Metadata menu and type **Lesson 6** in the Keywords text box. Make sure your settings are exactly as shown in the illustration below, and then click Import.

The three images are imported from the Lesson 6 folder and now appear in both the Grid view of the Library module and in the Filmstrip across the bottom of the Lightroom workspace.

Quick Develop

In the Library module, the Quick Develop panel in the right panel group provides a range of simple controls that enable you to make color and tonal corrections, apply developing presets, and crop an image without even switching to the Develop module.

Tip: You can select a series of images in the Grid view or the Filmstrip and apply a develop preset—or any other Quick Develop adjustment—to all of them at once.

1   In the Grid view, double-click the photo DSC_0653.NEF (an image of a mother and child) to see it in Loupe view.

2   In the right panel group, expand the Quick Develop panel.

3   From the Saved Preset menu, choose the BW Creative - Antique Grayscale, Color Creative - Direct Positive, and BW Creative - Sepia Tone presets in turn. The Loupe view shows the effect of each develop preset.

Tip: When saving and naming your own presets, you should keep it in mind that they will be listed in alphabetical order. You can group related presets in the list by adding a common prefix or sequential numbering to their names so that they will be listed in the order in which they should be applied.

Develop presets apply a combination of different developing settings to your images at the same time, enabling you to achieve dramatic results with a single click. As presets are listed in alphabetical order, these Lightroom presets with the prefix "Creative" appear high in the Saved Preset menu but it's actually preferable that you apply them as a last step after you've made any color and tonal corrections that are necessary.

4   To return the image to its original state, choose Default Settings from the Saved Preset menu.

5   Expand the White Balance pane in the Quick Develop panel. From the White Balance menu, choose the Daylight, Cloudy, and Shade presets in turn. You'll notice that the colors in the image become progressively warmer. Select the white balance you prefer; we chose the Daylight preset.

Adjusting the white balance—and most of the other develop settings—means making some very subjective choices.

If you wish to stay fairly close to the look of the original image, start with the As Shot setting in the Saved Presets menu, and then fine-tune the Temperature and Tint settings. If you feel that the white balance was set incorrectly when a shot was taken—perhaps as a result of artificial lighting—or if you wish to create a specific effect, use an appropriate preset from the menu as a starting point.

6   Expand the Tone Control pane and click the Auto Tone button. As the original photo was too bright, Auto Tone darkens the whole image considerably—exposing slightly more detail in the sky and water but effectively losing detail from the overly darkened faces. You can use the controls below the Auto Tone button to fine-tune the tonal balance of the image. In this case, you'll increase the detail visible in the shadowed areas of the image—including the faces—by adjusting the Fill Light control. Click the button on the far right three or four times to increase the fill light in relatively large increments.

You've already improved the image considerably with just a few clicks but you can do a lot more to enhance this photo in the Develop module later in this lesson.

While you're experimenting with the settings in the Quick Develop panel you can reset any control to its original state by simply clicking the name of the control. Clicking the Reset All button located at the bottom of the Quick Develop panel will revert the image to its original state.

In the next section of the lesson you'll explore the Develop module panels and learn how to use a variety of developing and editing tools. Once you have that background knowledge you can come back and apply what you've learned to get even better results from the Quick Develop panel.

7   Click Develop in the Module Picker or press the D key to switch to the Develop module.

The Develop module

The Develop module contains all the tools and controls you need to correct and enhance your images. To assist and guide your workflow, the tools in the Develop module panels are arranged from top to bottom in the order in which they would ordinarily be used. All of the controls are easy enough for a beginner to use and yet have the depth and power required by the advanced user. The Develop module offers two working views: the Loupe view and the split-screen Before/After view. The Toolbar across the bottom of the work area contains buttons for switching between the views and a slightly different suite of controls for each viewing mode.

At the top of the left panel group, the Navigator helps you find your way around a zoomed image, previews the effects of the developing presets, and reviews past stages in the developing history. The Navigator panel also contains controls for setting the zoom levels in the working views.

The Snapshots panel is used to record important stages in the development of a photo and the History panel keeps track of every modification made to the image—including the changes you made in the Library module.

At the top of the right panel group is the Histogram panel. Immediately below the Histogram is an array of tools for cropping, removing flaws and red eyes, applying graduated adjustments and painting develop settings directly onto an image selectively. Clicking any of these tools opens a drawer with controls and settings for that tool.

Below these editing tools is the Basic panel: your starting point for color correction and tonal adjustments. In many cases this may be the only panel you need to achieve the results you want. The remaining panels offer specialized tools for various image enhancement tasks.

For example, you can use the Tone Curve controls to increase the contrast in the mid-tones by fine-tuning the distribution of the tonal range or the Detail controls to sharpen an image and reduce noise.

It is not intended that you use every tool on every photo. In many circumstance you may make only a few adjustments to an image. However, when you wish to polish a special photo—or if you need to work with shots captured at less than ideal camera settings—the Develop module contains the all tools you need.

In the next exercise you'll crop and rotate the image, remove some spots, and then move on to the color adjustment tools.

Cropping and rotating images

The Crop Overlay tool makes it simple to improve your composition, crop unwanted edge detail, and even straighten your image.

1 If you're not already in Loupe view in the Develop module, press the D key or choose View > Go To Develop to switch to it now. Hide the Filmstrip and the left panel group to make more space in the work area.

2 Click the Crop Overlay tool (▦)button just below the Histogram panel, or press R. A crop overlay rectangle is placed over the image in the Loupe view and controls for the tool appear in the right panel group.

3 From the Aspect menu, choose Original. If the lock button shows an open lock icon, click the lock button to close the lock. The closed lock will constrain the aspect ratio while cropping.

You can specify a custom crop ratio by choosing Enter Custom from the Aspect menu. Your new Aspect Ratio will be added to the Aspect menu for later use; it will also be listed as a sorting and filter criteria.

4 Drag the top left handle of the crop overlay rectangle down and to the right. As you drag, you'll notice that the crop rectangle is resized from the center

while the image moves so that the cropped portion is always centered in the Loupe view. Release the mouse button when the horizon is roughly aligned with the guideline two-thirds of the way up the image as shown below.

5   Click outside the crop overlay rectangle and drag to rotate the photo. As you drag, additional grid lines appear to help you straighten the image. Release the mouse button when the horizon is aligned with the grid.

6   Click inside the crop overlay rectangle and drag to reposition the image. You'll notice that you cannot drag the image upwards or to the left because the image will move only until its edge touches the border of the cropping rectangle, which is different from what you might be used to in Photoshop.

7   Reduce the size of the crop overlay rectangle further by dragging the bottom right handle upwards and to the left. Drag the image to reposition it so that the horizon is aligned with the horizontal guide as shown in the illustration below.

8 To exit cropping mode, press R on your keyboard or click the Crop Overlay tool button again. The cropped image is displayed in the Loupe view.

▶ **Tip:** You can return and adjust a crop at any time by reactivating the Crop Overlay tool. The crop becomes "live" again—the entire image becomes visible once more and you can resize the cropping rectangle or reposition the image as you wish.

Undoing, redoing, and remembering changes

Lightroom offers several options for undoing and redoing changes and recalling key stages in the develop process.

Using the Undo and Redo commands

The Edit > Undo command (Ctrl+Z / Command+Z) lets you undo the last command executed; pressing Ctrl+Y / Command+Shift+Z will redo the last command undone. To jump backward and forward in the editing history by more than one step at a time, use the History panel.

The History panel

1 Press F7 or click the triangle in the left border of the workspace to show the left panel group. If necessary, collapse other panels to see the History panel.

● **Note:** If you return an image to a previous state by clicking an entry in the History panel, and then make any new adjustment to the image, all entries above your current position are replaced by the new command.

2 Expand the History panel. You can see a long list of commands that have already been performed; the most recent command appears at the top of the list. Even changes made in the Library module's Quick Edit panel are listed in the image's develop history.

3 Scroll down to the bottom of the list and click the first entry—Import [date and time of the import]—to see the image in its original state in the Loupe view.

4 Watch the Navigator panel as you move the pointer slowly up the list of commands in the History panel. The Navigator preview shows how the image looked at each stage of its developing history.

5 Scroll up to the top of the list and click the last entry—*Crop Rectangle*—to return the image to its most recent edited state.

Creating snapshots

As the list in the History panel quickly becomes long and unwieldy, it's a good idea to save key steps in an image's developing history as Snapshots for easy reference.

1 Scroll down in the History panel to the point just before you began using the Crop Overlay tool. Right-click / Control-click the most recent *Fill Light* entry (the highest in the list) and choose Create Snapshot from the context menu.

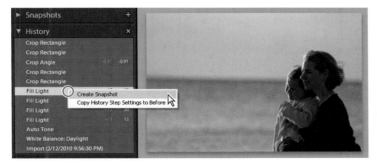

2 In the New Snapshot dialog box, type **Tonal Adjustments** as the name for your new snapshot, and then click Create.

3 In the History panel click the most-recent *Crop Rectangle* entry to return to your last editing step. Click the Create Snapshot button (+) in the header of the Snapshots panel to create a new snapshot. In the New Snapshot dialog box, type **Crop And Rotate** as the name for this snapshot, and then click Create.

4 Expand the Snapshots panel to see your two new entries. Click the listing for each of the snapshots in turn; in the History panel, even these actions are listed.

▶ **Tip:** To delete a snapshot, select its name in the Snapshots list and click the Delete Selected Snapshot button (-) in the header of the Snapshots panel or right-click / Command-click the snapshot and choose Delete from the context menu.

You now have a series of snapshots you can use to quickly return to important points in your developing process. In a later exercise, for example, we will return to an uncropped version of the image to demonstrate the spot removal tool.

Changing the Before image

By default, the original version of the image as it was imported is shown as the Before version in the Before / After view.

To designate a different state in the history of the image as the Before version, right-click / Control-click an entry in the History panel and choose Copy History Step Settings To Before. Repeat this step with the Import listing to reset the original state of the image as the Before view. To quickly toggle between the last edited state of an image and the Before view, press the Backslash key (\).

Creating virtual copies

There may be times when you wish to explore different treatments for an image without losing the work you've already done. You can create *virtual copies* of your photo and make modifications to each one independently just as if you had sepa-rate copies of the master file in your image library.

If a single photo is included in more than one collection, any changes you make to that image while you're working in any one of the collections will be visible in all the others. If you wish to modify an image for a specific collection without affecting the way the image appears elsewhere in your catalog you should use a virtual copy. You could include a full-frame, full-color version of a photo in a collection assem-bled for a slideshow and a tightly cropped, sepia-toned virtual copy of the same master file in another collection you've created for a print layout. Apply a unifying special effect to a whole collection of virtual copies without affecting the way the same images appear in your other collections and presentations.

The advantage in working with virtual copies is that you save a great deal of disk space. You'll still have only one copy of the original image file on your hard disk; when you make a virtual copy, Lightroom simply adds another entry for that image to the library catalog. Every change you make to the virtual copy is recorded in the new catalog entry so that not only the master file remains untouched but also your settings for any other virtual copy.

1   In the Snapshots panel, select the Tonal Adjustments snapshot that you created to record the last version of the image before it was cropped.

2   Choose Photo > Create Virtual Copy.

3   If necessary, press F6 to show the Filmstrip. You can see that there are now two
    copies of the same image visible in the Filmstrip.

4   Press G on your keyboard to switch to Grid view in the Library module. In Grid
    view and the Filmstrip, virtual copies are identified by a page peel icon in the
    lower left corner of the image.

By default, Lightroom will automatically
stack the virtual copy with the original in
the catalog. The image at the top of the
stack displays a stack icon.

5   Move the pointer over either of the
    stacked photos to see an image count.

6   To unstack the photos, select either image in the Grid view; then, right-click /
    Control-click the stack icon on either thumbnail and choose Unstack from the
    context menu.

You can use the Kind filter—one of the Attribute filters in the Filter bar—to filter
your library by file kind, isolating master images, virtual copies, or video files.

7   If you don't see the Filter bar at the top of the Grid view, choose View > Show
    Filter Bar, or press Backslash (\) on your keyboard. Click Attribute from the
    in the Filter bar; then click the second of the Kind filters—the icon with the
    turned-up corner. The Grid view displays only the virtual copy you just created.

8   Click None in the Filter bar to disable the Virtual Copies filter. Press D on your
    keyboard to switch back to Loupe view in the Develop module. Press F7 to hide
    the left panel group.

Removing spots

If you look at the photo carefully you'll notice three unsightly spots in the upper left of the image, caused by dirt on the lens. The Spot Removal tool is ideal for fixing blemishes like these.

1   In Loupe view in the Develop module, click the Spot Removal tool just below the Histogram panel, or press N. You'll notice that an extra pane opens below the tool buttons with controls and settings for the Spot Removal tool.

The Spot Removal tool works in either Clone mode or Heal mode. In Clone mode, the tool covers an imperfection in the photo (the target area) with an exact copy of another portion of the image (the sample area). Clone mode is ideal when you need to repair an area in the image which is patterned or where there are distinct repeated details such as bricks, stairs or even foliage. For areas in an image that have smooth color transitions—such as skin in a portrait shot or the sky in our example—use the Heal mode. In Heal mode, the Spot Removal Tool blends the sampled area with the target area rather than replacing it.

2   In the Spot Removal Tool settings, choose Heal from the two brush options.

3 Use the sliders to set the brush Size to about 80 pixels and the Opacity to 100%. Click the first blemish near the left margin of the image—but don't drag. Release the mouse button and move the pointer away; you'll notice that Lightroom automatically finds an appropriate area to sample. On your screen you should see something similar to what's shown in the illustration below: the lighter white circle with the cross-hairs is the target area centered on the blemish and the bolder white circle is the sample area.

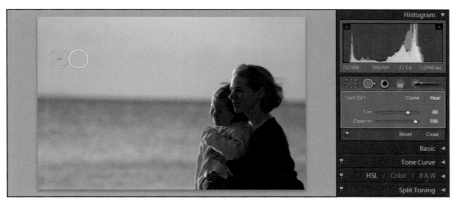

4 If you wish, you can manually specify the area to be sampled by the Heal brush. With the Spot Removal tool, click the next spot—but this time drag to find a sample that blends effectively; you can see the effect on the target area as you drag. Release the pointer when you're satisfied with the result. The white arrow indicates that data from the sample area has been applied to the target area.

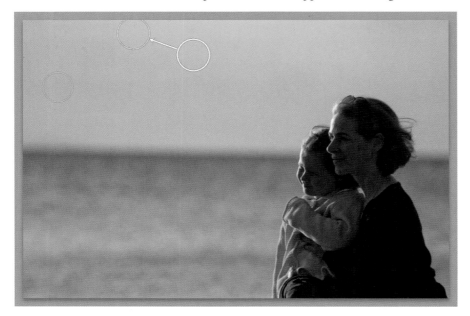

5   Remove the third spot using either of the techniques from the last two steps, and then press Q to disable the Spot Removal tool. The circular tool overlays disappear from the image in the Loupe view.

6   Click the Spot Removal tool, or press Q, to activate the tool again. The circular tool overlays for your three spot corrections reappear on the image in the Loupe view. These edits are all still "live"—you can adjust them at any time.

7   The best way to evaluate the results of the Heal operation—and many other image modifications—is to inspect the image at full size. Press F7 to show the left panel group if necessary. Click 1:1 in the header of the Navigator panel to set a pixel-for-pixel zoom ratio for the Loupe view; then, click in the Navigator preview image to focus on the site of any of your recent spot corrections.

▶ **Tip:** To cancel and remove the active spot correction, simply press Backspace / Delete.

8   To modify this spot correction, first click inside the target circle to activate it. Drag the circle to reposition it slightly and use the slider to adjust the size of the correction. Repeat the process for the sample circle.

9   Click the Spot Removal tool, or press Q, to disable the Spot Removal tool. To return to the Fit zoom level click the image in the Loupe view, or choose from the options in the header of the Navigator panel.

Applying basic color corrections

In the Develop module, the basic color corrections are generally best made in the following order:

- Apply tonal corrections to set the correct white point and maximize the tonal range in the image using the Histogram and the controls in the Basic panel.

- Adjust the overall brightness and contrast using the Brightness and Contrast controls and the Tone Curve panel.

- Apply sharpening and noise reduction in the Detail panel.

- Add special effects such as decorative lens vignetting, grain, or specific color adjustments, using the HSL / Color / B&W, Split Toning, and Effects panels.

The following exercise will take you through a typical image correction process.

Adjusting the white balance and the tonal range

You'll start by adjusting the white balance for the photo of the church using the Histogram and the controls in the Basic panel; then, you'll improve the tonal range by lightening the image—especially in the shadow areas.

1   In the Filmstrip, select the photo of the church: DSC_0706.NEF.

2   You can make more space in the Loupe view for for the this portrait-format photo by hiding the top panel (F5) and the Filmstrip (F6). Press T to hide the Toolbar. In the right panel group, expand the Histogram and Basic panels.

In the Basic panel you can see that the current White Balance (WB) setting is the default: As Shot. The Temp control shows that the shot was taken at color temperature of 4800 K (kelvin), which appears to be just about correct. However, by my recollection the color of the stonework was actually slightly warmer.

▶ **Tip:** When you're making fine corrections and adjustments in the Develop module, enlarge the right panel group to its maximum width; this will increase the length—and therefore the sensitivity—of the sliders.

3 Choose Daylight from the White Balance (WB) menu in the Basic panel. The Temp control now shows a color temperature value of 5500 K and the image looks a little too warm. Use the Temp slider to reduce the temperature to about 5250 K. Once you've made this adjustment, the current White Balance (WB) setting has changed to Custom.

The image is slightly too dark overall. You can see this reflected in the histogram; the tonal range looks somewhat weighted towards the left. The histogram shows the distribution of brightness—or *luminance*—in the image. The darker a pixel the further left it is

recorded in the histogram, a lighter pixel is mapped further to the right. A peak in the curve represents a large number of pixels of a similar brightness in the image.

While you're adjusting the tonal balance of an image, you can use the histogram as a reference as you work to achieve a more even distribution of tone over the full range from dark to light.

If you make an image too dark you'll notice that part of the distribution curve moves out of range to the left of the histogram. This is known as *clipping* and represents a loss of color information from the image. For the pixels in the truncated portion of

the curve, data recording differences in brightness has been lost and every pixel is mapped to black; the shadows have been clipped. The small triangles in the upper corners of the histogram are clipping indicators. If the curve is clipped at either end of the histogram the respective indicator turns white.

If you lighten the image too much, the highlights are clipped; the curve is truncated at the right end of the histogram and the affected pixels will all be mapped to white.

Once the histogram is spread over as much of the range as is possible without clipping of the highlights or shadows, you can redistribute the curve to produce a well balanced image.

4 You can see that there is already some truncation of the left end of the curve and a white triangle indicates that the shadows are being clipped. To see which areas of the image are affected, move the pointer over the clipping indicator. Clipped shadows are shown as bright blue in the image and clipped highlights as red. You can see that some color detail is being lost in the railings and planters in the foreground. Click the clipping indicator to highlight the clipped shadows permanently. To turn both clipping indicators on, right-click / Control-click in the histogram and choose Show Clipping from the context menu, or press J on you keyboard. Use the same method to turn Show Clipping off again, if you prefer, before continuing with the next step.

5 The Auto Tone command usually serves as a good starting point for adjusting the tonal range. Watch the histogram as you click the Auto button in the Tone pane in the Basic panel. You'll notice that the histogram curve shifts slightly to the right and the image becomes lighter overall. You can see at a glance that the left end of the curve is not as truncated; there is much less clipping of the shadows. Once you've applied the Auto Tone adjustment the button is disabled.

About white balance

To be able to display the full range of color information contained in an image file correctly, it's critical to set the right white balance for the photo. For this reason, it's important to understand what the white balance is. An image's white point reflects the lighting conditions in which the photo was taken. The white point is defined by values on two scales: temperature and tint.

If the red, green, and blue components of a pixel on the screen all have exactly the same values, the pixel appears as a neutral gray—ranging from white to black. The higher the red component, the warmer the image appears. The higher the blue component, the cooler the image. The tint accounts for color shifts in the direction of green or magenta.

The sensors in a digital camera record the amount of red, green, and blue light that is reflected from an object. A neutral gray reflects all color components of the light source equally. If the light source is not pure white but has a predominant red component for example, a higher amount of red will be reflected to the sensors. Unless the composition of the light source is known—and the *white balance* or *white point* is corrected accordingly—the image will have a red color cast.

Different types of artificial lighting have different white points; they provide lighting that is dominated by one color or deficient in another. Weather conditions also have an affect on the white balance.

When shooting in auto white balance mode, your camera tries to estimate the composition of the light source from the color information measured by the sensors. Although modern cameras are doing better at automatically setting the white balance to meet conditions, it is never fail-proof. It is preferable—if your camera supports it—to have the camera measure the white point of the light source; this is usually done by taking a picture of a light gray object under the same lighting conditions as the subject.

As well as the color information recorded by the camera sensors, a Raw image also contains the "As Shot" white balance information. This enables Lightroom to correctly interpret the recorded color information for a given light source. The recorded white point information is used as a calibration point in reference to which the white balance can be corrected and the colors in the image will be shifted accordingly.

About white balance (continued)

If there is an area in your photo that you know should appear as a light neutral gray on screen you can use that area to set the point around which the image can be calibrated. Use the White Balance Selector tool, located in the top left corner of the Basic panel, to sample the color information in that area and Lightroom will set the image's white balance accordingly.

As you move the White Balance Selector tool across the image you will see a magnified view of the pixels under the eyedropper and RGB values for the central target pixel. To avoid too radical a color shift, try to click a pixel where the red, green, and blue values are as close as possible. Do not use white or a very light color as target neutral; for a very bright pixel a color component might already have been clipped.

Color temperature is defined with reference to a concept known as *black-body radiation* theory. When heated, a black-body will first start glowing red, then orange, yellow, white, and finally blue-white. A color's temperature is the temperature—in kelvin (K)—to which a black-body must be heated to emit that particular color. Zero K corresponds to −273.15 °C or −459.67 °F and an increment of one unit kelvin is equivalent to an increment of one degree Celsius.

What we generally refer to as a warm color (with a higher red component) actually has a lower color temperature (in kelvin) than what we would call a cool color (with a higher blue component). The color temperature of a visually warm scene lit by candlelight is about 1,500 K. In bright daylight you would measure around 5,500 K and light from an overcast sky results in a color temperature in the photo of about 6,000 to 7,000 K.

The Temp slider adjusts the color temperature (in kelvin) of the designated white point, from low at the left side of the range to high on the right side. Moving the Temp slider to the left reduces the color temperature of the white point. In consequence, the colors in the image are interpreted as having a higher color temperature relative to the adjusted white point and are shifted towards blue. The colors displayed inside the Temp slider control indicate the effect a change in that direction will have on the image. Moving the slider to the left will increase the blue in the image, moving the slider to the right will make the image look more yellow and red.

The Tint slider works in the same way. For example, to remove a green cast in an image you would move the Tint slider to the right, away from the green displayed inside the slider control. This increases the green component in the white point so the colors in the image are interpreted as less green relative to the adjusted white point.

Adjusting the Temp and Tint sliders corresponds to shifting the white point in the color gamut.

6 Move the pointer slowly across the histogram from left to right. You'll see that the range of brightness values in the histogram is divided into four distinct zones, which are highlighted in turn as the pointer moves over them.
The name of the currently highlighted area is displayed in the lower left corner of the Histogram panel. You'll notice that the names of these areas: Blacks, Fill Light, Exposure, and Recovery, are shared by four of the controls in the Tone area in the Basic panel. As you move the pointer over each zone in the histogram, the relevant slider in the Tone controls is also highlighted.

To change the tonal balance within any of these areas you can either use the Exposure, Recovery, Fill Light, and Blacks sliders in the Basic panel, or drag the relevant portion of the curve directly in the histogram. Drag to the right to brighten that portion of the tonal range or to the left to darken it; the respective slider in the Tone controls will move to reflect your adjustment.

As you move either the Exposure or Fill Light sliders, the curve in the histogram will shift in the same direction as the slider. By comparison, the Recovery and Blacks sliders appear to work backwards. Increasing the Recovery value reduces the brightness in the Recovery area, shifting the curve to the left and thus recovering highlight information that might otherwise be clipped to white. Increasing the Blacks value also shifts the curve to the left, darkening the shadows and possibly resulting in more color information being clipped at the left end of the histogram.

Next you'll darken the brightly lit church wall and lighten the shadow area in the lower left of the image using the Exposure and Fill Light sliders.

7 To darken the brightest part of the church wall, drag the Exposure slider to about −0.38. Drag the Fill Light slider to about 25 to lighten the shadowed areas to the left of the building and in the foreground. You'll notice that this has also taken care of the clipped shadows.

8 Press the Backslash key (\) repeatedly to toggle between the edited and unedited versions of the image in the Loupe view. In this way you can quickly evaluate your current improvements against the original image.

The image is now much better lit but appears somewhat flat. For this exercise, we'll make a choice between a Clarity, Vibrance or Saturation adjustment.

The Saturation control alters the intensity of color in a photo—from washed-out and gray to extremely vivid and intense. A slight increase in color saturation can create a very pleasing effect, but over-saturating makes colors look artificial and color detail will be lost.

▶ **Tip:** Hold down the Alt / Option key while dragging the Exposure, Recovery, or Blacks slider to see the clipping mask in the Loupe view.

● **Note:** In general, clipped shadows are less of a problem than clipped highlights as the image artifacts resulting from clipping are usually more noticeable in the lighter areas of an image.

▶ **Tip:** Boosting the saturation before you convert an image to black and white can result in a far more dramatic final result.

The Vibrance slider alters the saturation in a non-linear manner—boosting the less saturated colors in a photo and having less effect on the bolder areas, while avoiding over-saturating skin colors.

For this image we'll leave the Vibrance and Saturation settings as they are and make an adjustment to the Clarity value instead.

Increasing the Clarity can add depth to an image by heightening *local contrast*, the differences in brightness between small adjacent areas of the image. The eye is very sensitive to changes in local contrast. On a larger scale, *contrast* describes the difference between significant bright and dark areas in the image. Later in the lesson, you'll adjust the contrast globally using the Tone Curve panel.

9 The Clarity setting is best adjusted at a magnification level of 100% or greater. Zoom the photo to 100% by clicking the 1:1 zoom ratio in the Navigator panel. Reposition the image so that you can focus on the colonnades and the lightest part of the curved stone wall. Then set the Clarity to about +50.

▶ **Tip:** You can set every control in the Basic panel using keyboard shortcuts. Press the Period (.) or Comma (,) keys to cycle forwards or backwards through all the controls in the panel. Use the Plus (+) and Minus (-) keys to change the settings; hold down the Shift key to adjust in higher increments. Press the Semicolon (;) to reset a control to its default value. Press Ctrl+U / Command+U for Auto Tone and Ctrl+Shift+U / Command+Shift+U for Auto White Balance. Press V to toggle between Grayscale and Color treatment. Press W to pick up and release the White Balance tool.

10 Undo and redo the last step a few times to quickly compare the image with and without the increased clarity setting. Drag the image in the Loupe view to review the effect in a different area. Before you continue, make sure the Clarity adjustment is applied.

Adjusting contrast using the tone curve

Working with the Tone Curve enables you to adjust contrast in different parts of the tonal range selectively. Tone curve corrections should not be applied until after the imaged has been processed as necessary with the controls in the Basic panel.

The tone curve maps the distribution of tonal values in the input image along the x-axis to a new distribution of tonal values in the output image along the y-axis. The dark end of the range is at the lower left and the light at the upper right.

A linear tone curve at a 45° incline from the lower left corner to the upper right corner has no effect on the image; each tone value in the input image is mapped to the identical tone value in the output image. Raising the tone curve above this line maps tone values to a lighter value; lowering it darkens the tonal values.

A tone curve section that is flatter than 45° compresses a range of tone values from the input image (X) to a narrower range in the output image (y). Some tone values which were distinguishable in the input image become indistinguishable in the output image and image detail is lost.

A tone curve section that is steeper than 45° expands tone values; the differences between tone values becomes more noticeable and the image contrast is increased.

In Lightroom, the tone curve is constrained so that the curve is always ascending. This means that if you increase the incline of one section of the curve you'll end up with a decreased incline somewhere else; you'll have to make a compromise. When using the tone curve, the trick is to increase the contrast in the range where you have the most tonal information; recognizable by a peak in the histogram. At the same time, try to place the flatter parts of the tone curve in ranges where there is less information in the image (troughs in the histogram) or where a lack of contrast is not as disturbing or noticeable.

A typical tone curve intended to increase mid-range contrast starts flat in the lower left corner (less contrast in the shadows), is steep in the center (more contrast in the mid-tones), and ends flat in the upper right corner (less contrast in the highlights).

For the image at hand we'll customize the tone curve to selectively increase the contrast in the well-lit wall area of the church, which is the focus of attention in the photo. For this substantial enhancement it will be worthwhile sacrificing a little of the contrast in the shadowed area at the lower left and in the sky.

1   If necessary, expand the Tone Curve panel in the right panel group. In the Navigator, set the Loupe view zoom level to Fit.

2   From the Point Curve menu at the bottom of the Tone Curve panel, choose Linear, Medium Contrast, and Strong Contrast in turn and notice the effect each setting has on the image. You can use a tone curve preset as a starting point for your adjustments; for this image, Medium Contrast works best.

Note the silhouette of the histogram plotted in the background in the tone curve display, This gives you an indication of the tonal ranges where an increase in contrast might be most effective.

● **Note:** The choice of point curve preset also constrains the amount of play in the adjustment controls.

3   Position the pointer over the tone curve. As you move from left to right you'll notice the names of the ranges you're moving over displayed at the bottom of the tone curve grid, while the corresponding slider is highlighted in the Region controls below.

▶ **Tip:** By default, the four tonal ranges are of equal width. You can change their width by dragging the controls below the tone curve to reposition the dividing lines between adjacent tonal ranges.

Whether you use the sliders, enter numeric values, or drag directly in the tone curve grid, the tone curve controls raise or lower the curve by moving the center points of these four ranges: Shadows, Darks, Lights, and Highlights. The overall shape of the tone curve changes to accommodate your adjustments, becoming flatter in one place and steeper in another.

The extent to which you can adjust each section of the tone curve is indicated by the gray area that appears when you position the pointer over that section.

4   To see which areas in the image correspond to the different tonal ranges, click the Target button (⊚) in the top left corner of the Tone Curve panel and move the pointer over the image in the Loupe view. As you move the pointer over the shadowed area in the lower left of the image you can see that these tones account for much of the first peak in the histogram around the 25% mark. Most of the tonal values in the blue sky are represented in the second peak in the histogram just below the 50% input level. The tones in the well-lit church wall are mostly spread between input levels of 60% to 90%.

Lowering the Lights value in the tone curve should produce the effect we're after: increasing the contrast in the well-lit church wall by steepening the curve for the input values above 60%. The compromise is a flattening of the curve for lower input values; reducing contrast in the sky and shadow areas where a loss of detail is less noticeable.

5   Watch the tone curve as you move the target cursor over the well-lit church wall. When you see that the Lights adjustment control is selected on the Tone Curve, click and drag downwards in the image. Release the mouse button when the Lights value is adjusted to −45. Remember: you can only adjust the tone curve by dragging directly in the image when you are using the Tone Curve Target mode.

6 Click the Target button in the top left corner of the Tone Curve panel again to turn off target mode.

7 To compare your image with and without the tone curve adjustment, switch the tone curve controls off and on by clicking the On/Off switch icon at the left side of the Tone Curve panel header. Review the effect in a few different areas of the image at 100% zoom level. Note how effectively your adjustment enhanced the image detail in the stone wall of the church.

The image was also darkened as a whole because the tone curve was pushed below the diagonal. This works quite well for the image at hand. In another case, you could lessen the effect, if you wished, by raising the Shadows value in the Tone Curve or by readjusting the levels using the controls in the Basic panel.

8 When you're done, set the zoom level to Fit and make sure the tone curve adjustment is turned on.

The image now looks quite acceptable. To improve it even further you can apply additional sharpening and reduce some of the noise that's visible in the sky area.

Sharpening detail and reducing noise

The Detail panel contains controls for sharpening image detail and reducing noise.

Sharpening helps make edges more pronounced and gives the image a crisper look. Lightroom applies a slight amount of sharpening to your Raw images by default, so you should apply additional sharpening with caution.

The Detail panel offers separate controls for reducing luminance noise and color noise. Noise is most noticeable in images shot under low lighting conditions or at a high ISO setting. The image for this exercise was shot at an ISO setting of 800 and contains a slight amount of noise, mostly noticeable the sky area.

● **Note:** Image sharpening and noise reduction are always best executed at 100% magnification.

1   In the Navigator panel, set the zoom level for the Loupe view to 1:1 (100%).

2   In the right panel group, scroll down or collapse other panels if necessary, and then expand the Detail panel.

3   For this image, the sharpening amount is already set to 25%. To quickly compare the image with and without this default sharpening, switch the Detail controls off and on by clicking the On/Off switch at the left of the Detail panel header. Review the effect in a few different areas of the image at 100% magnification. When you're done, make sure you've switched the Detail settings back on.

Though the default sharpening has already done a good job of emphasizing the edges in this image, you can still improve the crispness of the photo. Before you apply extra sharpening, however, it's best to create a mask that will restrict the effect of your adjustment to areas with edge detail. In the case of our lesson image, this will enable you to sharpen architectural detail while you avoid accentuating the noise in the sky area where it will be easily noticeable.

4   Position the photo in the Loupe view so that you can see some of the sky and part of the church at the same time. Hold down the Alt / Option key and drag the Masking slider to the right. The mask is displayed in the Detail panel preview and in the Loupe view when the zoom level is set to 1:1 or higher. Release the pointer when most of the sky area is masked (black) but the edge detail on the church is still unmasked (white). We used a value of 50.

5   To sharpen the image further, drag the Amount slider to the right. With the extensive mask in place, you can afford to increase the sharpening by a relatively large amount. We raised the setting to 100.

6   Compare the image with and without sharpening once again by clicking the On/Off switch icon at the left side of the header of the Detail panel. Review the effect in several areas of the image at 100% magnification.

7   In order to assess the effect of the sharpening mask, make sure the detail controls are turned on and drag the Masking slider all the way back to its default setting of 0. Then Undo and Redo to see the effect of applying sharpening with and without the mask. Pay particular attention to the sky area where unmasked sharpening accentuates noise. When you're done, return the Masking setting to 50.

Most of the noise apparent in this image is *luminance noise*—variations in the brightness of pixels which should be equally bright. Luminance noise looks a little like film grain and is in general less of a problem than color noise, or *chrominance noise*—bright blue, red and purple spots in an area that should be a uniform hue.

Under Noise Reduction at the bottom of the detail panel, you can see that a small amount of Color noise reduction has been applied to this raw image by default.

8 To assess the effect of the default reduction in color noise, focus on an area of sky in the image and drag the Color slider all the way to the left. Undo and Redo to compare the image with and without the default color noise reduction. If you can't see the effect clearly, use the menu at the right of the Navigator panel header to set a higher zoom ratio. When you're done, make sure to return the zoom ratio to 1:1 and the Color noise reduction value to 25.

You should use Noise Reduction with caution; both forms of noise reduction can result in blurring of some of the image detail. You can use the Detail slider associated with each of the Noise Reduction controls to help maintain the sharpness of the image, despite this smoothing effect.

9 Position the photo in the Loupe view so that you can some of the sky and part of the church wall at the same time, as shown in the illustration below. Drag the Luminance slider all the way to the right to a value of 100. The luminance noise in the sky has now disappeared—however, there is marked blurring of the detail in the church wall. You'll need to find a compromise between reducing noise and maintaining the sharpness. Drag the Luminance slider back to 0, and then slowly to the right until you notice that the sky area is improved with only slight blurring of the details on the church wall. We used a value of 40.

10 Use the Detail and Contrast controls below the Luminance slider to reduce the blurring effect of the noise reduction operation. We set Detail and Contrast values of 70 and 25 respectively.

Correcting lens effects

As well as the Transform sliders, the manual mode of the Lens Corrections panel provides controls for correcting Lens Vignetting and Chromatic Aberration—both unwanted effects that can be caused by your camera lens.

Lens vignetting is a phenomenon that results in reduced brightness or saturation of color towards the edges of an image—usually an accidental effect caused by a combination of the focal length, type of lens, and filters used. *Chromatic Aberration* is most noticeable with lower quality lenses or near the edges of an image shot with a wide-angle lens, resulting in color fringes where the lens has been unable to focus the different wavelengths of incoming light correctly on the sensor, There is only a very slight chromatic aberration noticeable in the image used for this exercise.

1 Set the zoom level to Fit. You'll notice that the sky is slightly darker towards the corners of the image. The same edge darkening is also present, though less noticeable, in the shadowed areas in the lower corners of the image.

2 In the right panel group, scroll down or collapse other panels if necessary and expand the Lens Corrections panel. Click Manual at the top of the panel. Under Lens Vignetting, drag the Amount slider to the right until the lens vignetting in the corners of the image appears to be corrected. We set a value of +20.

▶ **Tip:** For information on using the Profile mode to make lens corrections tailored to your camera, please refer to Lightroom Help.

3 In the Navigator panel, set the zoom ratio to 4:1. Click in the Navigator preview to focus on the arches visible above the roof-line in the upper left of the photo.

The color aberration in this photo is most apparent as a blue fringe along the top edge of the sunlit arches.

4 In the Chromatic Aberration controls, first drag the Red / Cyan slider to the right to see the existing aberration increased; then, drag the slider to the left until the color fringing disappears. We set value of -24.

Adding effects

In the last exercise, you used the controls in the Lens Corrections panel to remove accidental lens vignetting. Next, you'll use the controls in the Effects panel to deliberately create your own post-crop vignette.

A post-crop vignette can be used creatively to frame a photo (as you'll do here), to draw the viewer's attention to the center of an image, or even to simulate an accidental vignette in order to achieve an atmospheric or "antique" effect.

The Effects panel also offers a Grain effect that applies simulated film grain to give a digital image the distinctive look of a film photograph.

1 In the header of the Navigator panel, set the zoom level to Fit.

2 In the right panel group, scroll down or collapse other panels if necessary and expand the Effects panel.

3   In the Post-Crop Vignetting controls, set the Amount to −80, Midpoint to 0, Roundness to −100, and Feather to 20.

4   This example illustrates a fairly extreme application of the Post-Crop Vignetting feature. Experiment with the sliders to create different effects. Try each of the three options in the Post-Crop Vignetting Style menu, which affect the way the vignette is blended with the image.

5   In the Effects panel, double-click the words "Post-Crop Vignetting" to reset the Post-Crop Vignetting controls to their default settings.

6   Set the zoom level to 1:1, and then drag the Grain slider to the right to set a value of 50. If you wish, you can reset the Grain effect by double-clicking the word "Grain" in the Effects panel.

Updating the process version

Lightroom 3 uses updated technology to demosaic and render digital images, resulting in improved Detail adjustments—sharpening and noise reduction—and vignetting effects. Photos that are edited for the first time in Lightroom 3 use these new processes by default.

For a photo that was processed using a previous version of Lightroom, the Process Version feature is activated. An exclamation mark icon (!) is displayed to alert you to the fact that an image was edited using older processes; you can either leave the photo as it is, or take advantage of the latest processing technology by updating the image to the current *process version*.

The process version specifies which version of the Camera Raw demosaic, noise reduction, sharpening, and post-crop vignette functions are applied in rendering the photo. When you update the process version for a photo some characteristics will change more dramatically than others, depending on which processes were originally applied to the photo. You may find you need to modify some of the updated adjustments. Even if a photo has no previous sharpening, noise reduction, or post-crop vignetting, demosaicing improvements are applied to all updated images, so there will always be some change.

1 If you don't see the Filmstrip, press F6 or choose Window > Panels > Show Filmstrip. In the Filmstrip, select the image GreekRelief.NEF.

2 In the Navigator panel, set the zoom level to Fit. Note the exclamation mark icon (!) that appears at the lower right of the Loupe view, indicating that this image has been edited using an older process version.

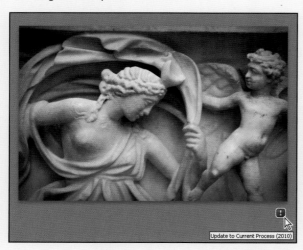

3 To update the process version, choose Settings > Update To Current Process (2010) or simply click the Update To Current Process icon in the Loupe view.

4 To apply an older process version, choose the version from the Settings > Process menu.

Making discrete color adjustments

You can use the controls in the HSL / Color / B & W panel to adjust discrete shades of color in your image, changing the hue, saturation, or luminance values for specific color ranges independently.

When converting an image to black and white, you can fine-tune the way that each color in the image will contribute to the grayscale mix. Use the Split Toning panel to apply creative duotone effects to a black and white image.

Understanding hue, saturation, and luminance

The color of each pixel in your image can be expressed either as a set of RGB values or as a combination of hue, saturation, and luminance values. Hue, saturation, and luminance values can be calculated from from RGB values, and vice versa.

Once you understand hue, saturation, and luminance, defining color in these terms seems far more natural than using RGB values, especially when it comes to describing changes made to color.

For example, darkening the blue colors in your image can be done by reducing the luminance value for the blue color component. Expressed in RGB values, a light blue might be composed of R: 42, G: 45, and B: 63, while a darker blue uses R: 35, G: 38, and B: 56—certainly not a very intuitive model for describing color adjustments.

When you describe a color by name—red, yellow, green, blue—you're referring to its hue. The full range of hues can be displayed as a color wheel. Adjusting the hue moves a given color around the wheel in one direction or the other.

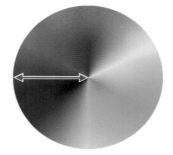

Saturation is the boldness or intensity of a hue, ranging from neutral and grayed to vivid and un-muted. Saturation can be visualized on a color wheel with fully saturated colors around the edge of the circle and less saturated colors closer to the center. As the saturation of a color is increased it moves from a neutral gray in the center of the wheel to a pure, vivid hue on the rim.

Luminance is the measure of brightness of a color, ranging from the minimum value for black to the maximum value for white. On the color wheel model, luminance can be represented by adding a third dimension, with a completely underexposed—or black—wheel below the color wheel and a completely overexposed—or white—wheel above it.

The terms tint, shade, and tone can all be expressed with reference to hue, saturation, and luminance.

A *tint* is a pure hue mixed with white; a hue with increased luminance and a reduced saturation. In our three-dimensional color wheel model the tints of a hue are found along the line from the pure hue on the rim of the wheel in the middle to the center point of the white wheel at the top.

A *shade* is a pure hue mixed with black; a hue with decreased luminance and saturation, located along a line from the pure hue on the rim of the wheel in the middle to the center point of the black wheel at the bottom.

A *tone* is a pure hue mixed with a neutral gray, located along a line from the pure hue on the rim of the wheel in the middle to the respective gray on the central axis.

Adjusting colors selectively

Understanding color in an image in terms of hue, saturation and luminance can help you both in identifying the changes you need to make to achieve the effect you want and in choosing the most effective way to make those changes.

In this exercise you'll darken the blue of the sky in the photo of the stone church you were working with earlier. You can do this by reducing the luminance of the blue color range while leaving the hue and saturation unchanged.

1   If you don't see the Filmstrip, press F6 or choose Window > Panels > Show Filmstrip. In the Filmstrip, select the photo of the church: DSC_0706.NEF.

2   In the Navigator panel, set the zoom level to Fit.

3   In the right panel group, scroll up or collapse other panels, if necessary, and then expand the HSL / Color / B & W panel. If not already selected, click HSL (Hue, Saturation, Luminance) in the panel header, and then click the Luminance tab.

4 Click the Target tool button () in the upper left corner of the Luminance pane.

5 In the Loupe view, click in the sky area and drag the pointer downwards to reduce the luminance of the color range under the pointer. Release the mouse button when the Luminance value for Blue reaches −20. You can see from the Luminance sliders that Lightroom also found some purple in the sky and has therefore made a slight adjustment to the luminance value for purple as well.

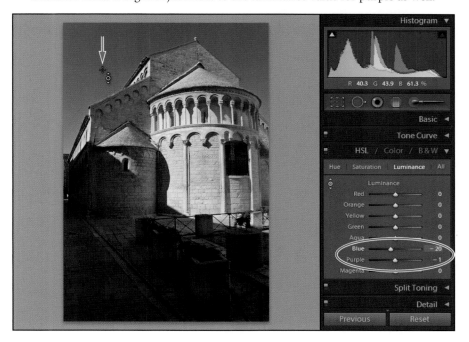

6 Click the Target button again to disable target mode.

7 To compare the image with and without the luminance adjustment applied, switch the HSL / Color / B & W adjustment off and on by clicking the On/Off switch icon at the left side of the panel header. Note that the adjustment has not affected the gradient from lighter blue near the horizon to darker blue at the top. It is important to understand that the luminance adjustment is not restricted to one discrete hue value but is applied across a range of colors to either side of the target hue. When you're finished reviewing the effect, make sure the HSL / Color / B & W adjustment is turned on.

You can adjust the hue or saturation in the same way. Select the Hue or Saturation tab, then use the Target tool to adjust the color in a specific area in the image. You could also use the respective slider controls. Click the All tab for access to all the sliders for Hue, Saturation, and Luminance at the same time. In the Color tab the sliders are grouped by color rather than by hue, saturation, and luminance. Click the All tab to see the sliders for all colors at the same time.

Converting an image to black and white

When Lightroom converts a photo to black and white (grayscale), each color in the image is mapped to a tone of gray according to a default mix.

To change the look of the resultant image you can adjust the predominance of each color in the mix. In other words, you can change the extent to which each color contributes to the black and white—or grayscale—information.

1 Click B & W in the header of the HSL / Color / B & W panel. You can see the result of the default black and white mix in the Loupe view.

If you wish, you can adjust the black and white mix selectively in different areas of the same image.

2 Click the Target button (⊚) in the upper left of the Black And White Mix pane.

3 In the Loupe view, click the area you wish to adjust, and then drag upwards or downwards to lighten or darken that part of the image. Click in the sky area and drag upwards to increase the value of Blue in the mix to about +30; then, click the bright church wall and drag downwards to reduce the value for Orange to about −20.

4 Click the Black And White Mix Target button (⊚) again to turn target mode off.

5 To compare the image before and after your adjustments to the grayscale mix, switch the Black And White Mix adjustments off and on by clicking the On/Off switch icon at the left side of the HSL / Color / B & W panel header. When you're done, make sure the Black And White Mix control is turned on.

Split toning

A split toning effect replaces the darker tones (shadows) in a black and white image with shades of one color and the lighter tones (highlights) with tints of another. The effect can be quite subtle and restrained or very striking and unusual depending on your choice of colors and your intention.

1 In the right panel group, expand the Split Toning panel. If possible, keep the HSL / Color / B & W panel open so you can see the settings for the grayscale mix at the same time.

2 Right-click / Control-click the image in the Loupe view, and then choose Settings > B&W Creative - Antique Grayscale from the context menu. Note the changes in the Split Toning panel. The Antique Grayscale effect uses a sepia tone for the highlights and a less saturated and slightly warmer color for the shadows.

3 In the right panel group, expand the Basic, Tone Curve, Detail, and Lens Corrections panels in turn, using Undo and Redo to see how the Antique Grayscale preset changes the settings. Collapse each panel when you're done with it.

If you wish to use some of the settings from a preset (or another image) and not others, you can copy the settings you want selectively. In this case, you'll copy just the color settings from the Split Toning panel.

4   Right-click / Control-click the antique grayscale image in the Loupe view, and then choose Settings > Copy Settings from the context menu. In the Copy Settings dialog box, first click the Check None button, and then activate only the Split Toning option. Click Copy.

5   Choose Edit > Undo Preset: Creative - Antique Grayscale to return to the black and white image with all your customized settings. Right-click / Control-click the image in the Loupe view and choose Settings > Paste Settings from the context menu. By checking the panels in the right panel group, you can see that this time only the settings in the Split Toning panel have been altered.

Antique Grayscale preset applied   Antique Grayscale Split Toning only

Synchronizing settings

In the last exercise, you used menu commands to copy and paste develop settings to a single image. You can copy, or *synchronize*, settings from one image to a multiple selection of images by using the Synchronize Settings command.

1   Select all four images in the Filmstrip. If necessary, click the image of the church so it's the active (the most selected) image. Synchronizing settings for the selected images will copy settings from the active image to all the other images in the selection.

2   Click the Sync button at the lower left of the right panel group or choose Settings > Sync Settings.

▶ **Tip:** The Synchronize Settings command in the Develop module copies absolute values from one image to the others. To apply relative changes to a selection of images—such as increasing exposure by 1/3 step independent of the current exposure settings in each of the destination images— you can use the Quick Development panel in the Library module.

3   In the Synchronize Settings dialog box (note the similarity to the Copy Settings dialog box), click the Check None button, and then activate both the Treatment (Black & White) and Split Toning options. Click Synchronize.

All four images have been converted to black and white and have had the duo-tone effect that you copied from the Antique Grayscale preset applied.

Local corrections

All the adjustments you've made in this lesson so far have been applied globally— across the entire image. For example, increasing Fill Light affects all the shadowed areas in a photo; you can't lighten one area selectively or some areas more than others. With the local correction tools—the Graduated Filter tool and the Adjustment Brush tool—you can do both.

Using the Graduated Filter tool

With the Graduated Filter tool you can created a gradient mask through which you can apply an adjustment so that the effect is stronger in one area and fades off across the rest of the image.

1   In the Filmstrip, select only the image of the stone church. Click the Graduated Filter button just below the Histogram panel (circled at right), or press M. Additional controls for the Graduated Filter tool appear below the tool buttons. If you don't see the Effect sliders as you do in the illustration at the right, click the triangle at the top right of the Effect pane.

2   Above the Effect pane, make sure New is selected as the Mask setting.

3   Adjust the Exposure setting to a value of **0.36**.

4   With the Graduated Filter tool, drag from a point near the lower left corner of the image upwards and to the right, as shown in the illustration below, and then release the pointer.

You have just created a basic gradient mask, through which your adjustment to the Exposure setting is being applied. You will go on to fine-tune both the mask and the adjustment, or effect, in the following steps of this exercise.

You can see the effect on the image at a glance; the exposure is gradually increased towards the lower left corner. In the Graduated Filter controls, the Mask setting has changed to Edit. You can still change the settings for the adjustment and reposition, rotate, resize, and fine-tune the gradient mask.

5   Increase the Exposure setting to **1.00**. Then adjust the gradient mask as shown in the illustration below. Drag the pin to reposition the center of the gradient beside the kerb-stone. Drag the center line to rotate the mask so that its orientation is parallel to the kerb, and then drag either of the outer lines to make the band of the gradient narrower or broader.

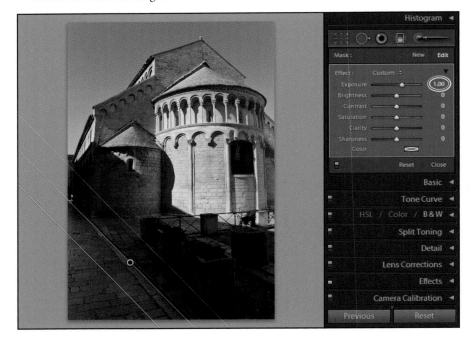

▶ **Tip:** You can use more than one graduated filter in a single image, each with its own position, direction, size, and adjustment settings.

The broader the band, the "softer" the gradient—the narrower the band, the more abruptly the adjustment is faded into the image. While you're dragging the outer lines, you can keep the center line fixed at its current position by holding down the Alt / Option key. The outer lines represent the boundaries beyond which the adjustment is applied at 100% of the specified value on one side and 0% on the other. Press the H key to hide or show the adjustment pin.

6   To evaluate the image with and without the graduated filter adjustment, click the On/Off switch icon in the lower left corner of the Graduated Filter controls pane. When you're done, make sure the graduated filter adjustment is activated.

7   Click the Graduated Filter button again to disable the Graduated Filter tool.

Using the Adjustment Brush tool

You can use the Adjustment Brush tool to paint adjustments directly onto different areas of the image selectively

1   Click the Adjustment Brush button below the Histogram panel (circled at right), or press K. The Adjustment Brush tool settings appear below the tool buttons. Make sure that Mask is set to New in the Adjustment Brush tool controls pane.

In addition to the Effect pane, with the same adjustment sliders that were available for the Graduated Filter tool, the Adjustment Brush tool settings also contain controls for setting up brushes. You can set a different size, softness, flow, and density for each of three brushes: two for applying the adjustment or effect and one to erase it.

For this exercise, you'll use the Adjustment Brush tool to apply a local adjustment to the sky area.

2   Reset the Exposure value to **0**. Click the color box to choose a color for a tint effect. We chose a strong, saturated red.

3   Click brush A and activate the Auto Mask option. When you begin painting with the Adjustment Brush, the Auto Mask option will detect the edges of the area you're painting based on similarity in color values, and will mask the image outside those edges.

4   Paint over the entire sky area. Even though the auto mask feature does a good
    job of detecting the edges of the sky, you should still avoid painting outside the
    area as much as possible. Hold down the Alt key / Option key while dragging to
    erase areas you've brushed over accidentally.

▶ **Tip:** You can use
the Adjustment Brush
to create more than
one adjustment area
in a single image, each
with its own settings. To
delete an adjustment
area, select its pin, and
then press delete.

5   Click the Adjustment Brush tool again to disable it.

Working with an external image editor

To do further pixel-based editing, you can open your image in an external editor
such as Photoshop or Photoshop Elements—from within the Lightroom workspace.

Simply select the photo you wish to edit with the external editor; then choose your
preferred image editing application from the Photo > Edit In menu.

You can also specify your preferred external editor and set file format preferences
in the External Editing tab of the Preferences dialog box.

If you have Photoshop CS3 (version 10.0.1) or later installed on your computer,
you have additional options for processing multiple photos, such as creating a
panorama, merging to HDR (High Dynamic Range), or combining them in a single
Photoshop document with each photo on its own layer. Right-click / Control-click
a multiple selection of images in the Filmstrip or the Grid view, and then choose
any of the Edit In options from the context menu.

Lightroom will render your Raw images into a pixel-based image file format—or ask the Photoshop Camera Raw plug-in to perform the conversion—and open the resulting image files in your external editor.

Don't rename the exported files or Lightroom will not be able to locate the edited versions in order to import them into the library. When saving from Photoshop or Photoshop Elements, make sure to activate the Maximize Compatibility option.

When you've finished editing your photos in the external editor, save your changes and return to Lightroom. The edited versions of your images will automatically be added to your photo library. The original image files will remain unchanged.

For more information, please refer to "Editing in other applications" in Lightroom Help.

You are now familiar with a wide variety of basic skills as well as some specialized techniques for more sophisticated image editing tasks. Experiment with the tools, settings, and options on your own to discover more of the depth and power of the Develop module.

Remember: all your edits are non-destructive—so enjoy!

Review questions

1 How do you undo changes or return quickly to a previous develop state?

2 What is white balance?

3 What does a tone curve represent and what is it used for?

4 What are the two kinds of noise you might encounter in a digital image and what can you do about them?

5 Which tools are used to perform local corrections?

Review answers

1 You can undo one modification at a time using the Undo command. You can jump back multiple steps at once in the History panel. You can create snapshots of important develop states so that you can return to them quickly.

2 An image's white balance reflects the composition of the red, green, and blue components in the light source when the picture was taken. It is used as a calibration benchmark to correctly interpret and render the color information recorded by the camera's sensors.

3 A tone curve adjusts the distribution of the tonal ranges in an image. The curve represents the way tonal information from the original image will be mapped to the adjusted image. It can be used to increase or decrease the contrast in specific tonal ranges.

4 Digital images may contain two kinds of noise: luminance noise, which is a result of variation in the brightness of pixels which should be of the same luminance, and color (chrominance) noise: bright blue, red and purple spots in an area that should be a uniform hue. Each kind of noise can be reduced using the appropriate noise reduction slider in the Detail panel.

5 You can restrict adjustments to selected areas of your image with the Graduated Filter tool and the Adjustment Brush tool.

7 CREATING SLIDESHOWS

Lesson overview

Now that you know how to import, review, organize, and enhance your photos, it's time to learn how Lightroom can help you to share them with friends and family or present them to a client. Choose a template as a starting point; then customize the layout, color scheme, and timing. Add backdrops, borders, and text, to create a presentation that will complement your work and captivate your audience.

In this lesson, you'll create your own slideshow by following these easy steps:

- Adding a text overlay
- Adding music and adjusting the playback settings
- Saving your customized template
- Previewing and playing your slideshow
- Exporting your presentation
- Grouping the images for your slideshow as a collection
- Viewing an impromptu slideshow
- Choosing a slideshow template
- Adjusting the slide layout
- Changing the background color and adding a backdrop image

 You'll probably need between one and two hours to complete this lesson.

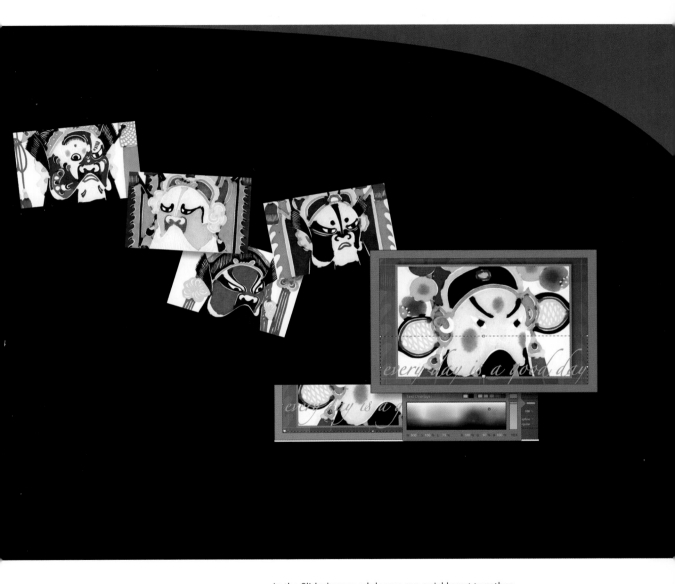

In the Slideshow module you can quickly put together an impressive on-screen presentation complete with stylish graphic effects, transitions, text overlays, and even music. Lightroom 3 makes it easier than ever to share your images with family and friends, clients, or the world at large by giving you the option of exporting your slideshow as a video.

Getting started

This lesson assumes that you are already familiar with the Lightroom workspace and with moving between the different modules. If you find that you need more background information as you go, refer to Lightroom Help, or review the previous lessons in this book.

Before you begin, make sure that you have correctly copied the Lessons folder from the CD in the back of this book onto your computer's hard disk and created the LR3CIB Library Catalog file as detailed in "Copying the Classroom in a Book files" on page 2 and "Creating a catalog file for working with this book" on page 3.

1   Start Lightroom.

2   In the Adobe Photoshop Lightroom - Select Catalog dialog box, make sure the file LR3CIB Library Catalog.lrcat is selected under Select A Recent Catalog To Open, and then click Open.

3   Lightroom will open in the screen mode and workspace module that were active when you last quit. If necessary, click Library in the Module Picker to switch to the Library module.

Importing images into the library

The first step is to import the images for this lesson into the Lightroom library.

1   In the Library module, click the Import button below the left panel group.

2   If the Import dialog box appears in compact mode, click the Show More Options button at the lower left of the dialog box to see all the options in the expanded Import dialog box.

3   Under Source at the left of the expanded Import dialog box, navigate to the Lessons folder you copied into the LR3CIB folder on your hard disk, and then select the Lesson 7 folder. Ensure that all nine images in the Lesson 7 folder are checked for import.

4   In the import options above the thumbnail previews, click Add to add the imported photos to your catalog without moving or copying them.

5   Under File Handling at the right of the expanded Import dialog box, choose Minimal from the Render Previews menu and ensure that the Don't Import Selected Duplicates option is activated.

6   Under Apply During Import, choose None from both the Develop Settings menu and the Metadata menu and type **Lesson 7** in the Keywords text box. Make sure your settings are exactly as shown in the illustration below, and then click Import.

The nine images, featuring details of Chinese papercuts, are imported from the Lesson 7 folder and now appear in both the Grid view of the Library module and in the Filmstrip across the bottom of the Lightroom workspace.

Playing an impromptu slideshow

Even before you leave the Library module you can play an impromptu slideshow, which is a convenient way to see a full-screen preview of the photos you've just imported. The Impromptu Slideshow can be launched from any of the Lightroom modules. The slide layout, timing, and transitions for the Impromptu Slideshow will reflect the current settings in the Slideshow module.

Tip: You can also start the impromptu slideshow from any module by choosing Window > Impromptu Slideshow. In the Library and Develop modules, click the Impromptu Slideshow button in the Toolbar.

1   In the Grid view of the Library module, choose View > Sort > File Name and View > Sort > Ascending.

2   Press Ctrl+A / Command+A or choose Edit > Select All to select all of the images you have just imported.

3   Press Ctrl+Enter / Command+Return to start the impromptu slideshow. Press the Right Arrow key to advance to the next slide or the Left Arrow key to return to the previous slide. Press the spacebar to pause and resume playback. The slideshow will cycle through the images until you either press the Esc key on your keyboard or click the screen to stop playback.

Setting up a slideshow

It's a good idea to group the images for your slideshow as a collection so that you can easily retrieve them when you want to work on your presentation, even though they may actually be stored in different folders on your hard disk. For example, you might assemble a collection of images featuring national monuments that includes a photo of the Statue of Liberty from your New York folder and a photo of the Golden Gate Bridge from your San Francisco folder. Once you have grouped the images as a collection you can call up the same selection at a single click. Grouping your images in a collection also has other advantages: you can make consistent adjustments across all the images, rearrange their display order and easily add or remove images from the grouping without deleting them from the catalog.

Creating a new collection

Tip: Once you have grouped a selection of photos as a collection, you can rearrange their order by simply dragging the thumbnails in the Grid view or the Filmstrip. The new display order will be saved with the collection—together with any settings you apply in the Slideshow, Print, or Web modules.

1   Check that all nine images for this lesson are still selected. If not, press Ctrl+A / Command+A or choose Edit > Select All.

2   In the left panel group, click the New Collection button (+) in the header of the Collections panel, and then choose Create Collection from the menu.

3   In the Create Collection dialog box, type **My Slideshow** in the Name box and choose None from the Set menu. Under Collection Options, activate Include Selected Photos and disable Make New Virtual Copies; then click Create.

4   If it's not already selected, click your new collection in the Collections panel.

5   Make sure the menu options View > Sort > File Name and View > Sort > Ascending are still activated from the previous exercise.

6   Switch to the Slideshow module by clicking Slideshow in the Module Picker or pressing Ctrl+Alt+3 / Option+Command+3.

The Lightroom Slideshow module

At center stage in the Slideshow module is the Slide Editor view where you can see how your images look in the current layout template and preview your slideshow. Choose a slideshow template from the Template Browser in the left panel group and the Slide Editor view is updated to display the new layout (the illustration below shows the Crop To Fill template). In the Preview panel above the Template Browser you can preview the templates by moving the pointer over the list. The Toolbar just below the Slide Editor view contains controls for navigating the images in your collection, previewing your slideshow, and adding text to your slides.

The settings and controls in the right panel group enable you to customize the slideshow template by tweaking the layout, adding borders, shadows, and overlays, changing the backdrop, adding title screens, and adjusting the playback settings.

Choosing a slideshow template

Each of the Lightroom slideshow templates provides a convenient starting-point for creating your own slide designs.

1   In the Template Browser panel, move the pointer over the list of slideshow templates in the Lightroom Templates folder. The Preview panel shows you how the selected image looks in each template layout. Select a different image in the Filmstrip and preview the templates again.

2   When you're done previewing the options in the Template Browser, click to select the Widescreen template.

3   Select the first image, Slideshow1.jpg, by clicking it in the Filmstrip. From the Use menu in the Toolbar, choose All Filmstrip Photos.

4   Click the Preview button at the bottom of the right panel group to preview your presentation in the Slide Editor view. When you're done, click in the Slide Editor view to stop the preview.

Template options for slideshows

As a convenient starting-point for creating your own slide layouts, you can choose from these customizable Lightroom templates:

Caption And Rating   This template centers the images on a grey background and displays the star rating and caption metadata for each photo.

Crop To Fill   Your photos fill the screen and may be cropped to fit the screen's aspect ratio, so this is probably not a good option for images in portrait format.

Default   This template is similar to the first, except that it incorporates your identity plate and displays the image file name rather than metadata information.

EXIF Metadata   The slides are centered on a black background and include star-ratings, EXIF (Exchangeable Image Format) information, and your identity plate.

Widescreen   Your images are centered and sized to fit the screen without being cropped: any empty space outside the image is filled with black.

Customizing your slideshow template

For the purposes of this lesson, you won't be adding an identity plate or metadata information to your slides, so the Widescreen template will serve as a good basis. You'll customize the template by tweaking the layout, creating a background, and overlaying text, and then liven up the show by adding a soundtrack.

Adjusting the slide layout

Once you've chosen a slide template you can use the controls in the right panel group to customize it. For this project you'll start by modifying the layout, and then change the background to set up the overall look of the design before you make decisions about the style and color of borders and overlaid text. The Layout panel enables you to change the size and position of the photo in the slide layout by setting the margins that define the image cell.

1   If the Layout panel in the right panel group is currently collapsed, expand it by clicking the triangle beside its name. Make sure that the Show Guides and Link All options are activated.

2   Move the pointer over the lower edge of the image in the Slide Editor view. When the pointer changes to a double-arrow cursor, drag the edge of the image upwards. As you drag, grey layout guide lines appear against the black background around the scaled-down image. All four guides move at the same time because the Link All option is activated in the Layout panel. As you drag upwards, watch the linked sliders and numerical values change in the Layout panel and release the mouse button when the values reach 50 px (pixels).

▶ **Tip:** To adjust the size of the image in the slide layout, you could also drag the sliders in the Layout panel or click the pixel values at the right and type **50**. In this case you would only need to drag one slider or enter one value because the settings are linked.

3   Collapse the Layout panel.

Setting the slide background

In the Backdrop panel you can set a flat background color for your slides, apply a graduated color wash, or place a backdrop image. When all of the background options are disabled, the slide background is black by default.

1   Expand the Backdrop panel in the right panel group.

2   Choose Edit > Select None.

3   In the Backdrop panel, activate the Background Image option, and then drag the image Slideshow7.jpg from the Filmstrip into the Background Image box.

4   Drag the Opacity slider to the left to reduce the value to 20%, or click the Opacity value and type **20**. You'll see the change in the Slide Editor view.

5 Activate the Background Color option, and then click the color swatch beside it. The Color Picker appears.

6 Drag the slider at the right of the Color Picker almost to the top, and then click a bright pink in the color field on the left. We chose a color with the RGB values: R: 70%, G: 0%, B: 60%. You can enter these values directly by clicking each number and typing the new value in the text box. If you see a hexadecimal value displayed in the lower right corner of the Color Picker rather than RGB values, click RGB below the color slider.

▶ **Tip:** A background image can be a stylish and effective device to set an overall theme for your slideshow, particularly when it's applied at less than full opacity and perhaps overlaid with text.

The color you specified appears in the color box at the top right of the Color Picker, in the Background Color swatch, and in the Background Image preview. The slide is now framed with a captivating pattern that, because it is derived from one of the papercut images, fits well with the rest of the series.

7 Click the Close button in the upper left corner of the Color Picker to close it.

8 Activate the Color Wash option. The Color Wash applies an angled gradient wash over the background color and the background image. The gradient fades from the background color to the color set in the Color Wash swatch.

9 Click the Color Wash swatch to open the Color Picker and set a wash color with the RGB values: R: 0%, G: 0%, B: 60%.

10 Close the Color Picker, and then use the Opacity slider to set the color wash opacity to 50%. Turn the Angle dial or drag the slider to experiment with the angle at which the color wash is applied.

11 Collapse the Backdrop panel.

Adjusting stroke borders and casting shadows

Now that you've established the overall layout and color scheme, you can "lift" the image to make it stand out more against the background by adding a stroke border and a drop shadow.

1   In the right panel group, expand the Options panel.

2   Activate the Stroke Border option, and then click the color swatch beside it to open the Color Picker.

3   We'll stay within our established color scheme, so that the design doesn't become too busy and compete with our images. Drag the slider at the right of the Color Picker to the top, and then click a bright pink in the large color field on the left. We choose a color with the RGB values: R: 80%, G: 0%, B: 80%.
Click outside the Color Picker to close it.

4   Increase the stroke width by dragging the Width slider to set a value of 10 pixels or type **10** in the box beside the slider.

5   Now activate the Cast Shadow option in the Options panel and experiment with the controls. You can adjust the opacity of the shadow, the distance that the shadow is offset from the image, the angle at which the shadow is cast, and the Radius setting, which affects the softness of the shadow's edge.

6   When you're finished experimenting, collapse the Options panel.

Adding a text overlay

In the Overlays panel you can add text or an identity plate to your slides and have Lightroom display the rating stars you've assigned to your images or the captions that you've added to their metadata.

● **Note:** For this exercise, you won't incorporate an identity plate in your slideshow. For more information on identity plates, refer to Lesson 2, Lesson 9, or the Lightroom Help topic "Add your identity plate to a slideshow."

Our text—a Chinese proverb—will be overlaid on every slide, becoming part of the imagery so that its role is atmospheric and decorative rather than informative.

1 Expand the Overlays panel and activate the Text Overlays option.

2 If the Toolbar is not visible just below the Slide Editor view, press the T key. In the Toolbar, click the Add Text To Slide button (ABC); the Custom Text box appears in the Toolbar.

3 Type the Chinese proverb **every day is a good day** in the Custom Text box.

4 Press Enter / Return. The text appears in the lower left corner of the Slide Editor view, surrounded by a bounding box. The Text Overlays settings are updated to show the font details (Myriad Web Pro is selected in the illustration below).

5 To choose a different font, click the double triangle beside the font name and choose a script font from the menu. We chose Zapfino, but any other script or calligraphic font such as Monotype Corsiva will suit our design. Zapfino is available only in Regular, so there are no other options available in the Face menu.

6 Enlarge the text by dragging the upper right handle of the bounding box. Release the mouse button when the text is the same width as the image.

To achieve the desired effect of ambience and subtlety, we'll choose a color in the same range of pinks as the background and border.

7 In the Overlays panel, click the Text Overlays color swatch to open he Color Picker.

8 In the Color Picker, drag the color slider on the right to the top, and then click a pink in the large color field on the left. We used a color with the RGB values: R: 100%, G: 50%, B: 100%. Click outside the Color Picker to close it.

9 Drag the text box to align the base line of the text with the border of the image as shown in the illustration below.

As you drag the text, Lightroom tethers the bounding box either to the nearest of various reference points around the edge of the slide, or to a point on the border of the image itself. To see this in operation, drag the text around the slide, both inside and outside of the image, and watch the white tether-line jump from point to point. When you're done, return the text to its original position. Throughout a slideshow, the text will maintain the same position either relative to the slide as a whole or

to the border of each image regardless of its size or orientation. You can use this feature to ensure that a caption, for instance, will always appear just below the left corner of each image no matter what its orientation while a title that applies to the presentation as a whole will remain in a constant position on the screen.
For the purposes of this exercise, you won't need to pay attention to this issue as there is no variation in the size or orientation of the images.

10 To integrate the text into the image even more effectively, drag the Opacity slider to 50, or type **50** in the Opacity box.

As a finishing touch you'll place a shadow behind the type to add depth and create the impression that the letters themselves are cut from paper and overlaid.

● **Note:** The Shadow option is available only on Mac OS.

11 On Mac OS, activate the Shadow option below the Text Overlays settings. Drag the sliders or type these values: Opacity: **64**, Offset: **20**, Radius: **8**, Angle: **0**.

12 Collapse the Overlays panel and deselect the text box in the Slideshow Editor view.

13 Select the first slide in the Filmstrip and click the Preview button at the bottom of the right panel group to preview your slideshow in the Slideshow Editor view. When you're done, press Esc to stop playback.

Using the Text Template Editor

In the Slideshow module, you can use the Text Template Editor to access and edit the information that is stored as metadata in your images and to specify which elements of that information you would like to display as text overlays on each slide.

You can add titles that differ from the original file names, or display captions, capture dates, image sizes, or any of numerous other options. You can save your choices as a text template preset and create presets with different sets of information for different types of presentation.

In the Slideshow module, click the Add Text To Slide button (ABC) in the Toolbar. Type anything at all in the Custom Text box and press Enter / Return. The text appears as an overlay in the Slide Editor. Make sure the text overlay is selected; then click the double triangle beside the Custom Text box in the Toolbar and choose Edit from the menu.

The Text Template Editor appears. In the Example text box, you will see a Custom Text *token*.

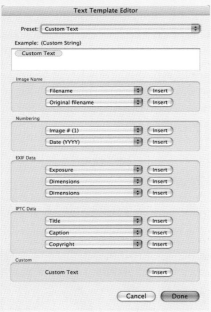

A token is a placeholder for whatever custom text you wish to specify. If you did not specify any other content for the token in the Text Template Editor the token would represent whatever custom text you already entered in the Toolbar.

Click the token to select it and type anything at all in the example box. Click Done and the new custom text replaces the original in the Slide Editor view.

Open the Text Template Editor again by clicking the double triangle beside the Custom Text box in the Toolbar and choosing Edit from the menu. This time you will replace the custom text with another token chosen from the options in the Text Template Editor. Select the custom text in the Example box and delete it. In the Image Name options, click the top Insert button. A Filename token appears in the Example box. Click Done and the file name appears in the Slide Editor view.

Drag the file name overlay to the upper left corner of the slide and click outside the bounding box to deselect it. Click the Add Text To Slide button (ABC) in the Toolbar; then click the double triangle beside the Custom Text box and choose Edit from the menu. The text <empty> appears on the slide as a new text overlay. In the Text Template Editor, select the new Custom Text token in the Example box and choose Image # (01) from the upper menu in the Numbering options. Click Done and the image number (in two-digit format) replaces the text <empty> on the slide in the Slide Editor view.

(continues on next page)

Adjusting the playback settings

In the Playback panel you can add a soundtrack to your presentation, set the duration for slides and transitions, or set the slideshow to display your images in random order. Adding a soundtrack can make your slideshow much more dynamic and compelling, so let's start with that.

Adding music to your slideshow

You'll find a sound file named Temple of the Moon.mp3 in your Lesson 7 folder. This piece of music will underline the Asian feel of the slideshow. However, feel free to choose any other file from your music library that you'd like to audition.

1   Expand the Playback panel in the right panel group, and activate the Soundtrack option.

2   Click the Select Music button; then navigate to your LR3CIB > Lessons > Lesson 7 folder, select the file Temple of the Moon.mp3, and click Choose.

> **Tip:** If you have more than one screen attached to your computer you'll see the Playback Screen pane in the Playback panel. You can choose which screen will be used when your slideshow is played at full-screen and whether to blank the other screens during playback.

The name of the sound file and its duration are now displayed in the Soundtrack pane of the Playback panel.

3   Click the Preview button at the bottom of the right panel group to preview the slideshow in the Slideshow Editor view. The music adds atmosphere to the slideshow. When you're done, press Esc to stop playback.

The next step is to fine-tune the timing of the slideshow by setting the duration of slides and fades to the length of the music file.

4   In the Soundtrack pane, click the Fit To Music button, keeping an eye on the default Slides and Fades values in the Slide Duration settings towards the bottom of the Playback panel as you do so.

Lightroom adjusts the Slides and Fades values to fit the duration of the music file.

5   Drag the Fades slider to the left to reduce the duration of the fade transitions by 0.5 seconds, and then click the Fit To Music button once more, keeping an eye on the Slides value in the Slide Duration settings as you do so.

Lightroom automatically re-calculates the duration for which each slide will be shown so that the slideshow still fits to the music file despite the shortened fades.

6   At the bottom of the Playback panel, disable both the Random Order and Repeat options, and then click the Play button at the bottom of the right panel group to see the slideshow in full-screen mode. While the slideshow is playing in full-screen mode, press the spacebar to pause and resume playback, the Right Arrow key to advance to the next slide, the Left Arrow key to return to the previous slide, and the Esc key to end the slideshow.

Saving the customized slideshow template

Having spent so much time customizing your slideshow template, you should now save it to become one more choice in the Template Browser menu.

Saving your customized slideshow template will save you a lot of time later should you wish to reuse this slideshow, extend it, or use the template as a starting-point to create another presentation. By default, your customized template will be listed with the User Templates in the Template Browser panel.

1   With your slideshow still open in the Slideshow module, click the Create New Preset button (+) in the header of the Template Browser panel, or choose Slideshow > New Template.

2 In the New Template dialog box, type **My Pink Slideshow** as the new template name. Leave the default User Templates folder selected as the destination folder in the Folder menu, and click Create.

▶ **Tip:** When saving a customized template it's a good idea to give it a descriptive name. This will make it easier to find as you add more choices to the Template Browser menu.

3 Check to see that your new customized template is now listed under User Templates in the Template Browser panel.

Exporting a slideshow

To send your slideshow to a friend or client, play it on another computer, or share it on the Web, you can export it as a PDF file or as a high-quality video file.

1 In the Slideshow module, click the Export PDF button at the bottom of the left panel group.

2 Review the options available in the Export Slideshow To PDF dialog box, noting the settings for size and quality, and then click Cancel.

● **Note:** PDF slideshow transitions work when viewed using the free Adobe Reader or Adobe Acrobat. However, slideshows exported to PDF will not include music, randomized playback order, or your customized slide duration settings.

3 In the Slideshow module, click the Export Video button at the bottom of the left panel group.

4 Review the Export Slideshow To Video dialog box, noting the range of options available in the Video Preset menu. Select each export option in turn to see a brief description below the Video Preset menu.

Lightroom exports slideshows in the popular H.264 movie format so that you can share your slideshow movies on popular video sharing sites or optimize them for playback on mobile media. Preset size and quality settings range from 320 x 240, optimized for personal media players and email, to 1080p, optimizes for high quality HD video.

5 In the Export Slideshow To Video dialog box, type a name for your exported video and specify a destination folder. Choose an option from the Video Preset menu, and then click Export.

A progress bar in the upper left corner of the workspace shows the status of the export process.

Modifying and organizing user templates

The Template Browser offers numerous options for organizing your templates and template folders:

Renaming a template or template folder

You cannot rename the Lightroom Templates folder, any of the Lightroom templates, or the default User Templates folder. To rename any of the templates or template folders that you have created, right-click / Control-click the template or folder in the Template Browser and choose Rename from the context menu.

Moving a template

If you wish to move a template into another folder in the Template Browser, simply drag the template to that folder. If you wish to move a template into a new folder, right-click / Control-click the template and choose New Folder from the context menu. The selected template will be moved into the new folder as it is created. If you try to move one of the Lightroom templates, the template will me copied to the new folder but will still remain in the Lightroom Templates folder.

Updating a custom template's settings

If you wish to modify one of your own custom templates select it in the Template Browser and make your changes using any of the controls in the right panel group. To save your changes, right-click / Control-click the template in the Template Browser and choose Update with Current Settings.

Creating a copy of a template

You may wish to create a copy of a template so that you can safely make modifications without affecting the original. If you wish to create a copy of the currently selected template in an existing template folder, click the Create New Preset button (+) in the Template Browser panel header. In the New Template dialog box, type a name for the copy, choose the destination folder from the Folder menu, and click Create. If you wish to create a copy of the currently selected template in a new folder, click the Create New Preset button (+) in the Template Browser panel header. In the New Template dialog box, type a name for the copy and choose New Folder from the Folder menu. In the New Folder dialog box, type a name for the new folder and click Create. The new folder appears in the Template Browser. Click Create in the New Template dialog box to dismiss it. The copied template will be created in the new folder.

Exporting a custom template

To export your custom slideshow template so that you can use it in Lightroom on another computer, right-click / Control-click the template name in the Template Browser menu and choose Export from the context menu.

Importing a custom template

To import a custom template that has been created in Lightroom on another computer, right-click / Control-click the User Templates header or any of the templates in the User Templates menu and choose Import from the context menu. In the Import Template dialog box, locate the template file and click Import.

(continues on next page)

Modifying and organizing user templates (continued)

Deleting a template

To delete a custom template, right-click / Control-click the template name in the Template Browser and choose Delete from the context menu. You can also select the template and click the Remove button at the bottom of the right panel group. You cannot delete the templates in the Lightroom Templates folder.

Creating a new templates folder

To create a new empty folder in the Templates Browser, right-click / Control-click the header of any other folder and choose New Folder from the context menu. You can drag templates into the new folder.

Deleting a templates folder

To delete a template folder, you'll first need to delete all the templates within that folder—or drag them to another folder. Right-click / Control-click the empty folder, and choose Delete Folder from the context menu or simply select the empty folder and click the Remove button at the bottom of the right panel group.

Well done! You have successfully completed another Lightroom lesson. In this lesson you learned how to view your image collection as an impromptu slideshow and then created your own stylish slideshow presentation.

In the process, you've explored the Slideshow module and used the control panels to customize a slideshow template—refining the layout and playback settings and adding a backdrop, text, borders, and a soundtrack.

In the next chapter you'll find out how to present your work in printed format, but before you move on, take a few moments to reinforce what you've learned by reading through the review questions and answers on the next page.

Review questions

1   How do you view an Impromptu Slideshow?

2   Which Lightroom slideshow template would you pick if you wished to display metadata for your images?

3   What options do you have when customizing a slideshow template?

4   What are the four Cast Shadow controls and what are their effects?

Review answers

1   To view an Impromptu Slideshow, press Ctrl+Enter / Command+Return. You can also choose Window > Impromptu Slideshow.

2   The EXIF Metadata template, which centers photos on a black background and displays star ratings and EXIF information for the images, as well as an identity plate.

3   In the right panel group you can modify the slide layout, add borders and text overlays, create shadow effects for images or text, change the background color or add a backdrop image, adjust the durations of slides and fades, and add a soundtrack.

4   The four Cast Shadow controls have the following effects:

   • Opacity: Controls the opacity of the shadow ranging from 0% (invisible) to 100% (fully opaque).

   • Offset: Affects the distance that the shadow is offset from the slide. As the offset is increased, more shadow becomes visible.

   • Radius: Controls how sharp (lower settings) or soft (higher settings) the edges of the shadow appear.

   • Angle: Sets the direction of the light source, which affects the angle at which the shadow is cast.

8 PRINTING IMAGES

Lesson overview

The Lightroom Print module offers all the tools you'll need to quickly prepare any selection of images from your library for printing.

You can print a photo singly or repeated at different sizes on the same sheet, or create an attractive layout for multiple images. Add borders, text, and graphics, and then adjust settings for print resolution, sharpening, paper type, and color management with just a few clicks.

In this lesson, you'll explore the Print module as you become accustomed to the steps in the printing workflow:

- Selecting and grouping your photos
- Choosing a layout template
- Creating a custom print template
- Creating a Custom Package print layout
- Adding borders and a background color
- Adding an identity plate
- Adding text
- Specifying print settings and printer driver options
- Saving print settings as an output preset

 You'll probably need between one and two hours to complete this lesson.

Whether you need to print a contact sheet or a fine art mat, Lightroom makes it easy to achieve professional results with a choice of highly customizable layout templates.

Getting started

This lesson assumes that you are already familiar with the Lightroom workspace and with moving between the different modules. If you find that you need more background information as you go, refer to Lightroom Help, or review the previous lessons in this book.

Before you begin, make sure that you have correctly copied the Lessons folder from the CD in the back of this book onto your computer's hard disk and created the LR3CIB Library Catalog file as detailed in "Copying the Classroom in a Book files" on page 2 and "Creating a catalog file for working with this book" on page 3.

1 Start Lightroom.

2 In the Adobe Photoshop Lightroom - Select Catalog dialog box, make sure the file LR3CIB Library Catalog.lrcat is selected under Select A Recent Catalog To Open, and then click Open.

3 Lightroom will open in the screen mode and workspace module that were active when you last quit. If necessary, click Library in the Module Picker to switch to the Library module.

Importing images into the library

The first step is to import the images for this lesson into the Lightroom library.

1 In the Library module, click the Import button below the left panel group.

2 If the Import dialog box appears in compact mode, click the Show More Options button at the lower left of the dialog box to see all the options in the expanded Import dialog box.

3 Under Source at the left of the expanded Import dialog box, navigate to the Lessons folder that you copied into the LR3CIB folder on your hard disk. Select the Lesson 8 folder. Ensure that all six images in the Lesson 8 folder are checked for import.

4 In the import options above the thumbnail previews, click Add to add the imported photos to your catalog without moving or copying them.

5 Under File Handling at the right of the expanded Import dialog box, choose Minimal from the Render Previews menu and ensure that the Don't Import Selected Duplicates option is activated.

6 Under Apply During Import, choose None from both the Develop Settings menu and the Metadata menu and type **Lesson 8** in the Keywords text box. Make sure your settings are exactly as shown in the illustration below, and then click Import.

The six images are imported from the Lesson 8 folder and now appear in both the Grid view of the Library module and in the Filmstrip across the bottom of the Lightroom workspace.

Creating a new collection

It's a good idea to group the images for your print job as a collection so that you can easily retrieve them even if they're actually stored in different folders on your hard disk. Grouping your images in a collection has other advantages: you can make consistent adjustments across all the images, rearrange their display order, and add or remove images. You can use the temporary Quick Collection in the Catalog panel, or create a new collection that will appear in the Collections panel.

1 Select all six images for this lesson by pressing Ctrl+A / Command+A or choosing Edit > Select All.

2 In the left panel group, click the New Collection icon (+) in the header of the Collections panel and choose Create Collection from the menu.

3 In the Create Collection dialog box, type **My Prints** in the Name box and choose None from the Set menu. Under Collection Options, activate Include Selected Photos and disable Make New Virtual Copies; then click Create.

The new collection is now listed in the Collections panel.

▶ **Tip:** To delete a collection, right-click / Control-click its name in the Collections panel and choose Delete from the context menu.

4 Click Print in the Module Picker to switch to the Print Module.

About the Lightroom Print module

In the Print module you'll find tools and controls for each step in the printing workflow. Organize your photos, choose a template and refine the layout, add borders, text, or graphics, and adjust the output settings; everything you need is at your fingertips.

In the Print module's left panel group are the Preview and Template Browser panels. By moving the pointer over the list of templates in the Template Browser you can see a thumbnail preview of each layout displayed in the Preview panel. The left panel group also contains the Collections panel for easy access to your images.

You can select the photos you wish to print in the Filmstrip. When you choose a new template from the list, the Print Editor view—at center-stage in the workspace—will be updated to show how the selected photos look in the new layout.

You'll use the controls in the right panel group to customize your layout template and to specify output settings.

The Template Browser contains templates of three distinct types: Single Image / Contact Sheet layouts, Picture Package layouts, and Custom Package layouts.

Four of the first twelve preset Lightroom templates in the menu are Picture Package layouts, which repeat a single image at a variety of sizes on the same page. The other eight are Single Image / Contact Sheet layouts, which can be used to print multiple photos at the same size on a single sheet. Single Image / Contact Sheet layouts are based on an adjustable grid of image cells. They range from contact sheets with many cells to single-cell layouts such as the Fine Art Mat and Maximize Size templates. The Custom layout templates further down the menu enable you to print multiple images at any size on the same page. All of the templates can be customized; you can save your modified layouts as user-defined templates, which will be listed in the Template Browser.

The suite of panels you see in the right panel group will vary slightly, depending on which type of template you have chosen. The Layout Style panel at the top of the group indicates which type of template you're working with.

The controls in the Image Settings panel enable you to add borders and to specify the way in which your photos are fitted to their image cells. For a Single Image / Contact Sheet template, you can use the Layout panel to adjust the margins, cell size and spacing, and to change the number of rows and columns that make up the grid. Use the Guides panel to show or hide a selection of layout guides. For a Picture Package or Custom package template, you'll modify your layout with the Rulers, Grid & Guides panel and the Cells panel. You can use the Page panel to watermark your printed images and to add text, graphics, or a background color to your layout. In the Print Job panel you can set print resolution, print sharpening, paper type, and color management options.

The photos in your collection are displayed in the Filmstrip across the bottom of the workspace, where you can select images for printing and drag their thumbnails to change the order in which they will appear in a multiple-image layout.

About layout styles and print templates

The Template Browser offers a wide choice of preset Lightroom print templates that differ not only in basic layout but may also include a variety of design features such as borders and overlaid text or graphics.

Templates may also differ in their output settings: the print resolution setting for a contact sheet will be lower than the resolution set for a template designed for producing finished prints.

You can save time and effort setting up your print job by selecting the print template that most closely suits your purpose. In this exercise you'll be introduced to the different types of template and use the panels in the right panel group to examine the characteristics of each layout.

1 In the left panel group, make sure that the Preview and Template Browser panels are expanded. If necessary, drag the top border of the Filmstrip down so that you can see as many as possible of the templates in the Template Browser. In the right panel group, expand the Layout Style panel and collapse the others.

2 Choose Edit > Select None, and then select just one of the images in the Filmstrip. The Print Editor view at the center of the workspace is updated to display the selected photo in the current layout.

3 If necessary, expand the Lightroom Templates folder inside the Template Browser panel. Move the pointer slowly over the list of preset templates to see a preview of each layout in the Preview panel.

4 Click the second template in the Template Browser: "(1) 4 × 6, (6) 2 × 3." The new template is applied to the image in the Print Editor view. Look at the Layout Style panel in the right panel group. You'll see that the Layout Style panel indicates that this template is a Picture Package layout. In the Template Browser, click the sixth Lightroom template "(2) 7 × 5." The Layout Style panel indicates that this is also a Picture Package layout.

5 Now choose the ninth preset template in the Template Browser: "2-Up Greeting Card." The Layout Style panel indicates that the template "2-Up Greeting Card" is a Single Image / Contact Sheet layout, and the Print Editor view at the center of the workspace displays the new template.

6 In the Layout Style panel, click Picture Package. The Print Editor view is updated to display the last selected Picture Package layout: "(2) 7 × 5." Click Single Image / Contact Sheet in the Layout Style panel and the Print Editor view returns to the last selected Single Image / Contact Sheet layout: "2-Up Greeting Card."

As you move between the Single Image / Contact Sheet and Picture Package layout styles you'll notice that a different suite of control panels become available in the right panel group. Panels common to both layout styles may differ in content.

7   In the right panel group, expand the Image Settings panel. In the Layout Style panel, click Picture Package and expand the Image Settings panel again. Toggle between the Picture Package and Single Image / Contact Sheet layouts and notice how the options available in the Image Settings panel change.

You can see that the selected photo fits to the image cell differently for each of these templates. In the Picture Package layout "(2) 7 × 5," the Zoom To Fill option is activated in the Image Settings panel so that the photo is zoomed and cropped to fill the image cell. In the Single Image / Contact Sheet "2-Up Greeting Card," the Zoom to Fill option is disabled and the photo is not cropped. Take a moment to examine the other differences in the Image Settings panel.

(2) 7 × 5 template

2-Up Greeting Card template

8   Select the Single Image / Contact Sheet layout style. Look at the page count at the right of the Toolbar below the Print Editor view: it reads "Page 1 of 1." Press Ctrl+A / Command+A or choose Edit > Select All to select all six images in the collection. The page count in the Toolbar now reads "Page x of 6." The template "2-Up Greeting Card" is now applied to all six photos, resulting in a print job of six pages. Use the navigation buttons at the left the Toolbar to move between the pages and see the layout applied to each image in turn.

► **Tip:** You can also navigate your multi-page print document by using the Home, End, Page Up, Page Down, and left and right arrow keys on your keyboard, or choosing from the navigation commands in the Print menu.

9   For the last step in this exercise, collapse the Image Settings panel and expand the Print Job panel. You'll notice that in the Print Job panel, the Print Resolution for the "2-Up Greeting Card" template is set to 240 ppi. Select the template "4×5 Contact Sheet" in the Template Browser. The Print Resolution option in the Print Job panel is disabled and the Draft Mode Printing option is activated.

Selecting a print template

Now that you've explored the Template Browser, it's time to choose the template that you will customize in the next exercise.

1 In the Template Browser, click the template "4 Wide." If you have customized your default identity plate, you may want to uncheck the Identity Plate option in the Page panel for now.

2 Choose Edit > Select None. In the Filmstrip, select the images Emma_1.jpg, Emma_2.jpg, and Emma_3.jpg. The Images will be arranged in the template in the same order in which they appear in the Filmstrip. Drag the images inside their grid cells to reposition them as shown in the illustration below.

> **Tip:** By default, each photo will be centered in its own image cell. To expose a different portion of an image that is cropped by the boundaries of its cell, simply drag the photo to reposition it within its image cell.

Specifying the printer and paper size

Before you customize the template, you'll need to specify the paper size and page orientation for your print job. Doing this now may save you the time and effort of readjusting the layout later.

1 Choose File > Page Setup.

2 In the Print Setup / Page Setup dialog box, choose the desired printer from the Name / Format For menu.

3 From the Paper Size menu, choose Letter (8.5 × 11 In.) / US Letter. Choose the portrait format option as Orientation, and then click OK.

> **Tip:** Lightroom automatically scales your photos in the print layout template to fit the paper size you have specified. In the Print Setup / Page Setup dialog box, leave the scale setting at the default 100% and let Lightroom fit the template to the page—that way, what you see in the Print Editor view will be what you'll get from your printer.

Customizing print templates

Having established the overall layout of your print job, you can use the controls in the Layout panel to fine-tune the template so that the images fit better to the page.

Changing the number of cells

For the purposes of this exercise, we need only three of the four preset image cells.

1   If necessary, expand the Layout panel in the right panel group. Under Page Grid, drag the Rows slider to the left or type **3** in the text box to the right of the slider.

2   Experiment with the Margins, Cell Spacing, and Cell Size sliders—making sure to undo (Ctrl+Z / Command+Z) after each change. Activate the Keep Square option below the Cell Size sliders. The Cell Width and Cell Height sliders are locked together at the same value. Disable the Keep Square option.

3   The black lines you might see around the photos are merely guides indicating the image cell boundaries; they will not appear on your printed page. These guides are helpful while you're adjusting the cell size and spacing but they'll be distracting when you add printable borders to your layout in the next exercise.

If necessary, expand the Guides panel below the Layout panel and disable the Image Cells option; then collapse the Layout and Guides panels.

Modifying the page layout of a print template

Layout controls for Single Image / Contact Sheet and Picture Package templates

Depending on which type of print template you are working with, you'll find a slightly different suite of panels in the right panel group. The Image Settings, Page, and Print Job panels are available for all template types but the controls for modifying the page layout differ. If you've chosen a Single Image / Contact Sheet template, you'll customize your layout using the Layout and Guides panels. For a Picture Package template, you'll use the Rulers, Grids & Guides panel and the Cells panel. For Custom Package layouts you'll also use the Rulers, Grids & Guides panel and the Cells panel—where you'll find a few minor differences from the options offered in the same panels for a Picture Package.

Picture Package templates and Custom Package layouts and are not grid-based so they are very flexible to work with; you can arrange the image cells on the page either by simply dragging them in the Print Editor view or by using the controls in the Cells panel. You can resize a cell using the width and height sliders or simply drag the handles of its bounding box. Add more photos to your layout with the Cells panel controls or Alt-drag / Option-drag a cell to duplicate it and resize it as you wish.

Lightroom provides a variety of guides to help you adjust your layout. Guides are not printed: they appear only in the Print Editor view. To show or hide the guides, activate Show Guides in the Guides panel, or choose View > Show Guides (Ctrl+Shift+H / Command+Shift+H). In the Guides panel you can specify which types of guides will be displayed in the Print Editor view.

Note: The Margins and Gutters guides and Image Cells guides—available only for Single Image / Contact Sheet layouts—are interactive; you can adjust your layout directly by dragging the guides themselves in the Print Editor view. When you move these guides, the Margins, Cell Spacing and Cell Size sliders in the Layout panel will move with them.

Using the Layout panel to modify a Contact Sheet / Grid layout

Ruler Units sets the units of measurement for most of the other controls in the Layouts panel and for the Rulers guide in the Guides panel. Click the Ruler Units setting and choose Inches, Centimeters, Millimeters, Points or Picas from the menu. The default setting is Inches.

Margins sets the boundaries for the grid of image cells in your layout. Most printers don't support borderless printing, so the minimum value for the margins is dependent on the capabilities of your printer. Even if your printer does support borderless printing, you may first need to activate this feature in the printer settings before you can set the margins to zero.

Page Grid specifies the number of rows and columns of image cells in the layout. The grid can contain anything from one image cell (Rows: 1, Columns: 1) to 225 image cells (Rows: 15, Columns: 15).

Cell Spacing and Cell Size settings are linked so that changes you make to one will affect the other. The Cell Spacing sliders set the vertical and horizontal spaces between the image cells in the grid; the Cell Size controls change the height and width of the cells. The Keep Square option links the height and width settings so that the image cells remain square.

(continued on next page)

Modifying the page layout of a print template (continued)

Using the Guides panel to modify a Contact Sheet / Grid layout

Rulers are displayed across the top and at the left of the Print Editor view. If Show Guides is activated, you can also show the rulers by choosing View > Show Rulers (Ctrl+R / Command+R). To change the ruler units, click the setting in the Layout panel.

Page Bleed shades the non-printable edges of the page, as defined by your printer settings.

Margins and Gutters guides reflect the Margins settings in the Layout panel; in fact, dragging these guides in the Print Editor view will move the respective sliders in the Layout panel.

Image Cells shows a black border around each image cell. When the Margins and Gutters guides are not visible, dragging the Image Cells guides in the Print Editor view will change the Margins, Cell Spacing, and Cell Size settings in the Layout panel.

Dimensions displays the measurements of each image cell in its top left corner, expressed in whatever units of measurement you have chosen for the Ruler Units.

Using the Rulers, Grids & Guides panel to modify a Picture Package layout

Rulers shows the rulers and lets you set the units of measurement just as you would in the Layout panel when you're working with a Contact Sheet / Grid template.

Grid displays a grid guide behind the image cells in the Print Editor view. As you drag the cells, you can have them snap to each other or to the grid (or turn the snap behavior off) by choosing Cells, Grid, or Off from the Snap menu options. The grid divisions are affected by your choice of ruler units.

Note: The snap behavior helps you to position the image cells accurately on the page. If you accidentally overlap your photos, Lightroom will let you know by showing a triangular yellow warning icon (!) in the top right corner of the page.

Bleeds and **Dimensions** are the Picture Package equivalents of the Page Bleed and Dimensions guides.

Using the Cells panel to modify a Picture Package layout

Add To Package offers six preset image cell sizes that can be placed in your layout at the click of a button. You can change which of the presets is assigned to each button by clicking its menu triangle. The default presets are standard photo sizes but you can edit them if you wish.

New Page adds a page to your layout, though Lightroom automatically adds pages if you use the Add to Package buttons to add more photos than fit on a page. To delete a page from your layout, click the red X in its upper left corner of the page in the Print Editor view.

Auto Layout optimizes the arrangement of the photos on the page for the fewest cuts.

Clear Layout removes all the image cells from the layout.

Adjust Selected Cell lets you change the height and width of an image cell using sliders or numerical input.

Creating stroke and photo borders

For our Single Image / Contact Sheet layout, the Image Settings panel offers options that affect the way your photos are fit to the image cells, and a control for adding borders. In this exercise you'll add a stroke border around each of the three images and adjust the width of the stroke.

1 Expand the Image Settings panel. For the 4 Wide template, the Zoom To Fill option is activated. This means that our photos are cropped in height to fit the proportions of the image cells.

▶ **Tip:** You can change the color of the border by clicking the Stroke Border color swatch and choosing a color from the Color Picker.

2 Click the checkbox to activate the Stroke Border option, and then drag the Width slider to the right or type **2.0** in the text box to the right of the slider. For your reference, 72 points (pt) are one inch.

3 In the Layout Type panel, click Picture Package. If necessary, expand the Image Settings panel. For a Picture Package template, the Image Settings panel offers two controls for borders. An Inner Stroke border is the Picture Package equivalent of a Stroke Border. Use the Photo Border control to specify the width of a blank frame between the edge of each photo and the boundary of its image cell.

4 Experiment with the Inner Stroke and Photo Border settings.

5 In the Layout Type panel, click Single Image / Contact Sheet to return to your modified 4 Wide template; then collapse the Image Settings panel.

Using the Rotate To Fit option

By default, Lightroom will place photos so that they are upright within their image cells. The Rotate To Fit option in the Image Settings panel will override this behavior so that your photos are rotated to match the orientation of the image cells. For presentation layouts you would not wish to have images displayed in different orientations on the same page but in some situations this feature can be very helpful and save on expensive photo paper too! The Rotate To Fit option is particularly useful when you wish to print photos in both portrait and landscape formats on the same sheet, as large as possible and without wasting paper, as shown in the illustration on the right.

Another situation where you might choose to use the Rotate To Fit setting is when you are printing contact sheets. As you can see in the next illustration, Rotate To Fit enables you to see all the photos at the same size regardless of the image orientation.

Customizing your identity plate

In the Page panel you have the option add an identity plate or text to your print layout. You can quickly edit your identity plate or add photo info, captions, page numbers, or crop marks to your prints. To begin with, you'll modify the identity plate to suit our sepia-toned images.

1   Expand the Page panel; then click the checkbox to activate the Identity Plate option. Click the triangle in the lower right corner of the identity plate preview pane and choose Edit from the menu.

2   In the Identity Plate Editor dialog box, activate the Use A Styled Text Identity Plate option. Choose Arial, Regular, and 36 point from the font menus. At this point, you could also change the default color for the identity plate text by clicking the color swatch to the right of the font size menu; we choose a light gray. Select the text in the text box and type **Manneken Photography** (or a name of your own choice); then click OK.

> ▶ **Tip:** If your text is too long to be fully visible in the text box, either resize the dialog box or reduce the font size until you've finished editing.

3   In the Page panel, drag the Scale slider to the right so that the identity plate text is the same width as the image. You can also scale the identity plate by clicking it in the Print Editor view and dragging the handles of its bounding box.

> ▶ **Tip:** By default the identity plate will be oriented horizontally. This setting (0°) is indicated at the top right of the Identity Plate pane in the Page panel. To re-orient your identity plate on the page, click on the 0° indicator and choose 90°, 180°, or −90° from the menu. To move your identity plate, simply drag it in the Print Editor view.

4 Now you'll change the color of the identity plate. Click the Override Color checkbox to set the color of the identity plate for this layout only—without affecting the defined color settings for the identity plate.

5 Click the Override Color swatch to open the Color Picker. Set the RGB values: R: **60%**, G: **45%**, B: **20%**, and then click outside the Color Picker to close it. The color of the identity plate is now matched to the sepia tones of the photos.

► **Tip:** If you see a hexadecimal value displayed in the lower right corner of the Color Picker rather than RGB values, click RGB below the color slider.

6 In the Identity Plate pane, use the Opacity slider or type **70** in the text box beside it to set an opacity value of 70% for the identity plate. This feature can be particularly effective if you wish to position your identity plate over an image.

Printing captions and metadata information

In this exercise, you will add a caption and metadata information—in this case, sequence numbers for the images—to your print layout using the Page panel and the Text Template Editor.

1 At the bottom of the the Page panel, click the checkbox to activate the Photo Info overlay option; then choose Edit from the menu to the right. Most of the other options in the Photo Info menu are drawn from the images' existing metadata.

256 LESSON 8 Printing Images

The text Template Editor enables you to access and edit the metadata embedded in your image files, and then to save your template as an easy-to-access preset.

2 In the Text Template Editor, choose Sequence from the Preset menu.

3 Click to place an insertion cursor just before the first token in the Example text box and then type **Emma Antique**. Be sure to add a space between your text and the first token. Click Done to close the Text Template Editor. The images in the Print Editor view are now captioned and numbered.

▶ **Tip:** You'll find more detailed information on the Text Template Editor in the section "Using the Text Template Editor" in Lesson 7, "Creating Slideshows."

4 Click the triangle beside Font Size at the bottom of the Page panel and choose 12 pt from the menu; then collapse the Page panel.

Saving your customized print template

Having started with a preset print template, you've created your own page design by modifying the layout and adding borders, an identity plate, and captions to the images. You can now save your customized layout for future use.

1   Click the Create New Preset button (+) in the header of the Template Browser panel header, or choose Print > New Template.

2   In the New Template dialog box, type **My Wide Triptych** in the Template Name text box. By default, new templates are saved to the User Templates folder. For this exercise, accept the default User Templates as the destination folder and click Create.

3   Your saved template appears in the User Templates folder in the Template Browser panel where you can access it quickly for use with a new set of images. With your new template selected in the Template Browser, select the last three images in the Filmstrip.

Creating a Custom Package print layout

If you prefer to create your own page layout from scratch, without using any of the Lightroom print layout templates as a starting point, you can use the Custom Package option in the Layout Style panel.

1   In the Layout Style panel, click Custom Package. If you clicked the print layout template Custom (2) 4 × 6 in the Template Browser earlier in the lesson, the page layout you see in the Print Editor view may already contain two 4 × 6 image cells. Delete the existing image cells by clicking inside each cell and pressing the Delete key on your keyboard.

2   Click the double tri-angle beside Grid Snap and choose Grid from the menu. This will make it easier to arrange the images in your print layout.

3   Choose Edit > Select None to deselect all the images in the Filmstrip, and then drag the image Emma_4.jpg from the Filmstrip to the Print Editor view, positioning it on the page as shown in the illustration.

4   Expand the Cells panel and make sure that the Lock To Photo Aspect Ratio option is activated. In the Adjust Selected Cell controls, click the Width value and type **3.6**; then press Enter / Return.

5   Hold down the Alt / Option key and drag the image in the Print Editor view to produce a copy. Repeat the process to produce a second copy, and then drag the images to position them on the page as shown in the illustration.

6   Drag the image Emma_5.jpg from the Filmstrip and drop it onto the photo at the top right of your layout.

7 Disable the Lock To Photo Aspect Ratio option at the bottom of the Cells panel.

8 Drag the image Emma_6.jpg from the Filmstrip and drop it onto the photo in the center of your layout.

With the Lock To Photo Aspect Ratio option disabled, the image Emma_6.jpg—which is in a square format—is cropped to fit the existing image cell.

9 Click the check box to activate the Lock To Photo Aspect Ratio option at the bottom of the Cells panel so that the image cell is resized to fit this photo's square aspect ratio.

10 Drag the image Emma_6.jpg in the page layout and use the corner handles of its bounding box to position and scale the photo as shown in the illustration.

Changing the page background color

In Lightroom 3, you can apply a background color to your print layout.

To save on printer ink, you may prefer not to print a page with large areas of bold color or black in the background on your home printer, but when you're ordering professional prints this can be a striking choice.

1   Expand the Page panel in the right panel group and activate the Page Background Color option.

2   Click the Page Background Color color swatch to open the Color Picker.

3   Move the pointer over the row of color swatches at the top of the Color Picker and use the eyedropper to sample the black swatch. Click the Close button (x) or click outside the Color Picker to close it.

The new color appears in the Page Background Color color swatch and in the page preview in the Print Editor view.

Configuring the output settings

The final step before you're ready to print your layout is to adjust the output settings in the Print Job panel.

1   Expand the Print Job panel in the right panel group.

From the Print To menu at the top of the Print Job panel you can choose to send the job directly to your printer or generate a JPEG file, which you can print later or send out for professional printing. The controls in the Print Job panel vary slightly depending on which option is selected in the Print To menu.

2   Choose Printer from the Print To menu at the top of the Print Job panel.

● **Note:** The terms "print resolution" and "printer resolution" have different meanings. "Print resolution" refers to the number of printed pixels per inch (ppi); "printer resolution" refers to the capability of the printer, called dots per inch (dpi). A printed pixel of a particular color is created by patterns of tiny dots of the few ink colors available.

Activating the Draft Mode Printing option will disable the other options in the Print Job panel. Draft Mode Printing results in high speed output at a relatively low quality, which is an efficient option for printing contact sheets or for assessing your layout before you commit it to high quality photo paper. The 4 × 5 Contact Sheet and the 5 × 8 Contact Sheet templates are preset for Draft Mode Printing.

The Print Resolution setting that is appropriate for your print job depends on the intended print size, the resolution of your image files, the capabilities of your printer, and the quality of your paper stock. The default print resolution is 240 ppi, which generally produces good results. As a rule of thumb, use a higher resolution for smaller, high quality prints (around 360 ppi for letter size). You can use a lower resolution setting for larger prints (around 180 ppi for 16″ × 20″) without compromising too much on quality.

3   The Print Resolution control has a range of 72 ppi to 480 ppi. For this exercise, type **200** in the Print Resolution text box.

● **Note:** The purpose of the Sharpening feature in the Develop module is to compensate for blurriness in the original photo, while Print Sharpening improves the crispness of printed output on a particular paper type.

Images tend to look less sharp on paper than they do on screen. The Print Sharpening options can help to compensate for this by increasing the crispness of your printed output. You can choose between Low, Standard, and High Print Sharpening settings, and specify a Matte or Glossy Media Type. You won't notice the effects of these settings on screen so it's useful to experiment by printing at different settings to familiarize yourself with the results.

4   If it's not already selected, choose Low from the Print Sharpening menu.

Using color management

Printing your digital images can be challenging: what you see on screen is not always what you get on paper. Lightroom is able to handle a very large color space but your printer may operate within a much more limited gamut.

In the Print Job panel, you can choose whether to have Lightroom handle color management or leave it up to your printer.

Color managed by your printer

The default Color Management setting in the Print Job panel is Managed By Printer. This can be the easiest option and, given the continuing improvement of printing technology, will generally produce satisfactory results.

Note: For Draft Mode Printing, color management is automatically assigned to the printer.

In the Print Setup / Print dialog box (File > Print Settings), you can specify the paper type, color handling, and other print settings. On Windows, click Properties in the Print Setup dialog box to access additional printer specific settings.

Note: The options available in the Print Setup / Print dialog box may vary depending on your printer.

If you choose Managed By Printer, enable the ICM Method for Image Color Management (Windows) or activate the ColorSync option in the Color Management settings for the printer driver software (Mac OS) so that the correct profile is applied before printing. Depending on the printer driver software, you can usually find the color settings in the Print Document dialog box under Setup / Properties / Advanced (Windows), or in the menu below the Presets in the Print dialog box (Mac OS).

Tip: If you choose a custom printer color profile rather than Managed By Printer from the Profile menu in the Color Management panel, make sure color management is turned off in the printer driver software; otherwise, your photos will be color managed twice, and the colors might not print as you expect them to.

Color management controlled by Lightroom

Letting your printer manage color may be acceptable for general printing purposes but to achieve really high quality results it's best to have Lightroom do it. If you choose this option you can specify a printing profile tailored to a particular type of paper or custom inks.

1   In the Print Job panel, choose Other from the Color Management Profile menu.

You can choose this option when the profile you want isn't listed in the Profile menu. Lightroom searches your computer for custom printer profiles, which are usually installed by the software that came with your printer. If Lightroom is unable to locate any profiles, choose Managed By Printer and let the printer driver handle the color management.

2   Depending on your printer and paper stock, choose one or more printer profiles. In this illustration a profile for the Epson Stylus Pro R800 using glossy photo paper has been selected. Each profile you choose will be added to the Profile menu under Color Management in the Print Job panel for easy access next time you print.

Once you've chosen a printer profile from the Profile menu, the Rendering Intent options are activated in the Print Job panel. The color space of an image is usually much larger than that within which most printers operate, which means that your printer may not be able to accurately reproduce the colors you see on screen. This may result in printing artifacts such as posterization or banding in color gradients as the printer attempts to deal with out-of-gamut colors. The Rendering Intent options help to minimize these problems. You can choose between two settings:

* **Perceptual** rendering aims at preserving the visual relationship between colors. The entire range of colors in the image will be re-mapped to fit within the color gamut your printer is able to reproduce. In this way, the relationships between all the colors are preserved but in the process even colors that were already in-gamut may be shifted as the out-of-gamut colors are moved into the printable range. This may mean that your printed image will be less vivid that it appeared on screen.

- **Relative** rendering prints all the in-gamut colors as they are and shifts out-of-gamut colors to the closest printable colors. Using this option means that more of the original color of the image is retained but some of the relationships between colors may be altered.

In most cases the differences between the two rendering methods are quite subtle. As a general rule, perceptual rendering is the best option for an image with many out-of-gamut colors and relative rendering works better for an image with only a few. However, unless you are very experienced it may be hard to tell which is which. The best policy is to do some testing with your printer. Print a very colorful, vivid photo at both settings and then do the same with a more muted image.

3   For the purposes of this exercise, choose Relative rendering as the muted tones of these images are very unlikely to be outside the printable range.

Saving print settings as an output collection

Your layout is ready to print. You can now save your print settings as an output collection to use for another print job. You'll be able to add photos to the collection later and the same output settings will be applied automatically.

An output collection is different from a normal photo collection. A photo collection is merely a grouping of images to which you can apply any template or output settings you wish. An output collection links a photo collection (or a selection of images from that collection) to a particular template and specific output settings.

For the sake of clarity: an output collection also differs from a custom template. A template includes all your settings but no images; you can apply the template to any selection of images. An output collection links the template and all its settings to a particular selection of images.

1   Now that you've saved your layout as a user template, selected the images you wish to print in the layout, and specified print settings, click the Create New Collection button (+) in the header of the Collections panel and choose Create Print from the menu.

2   In the Create Print dialog box, type **My Print Settings** as the name for your print output collection.

3 Activate the option Include Selected Photos / Include Referenced Photos and disable Make New Virtual Copies; then click Create.

▶ **Tip:** For more detailed information, please refer to the Lightroom Help topic "Save print settings as an output collection."

4 Your new output collection is now listed in the Collections panel. Note that your output collection has an icon representing a page layout, whereas an image collection is indicated by an icon representing a stack of photos.

Printing your job

1 Click the Print button at the bottom of the right panel group or choose File > Print.

2 Verify the settings in the Print dialog box and click OK / Print to print your page, or click Cancel to close the Print dialog box without printing.

Clicking the Print One button will send your print job to the printer queue without opening the Print dialog box. This is useful if you print repeatedly using the same settings and don't need to confirm or change any settings in the Print dialog.

To achieve the best results when you print, calibrate and profile your monitor regularly, always verify that print settings are specified correctly, and use quality papers. However, there is no substitute for experience. Experiment with a variety of settings and options—and if at first you do succeed, consider yourself very lucky!

Working with 16 Bit Output on Mac OS 10.5

If you are running Mac OS 10.5 (Leopard) and are using a 16-bit printer, you can activate the 16 Bit Output setting in the Print Job panel. This will result in less image degradation and color artifacts in files that have been extensively edited.
For detailed information on working with 16-bit output, consult the documentation for your printer or check with your output center.

Review questions

1 How can you quickly preview the preset print templates, and how can you see how your photos will look in each layout?

2 Which type of template would you choose to create a layout with a single photo repeated at various sizes on the same sheet, and how can you check which type of template you have chosen?

3 When you're working with the Print Setup / Page Setup dialog box, why is it better to leave the Scale setting at 100%?

4 For what purposes is Draft Mode Printing appropriate?

Review answers

1 Move the pointer over the list of templates in the Template Browser to see a thumbnail preview of each layout displayed in the Preview panel. Select your images in the Filmstrip and choose a template from the list; the Print Editor view shows how your photos look in the new layout.

2 Picture Package layouts repeat a single image at a variety of sizes on the same page. The Layout Style panel indicates whether a layout selected in the Template Browser is a Picture Package template or a Single Image / Contact Sheet template.

3 Lightroom automatically scales your photos in the print layout template to fit the specified paper size. Changing the scale in the Print Setup / Page Setup dialog will result in the layout being scaled twice so your photos may not print at the desired size.

4 Draft Mode Printing results in high speed output at a relatively low quality, which is an efficient option for printing contact sheets or for assessing your layout before you commit it to high quality photo paper. The contact sheet templates are preset for Draft Mode Printing.

9 PUBLISHING YOUR PHOTOS

Lesson overview

Lightroom 3 offers several easy-to-use options for sharing your photos. The new Publish Services feature enables you to share images directly from the Library module. You can create Publish Collections to help you manage the files you've handed off to a client, to sync photos to your iPhone, or to upload images directly to a photo sharing website. The Web module provides a range of customizable gallery layout templates and all the tools you need to build a striking website, preview it in a browser, and upload it to your web server.

In this lesson, you'll learn the techniques and skills you need to publish photos from the Library and to create your own web gallery:

- Publishing images to a photo sharing website

- Using Publish Collections and re-publishing updated images

- Distinguishing between HTML and Flash gallery templates

- Choosing and customizing a gallery layout template

- Rearranging the order of the images in your gallery

- Specifying the output settings and adding a watermark

- Previewing your web gallery

- Saving your customized templates and presets

- Uploading your gallery to a web server

 You'll probably need between one and two hours to complete this lesson.

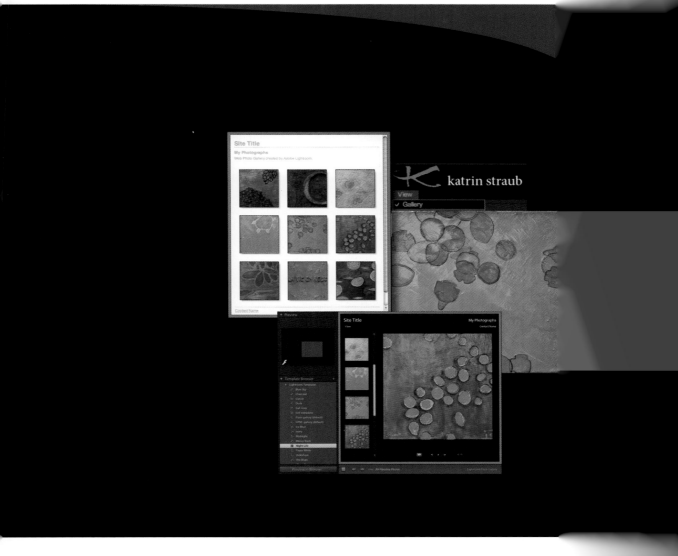

Use the Publish Services feature to share your photos directly from the Lightroom Library module, or choose from HTML and Flash templates in the Web module to quickly generate sophisticated interactive web galleries. Post images to a photo sharing site, sync photos to your iPhone, or upload an interactive gallery directly to a web server—all without leaving the Lightroom workspace.

Getting started

This lesson assumes that you are already familiar with the Lightroom workspace and with moving between the different modules. If you find that you need more background information as you go, refer to Lightroom Help, or review the previous lessons in this book.

Before you begin, make sure that you have correctly copied the Lessons folder from the CD in the back of this book onto your computer's hard disk and created the LR3CIB Library Catalog file as detailed in "Copying the Classroom in a Book files" on page 2 and "Creating a catalog file for working with this book" on page 3.

1 Start Lightroom.

2 In the Adobe Photoshop Lightroom - Select Catalog dialog box, make sure the file LR3CIB Library Catalog.lrcat is selected under Select A Recent Catalog To Open, and then click Open.

3 Lightroom will open in the screen mode and workspace module that were active when you last quit. If necessary, click Library in the Module Picker to switch to the Library module.

Importing images into the library

The first step is to import the images for this lesson into the Lightroom library.

1 In the Library module, click the Import button below the left panel group.

2   If the Import dialog box appears in compact mode, click the Show More Options button at the lower left of the dialog box to see all the options in the expanded Import dialog box.

3   Under Source at the left of the expanded Import dialog box, make sure that the option Include Subfolders is activated, and then navigate to the Lessons folder that you copied into the LR3CIB folder on your hard disk. Select the Lesson 9 folder. Ensure that all the images in the Lesson 9 folder are checked for import.

4   In the import options above the thumbnail previews, click Add to add the imported photos to your catalog without moving or copying them.

5   Under File Handling at the right of the expanded Import dialog box, choose Minimal from the Render Previews menu and ensure that the Don't Import Selected Duplicates option is activated.

6   Under Apply During Import, choose None from both the Develop Settings menu and the Metadata menu and type **Lesson 9** in the Keywords text box. Make sure your settings are exactly as shown in the illustration below, and then click Import.

The images are imported from the Lesson 9 folder and now appear in both the Grid view of the Library module and in the Filmstrip across the bottom of the Lightroom workspace.

Publishing photos from the Library

We live in a connected world where, for many of us, sharing our images with family and friends, posting to photo sharing websites, or handing off photos online to a client are almost daily occurrences.

The new Publish Services panel enables you to publish your images directly from the Library module by creating Publish Collections that help you manage your shared images by keeping track of whether or not they have been updated to the most current versions. A Publish Collection can be used to manage the images you have handed off to a particular client, to publish images to your iPhone sync folder, or to upload images directly to a photo sharing website.

Lightroom 3 ships with a direct connection from the Publish Services panel to the Flickr photo sharing site so that adding images to your Flickr Photostream is as simple as drag and drop. Adobe is working to support developers creating plug-ins that will enable direct access from the Publish Services panel to other popular photo sharing websites.

Setting up a Flickr account

In this exercise, you'll set up a Flickr account and publish a selection of photos.

1 In the left panel group, expand the Publish Services panel, if necessary, by clicking the triangle at the left of the panel name, and then click Set Up at the right of the Flickr header.

The Lightroom Publishing Manager dialog box appears.

2 Under Publish Service, type your name in the Description text box.

3 Under Flickr Account, click Log In. A dialog box appears, asking you to give Lightroom permission to upload images to Flickr. Click Authorize.

Your default web browser opens. You will be asked to sign in to Yahoo, and then your browser will open the Flickr sign-in page.

4 Type a screen name for your Flickr account and click Create A New Account.

5 Flicker asks you to confirm the request from Lightroom to link to your Flickr account. As you arrived at this page from Lightroom, click Next as shown in the illustration below.

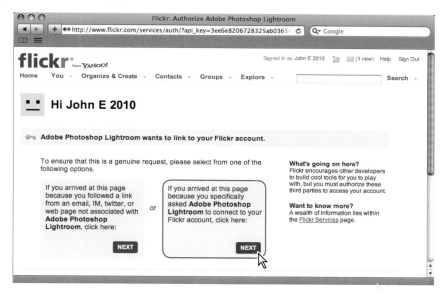

6 On the next screen, click "OK, I'll Authorize It" to authorize Lightroom to access all content in your Flickr account, to upload, edit, replace, and delete photos in your account, and to interact with other Flickr members.

7 Close the browser page, and then click Done to return to the Lightroom Publishing Manager dialog box.

8 Set up the options in the Lightroom Publishing Manager dialog box as follows:

- Under Flickr Title, choose Filename from the Set Flickr Title Using menu.

- Under File Settings, drag the Quality slider to set a value of 75.

- Scroll down, if necessary, to see the Output Sharpening options. Click the check box to enable sharpening, and then choose Screen from the Sharpen For menu, . Choose Standard from the Amount menu.

- Under Watermarking, disable the Simple Copyright Watermark option.

- Under Privacy and Safety, make sure the Public option is activated.

9 Leave the options for renaming, resizing, and metadata unchanged and click Save to close the Lightroom Publishing Manager dialog box.

In the Publish Services panel, the activated Flickr service displays the name you assigned in step 2. The service now contains a single Photostream. An image count of 0 at the right shows that the new Photostream does not yet contain any photos.

Publishing photos to Flickr

In this exercise you'll add a selection of images to your Flickr Photostream.

1 In the left panel group, expand the Folders panel. Collapse other panels, if necessary, so that you can see both the expanded Folders and Publish Services panels, as shown in the illustration below.

2 In the Folders panel, expand the Lesson 9 folder and click to select the subfolder named Batch1.

3 Choose Edit > Select All or Ctrl-click / Command-click to select all four images, and then drag the selected photos to your newly created Photostream under Flickr in the Publish Services panel.

4 Click the new Photostream entry under Flickr in the Publish Services panel.

The work area displays the four images in this Publish Collection under the header New Photos To Publish.

5 Click the Publish button at the bottom of the left panel group.

A progress bar appears in the upper left of the workspace as the images are uploaded to Flickr. The work area becomes a split screen, showing which images have been published and which are yet to be published.

6   Wait until all four images have been published to Flickr, and then right-click / Control-click the entry for your Photostream in the Publish Services panel and choose Show In Flickr from the menu.

Publishing photo comments

Your Publish Services connection allows for two-way interaction with Flickr.

1   On your Flickr web page, click the photo dockside_3.jpg to see the image enlarged. Type a comment in the text box below the enlarged image and click Post Comment.

2 Switch back to Lightroom and click the Refresh Comments button (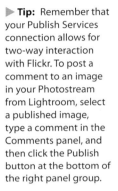) at the left of the header of the Comments panel in the right panel group. Watch the progress bar at the top left of the workspace as Lightroom connects to Flickr and updates your Publish Collection.

3 When the process is complete, click to select the image dockside_3.jpg under the Published Photos header in the work area.

4 In the right panel group, expand the Comments panel. The comment you posted on your Flickr page has been downloaded to Lightroom.

▶ **Tip:** Remember that your Publish Services connection allows for two-way interaction with Flickr. To post a comment to an image in your Photostream from Lightroom, select a published image, type a comment in the Comments panel, and then click the Publish button at the bottom of the right panel group.

Re-publishing a photo

Publish Services helps you keep track of images that have been modified since they were published, so you can easily make sure that you are sharing the latest versions.

1 With your Flickr Photostream selected in the Publish Services panel, and the image dockside_3.jpg selected in the work area, expand the Quick Develop panel in the right panel group.

2 In the Quick Develop panel, choose General - Grayscale from the Saved Preset menu. In the work area, the edited image is now displayed under the header Modified Photos To Re-Publish.

3 Click the Publish button to re-publish the modified photo. A dialog box appears asking you if you wish to replace the photo on Flickr, and informing you that with your free Flickr account, any comments or ratings attached to the image will be deleted when the image is replaced. Click Replace.

▶ **Tip:** With a Flickr Pro account, any comments and ratings attached to your photos on Flickr will be preserved when you re-publish images. For more detail on the advantages of a Flickr Pro account, click Help on the Flickr web page.

4 Right-click / Control-click your Photostream under Flickr in the Publish Services panel and choose Show In Flickr from the menu.

Your Flickr page has been updated to show the re-published black and white version of the image dockside_3.jpg.

▶ **Tip:** You may need to wait a few moments while your photostream is updated. If you don't see your re-published photo, try reloading the page in your browser.

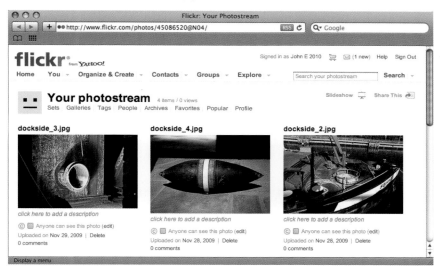

Creating a new Photoset on Flickr

The Publish Services panel offers several options for working with your Flickr account from within Lightroom.

1 In the Folders panel in the left panel group, expand the Lesson 9 folder and click to select the subfolder named Batch2.

2 Choose Edit > Select All or Ctrl-click / Command-click to select all six images in the Batch2 folder.

3 Right-click / Control-click your Photostream in the Publish Services panel and choose Create Photoset from the menu.

4   In the Create Photoset dialog box, type **Slow boat to China** as the name for the new set. Ensure that the Include Selected Photos option is activated and the Make New Virtual Copies option is disabled, and then click Create.

Your new Photoset appears under the Flickr service in the Publish Services panel and the work are displays the six slow_boat images under the header New Photos To Publish.

5   Click the Publish button, and then wait while the new set of images is uploaded to Flickr.

6   To view the newly published set of images online, right-click / Control-click the entry for your new Photoset in the Publish Services panel and choose Show In Flickr from the menu. Return to Lightroom when you're done.

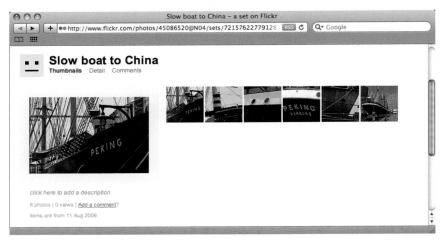

Publishing photos to your hard disk

The Publish services panel also enables you to create publish collections on your hard disk—Lightroom will keep track of which images have been updated since the collection was published, just as it does for a collection published online. You can create a new publish collection for each client to whom you hand off photos, making it easy to check whether they have the most current versions, or set up a publish collection that will enable you to publish images to your iPhone sync folder with drag and drop convenience.

1   In the Publish Services panel, click Set Up at the right of the Hard Drive header.

2   In the Lightroom Publishing Manager dialog box, type **Sync to iPhone** in the Description text box under Publish Service.

3   Under Export Location, choose My Pictures Folder / Pictures Folder from the Export To menu. Activate the Put In Subfolder option and type **iPhone** as the name for the new subfolder. Under File Settings, set a Quality value of 50. Review the other options in the Lightroom Publishing Manager dialog box, leaving the settings unchanged for the moment, and then click Save.

A listing for your new iPhone publish service appears under the Hard Drive header in the Publish Services panel.

4   In the Folders panel in the left panel group, expand the Lesson 9 folder and click to select the subfolder named Batch3.

5   Choose Edit > Select All or Ctrl-click / Command-click to select all six images in the Batch3 folder, and then drag the selected photos to your newly created iPhone entry in the Publish Services panel.

6   Click the iPhone entry in the Publish Services panel. The six cty_lights photos in the new publish collection displayed in the work area under the header New Photos To Publish. Click the Publish button at the bottom of the left panel group and wait while Lightroom processes the images.

7   Right-click / Control-click iPhone collection in the Publish Services panel and choose Go To Published Folder from the context menu.

An Explorer / Finder window opens showing the six published images in the new iPhone folder.

8   Close the Explorer / Finder window and return to Lightroom.

The Lightroom Web module

Another great way to share and showcase your photos is to use the Lightroom Web module to design, preview, and upload your own web gallery.

In the Web module, you'll use the Template Browser in the left panel group to preview the wide range of gallery layout templates. When you choose a template in the Template Browser, the Gallery Editor view in the central work area shows how your images look in the new gallery layout.

In the Gallery Editor view, your gallery is fully interactive, performing exactly as it will on the web.

● **Note:** For the purposes of the illustration below, the Lightroom Templates menu has been abridged; you'll actually find many more varied and versatile gallery designs there.

You'll use the panels in the right group to customize the gallery template. You can change the layout, the color scheme, or the background, and add text, borders, or effects. With a single click, you can preview your gallery in a web browser or upload it to your web server without leaving Lightroom.

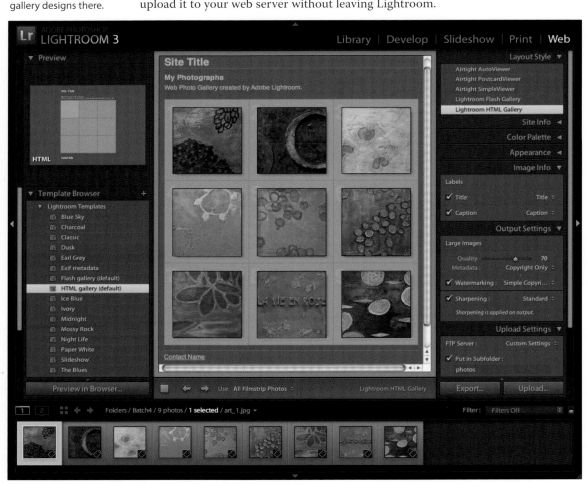

Creating a basic web gallery

In the following exercises you'll create a web portfolio based on one of the Lightroom Flash templates to showcase some photographs of paintings.

Creating a new collection

It's a good idea to group the images for your web gallery as a collection, so that you can easily retrieve the same selection of images should you wish to re-work or extend your presentation. Creating a collection has other advantages: you can make consistent adjustments across all the images, rearrange their display order, and easily add or remove images. You can use the temporary Quick Collection in the Catalog panel, or create a new collection that will appear in the Collections panel.

Note: A Collection is a groupings of photos in the library catalog. A Collection not only preserves the display order of the images it contains but also any settings applied in the Slideshow, Print, and Web modules.

1 If necessary, switch to the Library module. In the Folders panel in the left panel group, expand the Lesson 9 folder and select the subfolder named Batch4.

2 Choose Edit > Select All or Ctrl-click / Command-click to select all nine images in the Batch4 folder.

3 Click the New Collection button (+) in the header of the Collections panel, and choose Create Collection from the menu.

Tip: To delete a collection, right-click / Control-click its name in the Collections panel, and choose Delete from the context menu.

4 In the Create Collection dialog box, type **Web Portfolio** in the Name text box and choose None from the Set menu. Under Collection Options, activate the Include Selected Photos option and disable Make New Virtual Copies, then click Create.

A listing for your new collection, containing the nine images from the Batch4 folder, appears in the Collections panel in the left panel group.

Choosing a template in the Web module

1   In the left panel group, expand the Collections panel if necessary, and then click to select your Web Portfolio collection.

2   Switch to the Web module by clicking Web in the Module Picker. From the Use menu in the Toolbar below the Gallery Editor view, choose All Filmstrip Photos.

3   In the right panel group, expand the Layout Style panel. If it's not already selected, choose Lightroom HTML Gallery from the list in the Layout Style panel. The Gallery Editor view shows how your images will look displayed in the default HTML layout.

Note: For the purposes of the illustrations on this page and the next, the Lightroom Templates menu has been abridged; you'll actually find many more varied and versatile gallery designs in the list; you may need to scroll down to see the HTML Gallery (Default).

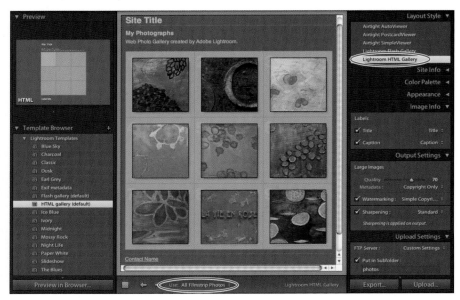

4   Hide the Filmstrip, if necessary, so that you can see both the Preview panel and the list of templates in the Template Browser. Move the pointer down the list to preview the different template designs in the Lightroom Templates folder. Note the HTML or Flash icon in the lower left corner of the layout preview indicating the gallery type for each template.

5   When you've finished previewing the gallery templates in the Template Browser, click to select the template Flash Gallery (Default).

The Gallery Editor view in the work area shows your images displayed in the new template layout.

Distinguishing between HTML and Flash templates

In the Template Browser you'll find both HTML and Flash templates. As you move the pointer down the list of gallery templates, you'll see a preview of each template layout in the Preview panel.

An icon in the lower left corner of the layout preview indicates the gallery type. Once you click to select a template in the Template Browser, the gallery type is also shown in the Layout Style panel in the right panel group and at the right of the Toolbar below the Gallery Editor view.

Templates of either type can be customized to show your work in its best light. You can add text and effects to your layout and change the color scheme, the background, and the image size.

The HTML gallery templates enable you to produce simple web sites that are compatible with most browsers. The HTML pages generated can be customized further in an HTML editor.

Flash templates can produce more sophisticated web galleries, including animations, slideshows with smooth transitions, and other special effects. However, Flash galleries require that the viewer has the appropriate Adobe Flash Player plug-in installed. Should security settings be in place to block scripts and ActiveX controls, your audience may have to click through warning messages in the web browser before being able to see the gallery.

6 In the Gallery Editor view you'll notice that the default Lightroom Flash gallery has its own navigation controls below the large image. Click the Play button to view the gallery slideshow.

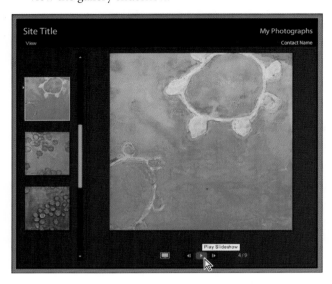

7 To stop the slideshow, press the spacebar or click the Pause button.

Rearranging the order of your images

Note: The order of the images in the Grid view and the Filmstrip determines their display order in a Web gallery.

After seeing your slideshow in action, you may wish to change the order in which the images appear in the web gallery. In this exercise, you'll move two of the images so that the slideshow alternates between cool and warm colors.

1 Click the Library Grid button (▦) at the top left of the Filmstrip, or press G on your keyboard, to return to the Grid view in the Library module.

2 Make sure that your Web Portfolio collection is still selected in the Collections panel, and then choose Edit > Select None.

Note: Dragging an image that is part of a multiple selection will move all the selected images. If all images in a collection are selected you will not be able to rearrange their order.

3 In the Grid view, drag the image art_6.jpg one position to the left. Release the mouse button when the vertical black line appears to indicate an insertion point between the images art_4.jpg and art_5.jpg.

4 In the Filmstrip, drag the third image, art_3.jpg, one position to the left. Release the mouse button when a vertical black line appears to indicate an insertion point between the first two images art_1.jpg and art_2.jpg.

● **Note:** You can rearrange the order of images in the Filmstrip or the Grid View only if the images have been grouped as a collection.

5 Click Web in the Module Picker and review the slideshow again in the Gallery Editor view. Notice that with the new image order the images now alternate between cool and warm colors. Press the spacebar to stop the slideshow.

6 (Optional) In the Web module, create a new image order by dragging one or more thumbnails to new positions in the Filmstrip. If the Gallery Editor view in the work area is not updated automatically, choose Web > Reload. Switch to the Library module to confirm that the images in the Grid view are displayed in the same order as in the Filmstrip. Switch back to the Web module.

Customizing your web gallery

You can save time creating your web gallery by starting with the layout template closest to the design you have in mind. Once you've made your choice, you can use the Site Info, Color Palette, Appearance, Image Info, and Output Settings panels in the right panel group to customize the template. You can add text, choose backgrounds and color schemes, and tweak the layout to change the look and feel of your gallery. In the following exercises, you'll customize the text in your gallery template, adjust the layout, place a logo, and add a watermark to the images.

Replacing text

In the Site Info panel you can add a website title, a collection description, contact information, and web or e-mail links. The information you enter in the Site Info panel will appear on your website.

1 If the Site Info panel is currently collapsed in the right panel group, expand it by clicking the triangle beside its name.

2 Click the default Site Title text in the Site Info panel and type a title for your site. Press Enter on your keyboard to update the title displayed in your layout in the Gallery Editor view. In a web browser, the site title will also appear in the title bar of the browser window.

3 Click the triangle beside Site Title and note the entries in the Site Title menu. Lightroom keeps track of your entries for each of the text boxes in the Site Info panel. Instead of retyping information each time you create a new web gallery, you can choose previously entered details from this list.

4 As an alternative to working with the Site Info panel, you can edit the text in your gallery directly in the Gallery Editor view in the work area. Click the Collection Title (My Photographs) in the top right corner of the Gallery Editor view and type a new title. Press Enter and both the gallery preview and the corresponding entry in the Site Info panel will be updated.

5 In the Site Info panel, delete the default text under Collection Description. Additional information about the images in your web gallery can be entered here. In this particular template, the viewer can access those details by clicking View below the site title and choosing About These Photos from the menu.

The last two items in the Site Info panel are Contact Info and Web Or Mail Link. Your web or email address will become an active link on your website, so the viewer's browser will either jump to the specified web page or launch their default e-mail application.

Enter an e-mail address like this: mailto:user@domain.com, or a web address in the following format: http://www.domain.com.

► **Tip:** As illustrated here, you could create a link to a Home page where you can offer the viewer links to the other galleries that you've created in Lightroom.

Changing colors

The controls in the Color Palette panel enable you to change the color scheme for your website. You can set the color for every element in your layout: background, borders, header, menu bar, and text.

Choosing colors that work well together and look good on any system may seem a major challenge, but a few simple rules might help you to stay within a safe color palette:

• Use dark text on light backgrounds.

• Use light text on dark backgrounds.

• Don't rely on differences in color to convey essential information.

In this exercise you'll change the color of the text for the site and collection titles, but the same technique applies to any of the color settings.

1   Expand the Color Palette panel by clicking the triangle next to its name. If necessary, you can collapse other panels to make more space.

2   In the Color Palette, click the Header Text color swatch to open the Lightroom Color Picker.

► **Tip:** When choosing colors, particularly for base elements such as the background, borders, and headers, remember that neutral colors will compete less with your images. If you want to get serious about designing color schemes, kuler from the Adobe labs can be an invaluable tool (http://labs.adobe.com/technologies/kuler/).

► **Tip:** To simplify working with the side panel groups, right-click / Control-click any panel header, and activate Solo Mode in the context menu. In Solo Mode, you can open only one panel in the group at a time.

► **Tip:** If you see a hexadecimal value displayed in the lower right corner of the Color Picker rather than the RGB values shown in the illustration at the right, click RGB below the vertical color slider.

3   In the Color Picker, drag the slider at the right almost to the top, and then click a bright red in the large color field on the left. We chose a color with RGB values of R: 90%, G: 10%, B: 15%. You can enter these RGB values directly by clicking the number and typing a new value. The new color appears in the Header Text color swatch in the Color Palette panel and is applied to both the site and collection titles in the Gallery Editor view.

4   Close the Color Picker and collapse the Color Palette panel.

Tweaking the layout of a web gallery

You can adjust your gallery layout using the Appearance panel. The options available in the Appearance panel differ for Flash and HTML galleries.

For an HTML gallery, the Appearance panel offers the options shown in the illustration to the right. You can add borders or drop shadows to your images and display an index number in the background of each image cell. Change the number of rows and columns used on the index page with the Grid Pages controls, which will indirectly determine the size of the thumbnail images in the grid. The minimum grid is three by three—if your gallery contains more than nine images additional index pages will be generated. You can also set the size of the page and the width of a photo border for the enlarged view of an image.

These options give you great flexibility in customizing the look and feel of your HTML gallery. For a Flash gallery the options in the Appearance panel are more restricted.

1 In the right panel group, expand the Appearance panel; then click the double triangle beside Layout, and choose the Scrolling layout option from the menu.

The Scrolling layout displays a scrollable row of index thumbnails beneath an enlarged image view.

2 In the Appearance panel, click the double triangle beside Layout, and choose the Paginated layout option from the menu.

The Paginated layout displays thumbnails organized as an index beside an enlarged image view. Navigation controls below the thumbnails provide easy access to additional index pages.

3 Under Thumbnail Images in the Appearance panel, click the double triangle beside Size and choose Medium from the menu.

The gallery preview is updated in the Gallery Editor view. Depending on the number of images in your collection and the size of your Lightroom workspace window, the new thumbnail size may affect the number of index pages for your gallery.

4 In the Appearance panel, click the double triangle beside Layout, and choose the Slideshow Only layout option from the menu.

The Slideshow Only layout, displays only the enlarged image view, with controls for navigating through the collection and playing a gallery slideshow.

5 In the Appearance panel, click the double triangle beside Layout, and choose the Left layout option from the menu to return to the default layout for this gallery template, with a scrolling column of thumbnails to the left of the enlarged image view.

6 Click the View Slideshow button () below the enlarged image view to hide the index thumbnails and view a slideshow that will display only the enlarged images.

The View Slideshow button switches the gallery temporarily to Slideshow Only mode—it is available in all of the Flash gallery layout options except the Slideshow Only layout. When the View Slideshow button is clicked, it changes to the View Gallery button ().

7 Click the View Gallery button () to return to the selected gallery layout, complete with index thumbnails.

Personalizing your web gallery

Next, you'll personalize your web gallery by placing a logo in the header area.

1 In the Appearance panel, activate the Identity Plate option; then click the white triangle at the lower right of the Identity Plate preview pane and choose Edit from the menu.

2 In the Identity Plate Editor dialog box, activate the option Use A Graphical Identity Plate, and then click the Locate File button.

3 In the Locate File dialog box, navigate to the Lesson 9 folder and select the file Web_Identityplate.png. Click Choose, and then click OK.

▶ **Tip:** For best results use an image that is no more than 60 pixels high so that it will not need to be scaled to fit your layout template. In this case we used an image with a height of 46 pixels.

The new identity plate appears in the gallery preview and in the Identity Plate preview in the Appearance panel. The identity plate will replace the site title on your web page, but when the gallery is viewed in a web browser, the text you entered as the Site Title will still be displayed in the title bar of the browser window.

Working with identity plates

You can personalize your slideshows, Web presentations, and print layouts—and the Lightroom workspace itself—by adding your own identity plate.

A **Styled Text Identity Plate** will display the text you enter in the Identity Plate Editor dialog box. You can choose from the menus below the text box to specify the font characteristics.

A **Graphical Identity Plate** uses a graphic that is no more than 60 pixels high, in any of the following file formats: PDF, JPG, GIF, PNG, TIFF, or PSD (Windows) and JPG, GIF, PNG, TIFF, or PSD (Macintosh). The resolution of graphical identity plates may be too low for printed output. Choose Save As from the Enable Identity Plate menu, and give your identity plate a name.

To display your identity plate in the Lightroom workspace, choose Edit > Identity Plate Setup / Lightroom > Identity Plate Setup. In the Identity Plate Editor dialog box, activate the Enable Identity Plate option and choose one of your saved identity plates from the menu to the right.

Choose from the pop-up menus on the right side of the dialog box to change the font style, size and color for the Module Picker. The first color swatch sets the text color for the active module; the second swatch sets the text color for the others.

—From Lightroom Help

Providing more information

You can display information about the images in your web gallery by choosing from a range of options in the Title and Caption menus in the Image Info panel. Show specific details retrieved from the metadata of each image, apply the same text to all the images at once, or display your images without any text information at all.

You can also set up a text template that will combine information drawn from different sources to compose titles and captions for your images automatically. In this exercise, you'll add a title and caption to the first image in the collection.

1 Expand the Image Info panel in the right panel group. Make sure that both the Title and Caption options are activated.

2 Click on the double triangle beside Title to see the list of options. The same choices are available in the Caption menu. Most of the options display information retrieved from an image's metadata.

● **Note:** The title text will be displayed immediately below the enlarged image view. The caption appears below the title in a smaller font size.

▶ **Tip:** Choose the Custom Text option to add "boilerplate" text that will be displayed with every image.

3 From the Title menu, choose Title. From the Caption menu, choose Caption.

Next, you'll need to edit the image metadata from which the Title and Caption information will be drawn. You can do this in the Library module.

4 Press G to switch to the Grid view in the Library module.

5 In the Grid view, select the first image. If you've arranged the images differently than shown in the illustration below, that's fine. Expand the Metadata panel in the right panel group. In the Title text box, type **Soliloquy I** and for the Caption type **mixed media on canvas**; then press Enter / Return.

6 (Optional) Enter titles and captions for the other images.

7 Switch back to the Web module by pressing Ctrl+Alt+5 / Command+Option+5. The new details are now displayed under the enlarged view of the first painting.

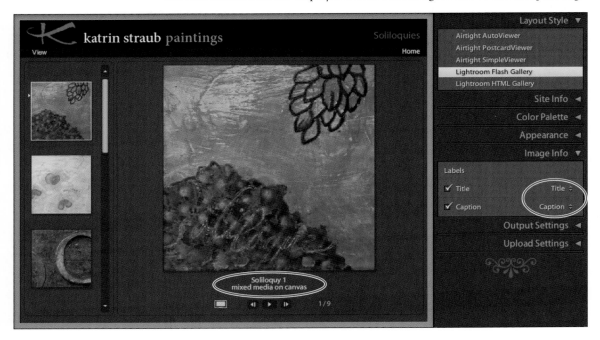

Specifying output settings

In the Output Settings panel you can control the image quality and the sharpness of the JPEG images generated for your web gallery. You can also choose to add a watermark to your images—a minimal protection when making your work available to the public.

1 In the right panel group, collapse the Image Info panel and expand the Output Settings panel. Drag the Quality slider to set the image quality to 70%, or alternatively, click the value to the right, type **70** and press Enter. In most cases, an image quality setting of 70% to 80% strikes a good balance between file size and image quality.

▶ **Tip:** It's always worth experimenting with the image quality settings; for some images a lower setting might be sufficient, resulting in a website that loads faster.

2 Activate the Sharpening option at the bottom of the Output Settings panel. Click the double arrow to open the Sharpening menu and choose Standard.

You won't see the changes to these settings reflected in the images in the gallery preview; both the image quality and sharpening settings will not be applied until Lightroom exports the image files for your website.

Watermarking images

With the new Watermark Editor interface, Lightroom 3 makes it easier than ever to watermark your images for export, printing, publishing, or for a web gallery.

You have the choice of applying a simple text watermark—ideal for a copyright message or your business name—or importing an image file such as your company logo to be applied as a graphic watermark.

For a text watermark you can specify a font and the text color, and for both watermark styles you can adjust the opacity and either use precise scaling and positioning controls or work directly with your watermark in the watermarking preview.

1 In the Filmstrip, select all the images in your web gallery. In the Output Settings panel, activate the Watermarking option. Click the double arrow to open the Watermarking menu and choose Edit Watermarks to open the Watermark Editor dialog box.

The default watermark style is a simple text copyright watermark. In the Watermark Editor dialog box you have the opportunity to enter your own message and specify the font, style, alignment, and color of your text. On Mac OS, you also have the option to set up a drop-shadow effect for your watermark text.

Tip: For both watermark styles you can use the Watermark Effects controls at the right of the Watermark Editor dialog box, where you can adjust the opacity of your watermark as well as its size and placement. Alternatively, you can move or resize your watermark directly in the watermarking preview; a bounding box and handles will appear around the watermark when you move the pointer over the preview. Use the left and right arrows at the top of the dialog box to change the image in the preview pane.

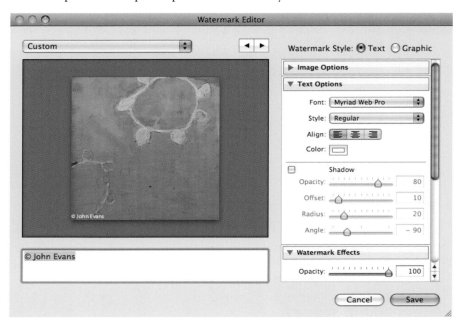

2   Under Image Options at the top right of the Watermarks Editor dialog box, click Choose to select an image file to be used as a graphic watermark.

3   In the Open / Choose A File dialog box, navigate to and open the Lesson 9 folder. Select the file watermark_K.png, and then click Choose.

4 At the right of the Watermarks Editor dialog box, scroll down if necessary and expand the Watermark Effects controls. Use the sliders or type new values to set up the Watermark Effects controls as shown in the illustration below. Set the opacity value to **40**, proportional sizing value to **25**, and both the horizontal and vertical inset values to **3**. Leave the Anchor setting at the default so that the watermark appears in the lower left corner of the image. For our purposes, you won't need to use the Rotate buttons to reorient the watermark image.

5 Use the left and right arrow buttons at the top of the Watermarks Editor dialog box to cycle the image in the watermarking preview and decide whether the settings are effective for all the images in the collection. Make any adjustments you wish to make.

6 Choose Save Current Settings As New Preset from the Custom menu above the watermarking preview.

7 In the New Preset dialog box, type **web portfolio** as the name for your new preset, and then click Create.

You will now be able to use the watermarking presets menu to apply the same watermark settings to another collection of images quickly and easily.

8 Click Done to close the Watermark Editor dialog box. The watermark appears on the images in the gallery preview and the web portfolio preset is indicated beside Watermarking in the Output Settings panel.

This concludes the section on customizing the look and feel of your web gallery. You've changed the site title text, added a link to your Home page, learned how to adjust the color scheme and modify the layout, personalized your web page by placing a graphic identity plate, and finally added titles, captions and a watermark to the images. It's time to save all these modifications as a custom template that you can use as a starting point the next time you create a web gallery, but first let's preview your gallery in your web browser.

Previewing the gallery

To enable you to preview your gallery as it will appear on the Web, Lightroom generates the web pages and all the necessary image files in a temporary folder on your hard disk, and then opens the main page of the gallery in your default web browser.

1 To preview the gallery in your default web browser, click the Preview In Browser button below the left panel group, or choose Web > Preview In Browser.

While Lightroom generates the necessary files, a progress bar appears in the upper left corner of the Lightroom workspace. You can cancel the Preview In Browser command at any time by clicking the small cross icon (x) at the right end of the progress indicator—but for this exercise, let the process run its course.

2 Once Lightroom has finished generating the necessary files, your web gallery opens in your default browser.

Tip: You should always preview your gallery in this way before uploading it to your website. Check that the navigation controls work as expected, examine the image quality, and confirm that your photos appear in the correct order. Finally, you should resize the browser window to see how well the gallery layout adapts to different display sizes.

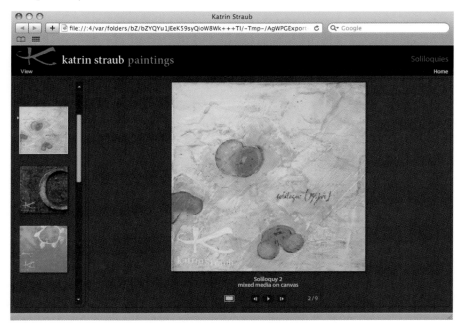

3   To check how your web gallery performs in the browser, run these simple tests:

- Click the Play button in the group of navigation controls below the large image to start the gallery slideshow.

- Click the Pause button or press the spacebar to stop playback.

- Use the scrollbar to scroll down the list of small thumbnail images on the left. Click a thumbnail to view the enlarged image on the right.

- Click the word View just below the identity plate at the upper left of the gallery layout, and then choose Slideshow from the menu.

- Use the arrow keys on your keyboard to move from one image to the next.

- Click the View Gallery button at the left of the navigation controls below the large image to leave the slideshow mode and return to the gallery layout with the column of thumbnail images on the left.

- Resize your browser window to see how the gallery works at different sizes.

- Examine the image quality.

- Make sure the titles, captions, and watermarks are displayed correctly.

- Click the Home button to see if it links correctly to your home page. (You'll need an active Internet connection to test this.)

4   When you're done, close the browser window and return to Lightroom.

Saving your custom template

Having spent time and effort modifying the gallery layout, changing the color scheme and text style, adding titles, captions, an identity plate, and watermarks, you should save your design as a custom web gallery template. The new template will be listed under User Templates in the Template Browser panel, where you can access it easily in case you need to rework or extend your gallery, or should you wish to use your customized template as a starting point for creating a new layout. You can create additional folders in the Template Browser to help you manage your custom templates.

1   With your customized web gallery still open in the Web module, click the Create New Preset button (+) in the header of the Template Browser panel in the left panel group. Alternatively, choose Web > New Template.

2 In the New Template dialog box, type **My Flash Web Portfolio**. Leave the default User Templates folder selected in the Folder menu and click Create.

Tip: To delete a custom template, select the template and click the Delete Selected Preset button (-) in the header of the Template Browser. You cannot delete the Lightroom templates.

Your customized web gallery template is now listed under User Templates in the Template Browser panel.

3 In the Template Browser panel right-click / Control-click the User Templates folder and choose New Folder from the context menu.

4 In the New Folder dialog box, type **My CIB Templates** as the name for the new folder; then click Create.

The new folder is listed in alphabetical order in the Template Browser panel.

Tip: In order to delete a folder from the Template Browser panel, first delete all the templates inside it—or drag them into another folder; then right-click / Control-click the empty folder and choose Delete Folder from the context menu. You cannot delete either the Lightroom Templates folder or the default User Templates folder.

5 In the Template Browser panel, drag the My Flash Web Portfolio template from the User Templates folder into your new My CIB Templates folder.

Exporting your gallery

Now that you're happy with your gallery and you've saved the template, you can export the website to your hard disk. You can run the exported website from your laptop if you need to present your work where there is no Internet connection, or burn the exported files to a CD-ROM as a working backup or to send to a client.

1 Select My Flash Web Portfolio from the My CIB Templates folder in the Template Browser panel and click the Export button below the right panel group, or choose Web > Export Web Photo Gallery.

2 In the Save Web Gallery dialog box, navigate to your Lesson 9 folder. Type **My Web Gallery** in the File Name / Save As text box, and then click Save.

Tip: Before burning your web gallery to a CD-ROM for a client, create an alias of the index.html file, place it beside the folder containing the files for the website, and rename it **Start here**. This will make it easy for your client to launch your presentation.

Lightroom will create a folder named My Web Gallery inside the Lesson 9 folder and generate all the necessary image files, web pages, subfolders and support files within that folder. If you have many images in your gallery, this operation might take a while—a progress bar at the upper left of the Lightroom workspace provides feedback as Lightroom completes the process.

3 When the export is complete, double-click the file index.html in the folder My Web Gallery inside your Lesson 9 folder. Your gallery opens in your default web browser. When you're finished reviewing the exported gallery, close the web browser window and return to Lightroom.

Uploading your gallery to a web server

In the last exercise of this lesson you'll learn how to upload your web gallery to a server from within Lightroom. To do this, you'll need to know your FTP server access information. You can get these details from your Internet service provider.

1 In the Web module, expand the Upload Settings panel in the right panel group.

2 From the FTP Server menu in the Upload Settings panel, choose Edit.

3 In the Configure FTP File Transfer dialog box, enter the server address, your username and password, and the server path.

> ▶ **Tip:** For security reasons, don't activate the Store Password In Preset option unless you are the only person with access to the computer you're using.

4 From the Preset menu, choose Save Current Settings As New Preset.

5 In the New Preset dialog box, enter a name for your FTP server preset, and then click Create.

6 Click OK to close the Configure FTP File Transfer dialog box. You'll notice that the name of your new FTP server preset now appears in the Upload Settings panel, where you can access it at any time from the FTP Server Presets menu.

▶ **Tip:** To avoid possible compatibility issues with your web server, you should use only lowercase letters, the minus sign (-), and the underscore character (_) in the subfolder name. Avoid using spaces in the folder name.

7 To place the gallery inside a subfolder on your FTP server, activate the option Put In Subfolder and type a name for the subfolder that's relevant to the content of the gallery. This subfolder name will become part of the URL of your web gallery. For example, we used **soliloquies** as subfolder name, so the complete URL might look like this: http://www.katrinstraub.com/soliloquies.

8 Click the Upload button below the right panel group. If you didn't save your FTP server password in the Configure FTP File Transfer dialog box, you'll need to enter it now in the Enter Password dialog box, and then click Upload.

Uploading your web gallery to an FTP server generally takes much longer than exporting it to your local hard disk. You can watch the upload status in the progress bar at the upper left of the Lightroom workspace.

Once the upload is complete, you can enter the URL of your gallery in your web browser and admire your site live on the Internet. Don't send the URL to a client or friends before you've confirmed that everything works as expected!

Congratulations—you've completed this lesson on publishing images. You've learned how to use the new Publish Services feature to publish images to a photo sharing website or to your hard disk. You've built your own web gallery, saved a custom gallery template and created new watermarking and FTP upload presets. Finally, you learned how to export your web gallery or upload it to a web server. Before you move on to the next lesson, take a moment or two to review some of your new skills by reading through the questions and answers on the facing page.

Review questions

1 Why would you use Publish Services to publish images to your hard disk?

2 Why is it useful to create a collection to group the images that you intend to use for a web gallery?

3 What is the difference between HTML and Flash galleries?

4 Which panels would you use to customize the Lightroom web templates?

5 How do you add a graphic watermark to the images in your web gallery?

Review answers

1 You can create a new publish collection on your hard disk for each client to whom you hand off photos, making it easy to check whether they have the most current versions, as Lightroom will keep track of which images have been updated since the collection was published. You can also set up a publish collection that will enable you to publish images to your iPhone sync folder with drag and drop convenience.

2 Grouping your images as a collection not only keeps them all in one place for easy reference—it will also make the process of updating and adjusting your web gallery much more efficient. Once a selection of images has been saved as a collection it is possible to rearrange the order in which they will appear in the gallery.

3 HTML gallery templates produce simple web sites that are compatible with most browsers. Flash templates can produce more sophisticated web galleries, including animations, slideshows with smooth transitions, and other special effects. However, Flash galleries require that the viewer has the appropriate Adobe Flash Player plug-in. Viewers may need to click through security messages in the web browser before being able to see the gallery.

4 The panels in the right panel group—the Site Info, Color Palette, Appearance, Image Info, Output Settings, and Upload Settings panels—contain controls for modifying the gallery layout templates available in the Template Browser.

5 In the Web module, activate the Watermarking option in the Output Settings panel. Click the double arrow to open the Watermarking menu and choose Edit Watermarks to open the Watermark Editor dialog box. Under Image Options in the Watermarks Editor dialog box, click Choose to select an image file to be used as a watermark.

10 CREATING BACKUPS AND EXPORTING PHOTOS

Lesson overview

Lightroom makes it easy to back up and export all the data connected with your image library. You can create backup copies to external storage during import, have Lightroom schedule automatic backups of your catalog file, and perform full or incremental backups of both your photos and develop settings. Export files in a range of formats—from images optimized for on-screen viewing to archival copies.

In this lesson you'll learn a variety of techniques to help you to manage your image library, minimize the impact of accidental data loss, and streamline your workflow:

- Backing up your catalog file
- Backing up the entire image library
- Making incremental backups
- Exporting metadata
- Exporting photos for on-screen viewing
- Exporting photos to be edited in another application
- Exporting photos for archival purposes
- Using export presets
- Setting up automated post-export actions

 You'll probably need between one and two hours to complete this lesson.

Safeguard your photographs and develop settings
against loss using Lightroom's build-in backup tools.
Back up just your catalog file, or your entire photo
library, complete with develop settings and copies of
your master files. Export photos in different file formats for multimedia presentations, for further editing
in an external image editor, as e-mail attachments, or
to be burned to CD or DVD for archival purposes.

Getting started

This lesson assumes that you are already familiar with the Lightroom workspace and with moving between the different modules. If you find that you need more background information as you go, refer to Lightroom Help, or review the previous lessons in this book.

Before you begin, make sure that you have correctly copied the Lessons folder from the CD in the back of this book onto your computer's hard disk and created the LR3CIB Library Catalog file as detailed in "Copying the Classroom in a Book files" on page 2 and "Creating a catalog file for working with this book" on page 3.

1   Start Lightroom.

2   In the Adobe Photoshop Lightroom - Select Catalog dialog box, make sure the file LR3CIB Library Catalog.lrcat is selected under Select A Recent Catalog To Open, and then click Open.

3   Lightroom will open in the screen mode and workspace module that were active when you last quit. If necessary, switch to the Library module.

4   For the purposes of exercises to follow, we need to be sure that Lightroom won't automatically write changes made during import into the image files' XMP data. Choose Edit > Catalog Settings / Lightroom > Catalog Settings. On the Metadata tab, make sure that the Automatically Write Changes Into XMP option is disabled, and then close the Catalog Settings dialog box.

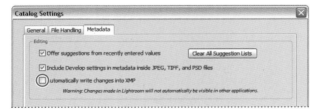

Importing images into the library

The next step is to import the images for this lesson into the Lightroom library.

1   In the Library module, click the Import button below the left panel group.

2 If the Import dialog box appears in compact mode, click the Show More Options button at the lower left of the dialog box to see all the options in the expanded Import dialog box.

3 Under Source at the left of the expanded Import dialog box, navigate to the Lessons folder that you copied into the LR3CIB folder on your hard disk. Select the Lesson 10 folder. Ensure that all four images in the Lesson 10 folder are checked for import.

4 In the import options above the thumbnail previews, click Add to add the imported photos to your catalog without moving or copying them.

5 Under File Handling at the right of the expanded Import dialog box, choose Minimal from the Render Previews menu and ensure that the Don't Import Selected Duplicates option is activated.

6 Under Apply During Import, choose None from both the Develop Settings menu and the Metadata menu and type **Lesson 10** in the Keywords text box. Make sure your settings are exactly as shown in the illustration below, and then click Import.

The four images are imported from the Lesson 10 folder and now appear in both the Grid view of the Library module and in the Filmstrip across the bottom of the Lightroom workspace.

Preventing data loss

The importance of a good backup strategy is often only understood too late. How much damage would be done if your computer was stolen right now? How many files would be irrecoverably lost if your hard disk failed today? How much work and money would that cost you? You can't prevent a disaster from happening but it is in your power to reduce the risks and the cost of recovery. Backing up regularly will reduce the impact of a catastrophe and save you time, effort, and money.

Lightroom delivers a range of options that make it easy to safeguard your photo library; as for the rest of the files on your computer, you really should have your own backup strategy in place.

Backing up the catalog file

The Lightroom catalog file stores a great deal of information for the photos in your library—not only the locations of the image files, but the metadata attached to them, including titles, captions, keyword tags, flags, labels, and ratings, together with all your developing and output settings. Every time you modify a photo in any way, from renaming the file during import to color correction, retouching, and cropping—all your work is saved to the catalog file. It records the way your images are grouped and ordered in collections, and records the publishing history, slide-show settings, web gallery designs, and print layouts associated with them as well as your customized templates and presets.

Even if you have copies of your original images stored safely on removable media—unless you back up your catalog, you could still lose hundreds of hours of work in the event of a hard disk failure, accidental deletion, or a corrupted library file. You can set Lightroom to initiate a regular backup of your catalog file automatically.

1   Choose Catalog Settings from the Edit / Lightroom menu. on the General tab, choose When Lightroom Next Exits from the Back Up Catalog menu.

2 Click OK / the Close button (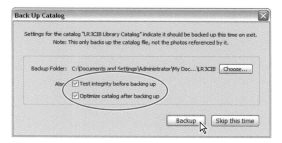) to close the Catalog Settings dialog box; then quit Lightroom.

3 In the Back Up Catalog dialog box, click the Choose button to change the folder where the backed up catalog will be stored. Ideally the backup should be located on a different disk than your original catalog file; for the purpose of this exercise you can select the LR3CIB folder on your hard disk. In the Browse For Folder / Choose Folder dialog box, select the LR3CIB folder as the backup directory and click OK / Choose.

4 Make sure the options Test Integrity Before Backing Up and Optimize Catalog After Backing Up are activated. It's a good idea to keep these options activated whenever you back up your catalog; it would defy the purpose of making a backup if your original catalog file was not in good working order. Click Backup.

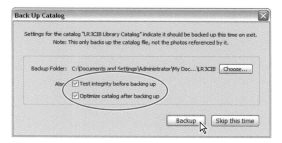

Each time you back up your catalog, Lightroom will create a complete copy of the catalog file in the directory you specified, inside a new folder with a name composed from the date and time of the backup.

Should your catalog be accidently deleted or become corrupted, you can now restore it either by copying the backup file to your catalog folder or by creating a new catalog and importing the contents of your backup file.

To avoid inadvertently modifying your backup file, it's preferable not to open it directly from the Lightroom File menu.

5 Start Lightroom. In the Adobe Photoshop Lightroom - Select Catalog dialog box, make sure that the file LR3CIB Library Catalog.lrcat is selected under Select A Recent Catalog To Open, and then click Open.

6 Choose Edit > Catalog Settings / Lightroom > Catalog Settings.

7 In the Catalog Settings dialog box, click the General tab and reset your preferred backup frequency by choosing from the Back Up Catalog menu.

8 Click OK / the Close button (⬤) to close the Catalog Settings dialog box.

▶ **Tip:** To save space on your backup drive, you can either delete your older backup files or compress them. Catalog files compress very effectively; you can expect a compressed catalog to be as small as 10% of the size of the original. Make sure to decompress the file before attempting to restore your catalog from the backup.

⬤ **Note:** Backing up the catalog file in this way does not make backup copies of the original image files or the preview images that Lightroom displays in the workspace. The previews will be regenerated as your catalog file is restored from the backup, but you'll need to back up your original image files separately.

Exporting metadata

The catalog is a central storage location for all the information associated with every image in your library; exporting and distributing the catalog file's content is another strategy that will lessen the impact if your catalog file is lost or damaged. You can save a copy of the information from the catalog file that is specific to each photo back to the respective image file on your hard disk.

If you keep this exported information in sync with your catalog file—something that can be done automatically—you have what is, in effect, a distributed backup of the metadata and develop settings for each of your photos.

When a photo has changes to its metadata that have not yet been saved to the original image file—such as the keyword tag you applied to the images for this lesson during the import process—its image cell in the Grid view and the Filmstrip is marked with the Metadata File Needs To Be Updated icon (≡↓).

1 If you don't see the Metadata File Needs To Be Updated icon (≡↓) in the Grid view image cells, choose View > View Options. On the Grid View tab in the Library View Options dialog box, activate the Unsaved Metadata option under Cell Icons. Click the Close button to close the Library View Options dialog box.

2 Select the first image in the Grid view. Right-click / Control-click the thumbnail and choose Metadata > Save Metadata To File from the context menu. After a brief processing time, the Metadata File Needs To Be Updated icon disappears.

3 Ctrl-click / Command-click to select the other three photos, and then click the Metadata File Needs To Be Updated icon (≡↓) in the image cell of any of the selected images. Click Save in the confirmation dialog box to update the image files on your hard disk. The Metadata File Needs To Be Updated icon disappears from each of the image cells after a brief processing time.

For files in DNG, JPEG, TIFF, and PSD format, Lightroom writes metadata into the image file itself. These formats have well-defined spaces within the file's structure where XMP information can be stored without having any affect on the image data.

Changes made to the camera raw image amongst the lesson files, however, are written into a separate *XMP sidecar file*, which is stored alongside the original file. The XMP file will record all the exported metadata and develop settings associated with the image.

4   To see the XMP file, right-click / Control-click the image 4_Winter.NEF and choose Show In Explorer / Show In Finder from the context menu. In the Explorer / Finder window, the sidecar file has the same name as the selected image, followed by an .xmp file extension.

4_Winter.NEF   4_Winter.xmp

▶ **Tip:** On Windows, if you don't see the file name extensions in the Explorer window, choose Tools > Folder Options and disable the option Hide Extensions For Known File Types on the View tab.

Many camera manufactures use proprietary and undocumented formats for their Raw files, some of which become outdated as new ones appear. Because of this, storing the metadata in a separate file is the safest approach, avoiding both possible corruption of the Raw file or loss of the exported metadata.

Applications such as Adobe Bridge and the Photoshop Camera Raw plug-in can read XMP metadata and will allow you to edit it. When you edit or add to an image's metadata in another application, Lightroom will show the Metadata Was Changed Externally icon (≡⬆) above the thumbnail in the Grid view. To accept the changes and update your catalog file accordingly, choose Metadata > Read Metadata From File. To reject the changed metadata and overwrite it with the information in your catalog file, choose Metadata > Save Metadata To File.

You can update the metadata for a batch of modified images—or even for the entire catalog with all its folders and collections—by selecting the images or folders to be updated and choosing Metadata > Save Metadata To File as you did with a single file in step 4. You can also configure Lightroom to export the metadata automatically whenever an image is modified. Although you might notice some slowing in performance as Lightroom writes information to the hard disk, the advantage is that you will always have an up-to-date copy of the metadata from your catalog stored either in the image files themselves or in their sidecar files.

However, XMP information exported in this way contains only the metadata attached to the individual images: keywords, flags, labels, ratings, and develop settings. It does not include higher-level data relevant to the catalog as a whole such as information relating to stacks, virtual copies, and settings used in presentations.

5   In Lightroom, choose Edit > Catalog Settings / Lightroom > Catalog Settings. In the Catalog Settings dialog box, activate Automatically Write Changes Into XMP under Editing on the Metadata tab. Click OK / the Close button (⬤) to close the Catalog Settings dialog box.

Backing up the library

In the first exercise you backed up your catalog without the image files. In the second you updated your images files with just part of the information stored in the catalog. In this exercise you'll export your entire Lightroom library: images, catalog, stacks, collections—the works!

Exporting images as a catalog

When you export your photos as a catalog, Lightroom creates a copy of the catalog file and gives you the option to make copies of the master files and the image previews at the same time. You can choose to export the entire library, or just a selection of your images, as a catalog. Exporting images in this way is ideal for moving your photos together with all the associated Lightroom catalog information from one computer to another. You can use the same technique to restore your entire library from a backup after a data loss.

1   In the Catalog panel, click All Photographs, and then choose File > Export As Catalog.

Ideally, you should save your backup files to a different hard disk than the one that stores your catalog and the master image files—but for this exercise, you can save the backup files to the LR3CIB folder on your hard disk.

2   In the Export As Catalog dialog box, navigate to the LR3CIB folder you created on your hard disk. Type **Backup** in the File Name / Save As text box, disable Export Selected Photos Only and activate Export Negative Files and Include Available Previews. Click Save / Export Catalog.

An initial progress bar is displayed while the new catalog is being created, which should only take a few seconds.

Lightroom then begins copying all the image files associated with this catalog to the new location as a background task.

3 While you wait for the export to be completed, watch the progress bar in the upper left the Lightroom workspace.

4 When the export process is complete, switch to Windows Explorer / the Finder and navigate to the LR3CIB folder. Open the new Backup folder.

● **Note:** You may see a different set of folders than is shown in the illustration, depending on which lessons you've already completed.

You can see that the folder structure nested inside the Backup folder replicates the arrangement of folders you see in the Folders panel. All the master images in your Lightroom library have been copied into these new folders and the file Backup.lrcat is a fully functional copy of your original catalog.

5 In Lightroom, choose File > Open Catalog. In the Open Catalog / Open dialog box, navigate to the new Backup folder inside the LR3CIB folder. Select the file Backup.lrcat, and then click Open. If the Open Catalog dialog box appears, click Relaunch. Lightroom will open the backup catalog.

6 Other than the filename in the title bar of the workspace window, this catalog will be almost indistinguishable from your original. Only some minor status information has been lost. For example, you can see that the Previous Import folder in the Catalog panel is now empty.

7 Some of your preferences have been reset to default values which may differ from the choices you've made for your LR3CIB catalog. Choose Edit > Catalog Settings / Lightroom > Catalog Settings. In the Catalog Settings dialog box, click the General tab. The backup frequency has been reset to the default:

Once A Week, When Exiting Lightroom. Click Cancel / the Close button (⬤) to close the Catalog Settings dialog box.

8 Choose File > Open Recent > LR3CIB Library Catalog.lrcat to return to your original catalog. If the Open Catalog dialog box appears, click Relaunch.

9 If the Back Up Catalog dialog box appears, click Skip Now.

Doing incremental backups

In the usual course of events the majority of the images in your library will remain unchanged between backups. An incremental backup will save you time by replacing only the backup copies and catalog entries of images that have been modified since the last backup.

Although Lightroom does not have an incremental backup command, you can achieve the same effect by regularly updating your existing backup with just those files in your main catalog that have been modified since the last backup.

1 In the Folders panel, select the Lesson 10 folder. Change the star rating for one of the images in the Grid view. This will be the incremental change to your library for the purposes of this exercise.

2 Choose File > Open Recent > Backup.lrcat to switch to the Backup catalog. If the Open Catalog dialog box appears, click Relaunch.

3 Choose File > Import From Catalog. In the Import From Lightroom Catalog dialog box, navigate to the LR3CIB folder. Drill down to the LR3CIB Library/ LR3CIB Library Catalog folder. Inside that folder, select LR3CIB Library Catalog.lrcat, and then click Open / Choose.

4 In the Import From Catalog dialog box, make sure the Show Preview option is activated. Choose Metadata And Develop Settings Only from the Replace menu under Changed Existing Photos. Scroll down in the Preview panel to confirm that only the image you modified in step 1 is selected for import.

Note: When you're adding new images to your backup library, choose Copy New Photos To A New Location And Import from the File Handling menu. Click the Choose button to specify your current Backup folder as the destination for the copied files.

5   Click Import. You can see that the modified image has been updated with the rating you changed in the master catalog. You have just performed an incremental backup.

6   (Optional) In the Catalog panel, click All Photographs and choose Edit > Select All or press Ctrl+A / Command+A. Choose Metadata > Save Metadata To Files or press Ctrl+S / Command+S. This will export the metadata and develop settings for each photo in the backup library to the backup image file or its XMP sidecar, as an extra precaution against data loss.

7   To return to your original catalog, choose File > Open Recent > LR3CIB Library Catalog.lrcat. If the Open Catalog dialog box appears, click Relaunch.

8   If the Back Up Catalog dialog box appears, click Skip This Time.

Exporting photos

The backup techniques we have discussed so far all produce backup files that can be read only by Lightroom or another application that is capable of reading and interpreting the exported XMP metadata.

If you wish to send your work in a usable format to somebody who doesn't have Lightroom installed on his or her computer you'll first need to convert the images to an appropriate file format. This is comparable to saving a Word document as plain text or as a PDF document for distribution; some of the functionality is lost but at least the recipient can see what you're working on.

Your choice of file format for the exported photos will depend on the purpose for which the images are intended. To export an image for use as an e-mail attachment intended to be viewed on screen, use the JPEG file format and minimize the file size by reducing the resolution and dimensions of the image. To export an image to be edited in another application, use the PSD or TIFF file format at full size. For archival purposes you can export the images in their original file format or convert them to DNG.

Exporting JPEG files for on-screen viewing

For this exercise, you'll convert the images to grayscale before you export them so you'll be able to see at a glance that your develop settings have been applied to the images as they were exported.

1   In the Folders panel, select the Lesson 10 folder. Choose Edit > Select All, and then choose Photo > Develop Settings > Convert To Black & White. If you prefer using keyboard shortcuts, press Ctrl+A / Command+A, and then press the V key on your keyboard.

2   With all four images still selected in the Grid view, choose File > Export.

3 Under Export Location in the Export dialog box, choose Specific Folder from the Export To menu, and then click the Choose button below it to specify a destination folder *(see illustration after step 4)*. Navigate to your Lessons folder, select the Lesson 10 folder, and click OK / Choose.

4 Activate the Put In Subfolder option and type **Export** as the name for the new subfolder. Disable the option Add To This Catalog.

5 Under File Naming in the Export dialog box, click the checkbox to activate the Rename To option; then, choose Filename from the menu.

6 Under File Settings, choose JPEG from the Format menu and set a Quality value of between 70% and 80%—a range that generally makes an acceptable compromise between image quality and file size. From the Color Space menu choose sRGB. The sRGB color space is a good choice for images intended to be viewed on the web—or in other circumstances where you are unsure what form of color management is used, if any at all.

7 Scroll down in the Export dialog box, if necessary, so that you can see the Image Sizing controls. Activate the Resize To Fit option and choose Width & Height from the menu. Enter **750** for both width (W) and height (H) and choose Pixels from the units menu. This will proportionally scale each image so that its longest side is 750 pixels. Activate Don't Enlarge to avoid smaller images being upsampled. Set the Resolution to **72** Pixels Per Inch—although resolution settings are in general ignored for on-screen display. The reduction in file size is the result of reducing the total number of pixels that make up the image.

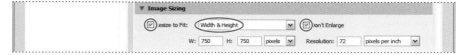

8 In the Output Sharpening settings, disable the Sharpen For option. In the Metadata options, activate only Minimize Embedded Metadata. Disable the Watermark option. Choose Show In Explorer / Show In Finder from the After Export menu under Post-Processing, and then click Export.

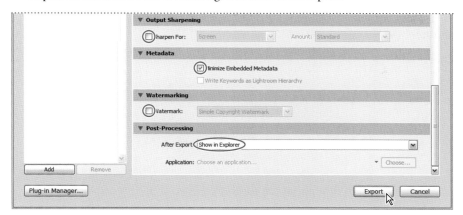

9 Watch the progress bar on the left side of the top panel in the Lightroom workspace. When the export process is complete, your Export folder inside the Lesson 10 folder will open in Windows Explorer / the Finder.

● **Note:** To have Lightroom notify you by playing a sound when the export process is complete, choose a sound from the menu under Completion Sounds on the General tab in the Preferences dialog box.

Using export plug-ins

You can use plug-ins to extend Lightroom's functionality.

For example, you can download and install an iPhoto plug-in that extends the options in the Export dialog box. The Lightroom iPhoto plug-in enables you to export images in your preferred file format and then import them into iPhoto as an album.

You can then take advantage of iPhoto's close integration with the Mac OS to browse your photos from within other applications or to transfer them to an iPod or iPhone.

There are export plug-ins available to enable you upload photos directly from within Lightroom to your SmugMug, Zenfolio, or Picasa Web accounts.

Other export plug-ins let you create entire web galleries from the selected images and upload them to your FTP server. Worth mentioning are the plug-ins for PixelPost Photoblob, SlideShowPro, and IStockPhoto, to name just a few.

Search the Internet for Lightroom plug-ins or browse the Adobe Store (www.adobe. com/go/store) where you have access to thousands of plug-ins from third-party developers, either offering additional export functionality or helping you to auto-mate tasks, customize workflows, create specialized professional effects, and more.

10 In Windows Explorer, use the Filmstrip or Thumbnail view to see a preview of the images in the folder. In the Finder, select an image in Column view or in Cover Flow to see its preview. You can see that the images are in black and white; your develop settings have been applied to the during the export process. The width of the images is 750 pixels and the file sizes are much reduced.

11 In Windows Explorer / the Finder, delete the four black and white images in the Export folder, and then return to Lightroom. Press the V key, or choose Photo > Develop Settings > Reset or to revert the images to their original colors.

Exporting as PSD or TIFF for further editing

1 In the Grid view, choose Edit > Select None, and then click to select the camera raw image, 4_Winter.NEF. In the right panel group, expand the Quick Develop panel and choose BW Creative - Cyanotype from the Saved Preset menu.

● **Note:** For the purposes of this illustration, the Saved Preset menu has been abridged; you'll actually find the BW Creative - Cyanotype preset quite a long way further down the menu.

2   Choose File > Export. In the Export dialog box, you'll notice that all your settings from the previous exercise are still in place.

3   In File Settings, choose TIFF from the Format menu. When saving in TIFF format, you have the option to apply ZIP data compression—a lossless form of compression—to reduce the resulting file size. Notice that AdobeRGB (1998) is automatically selected in the Color Space menu.

► **Tip:** To export more images using the same settings that you used for the previous export (and without calling up the Export dialog box) choose File > Export With Previous.

When you intend to edit an image in an external application after exporting it, you should use the AdobeRGB (1998) color profile rather than the sRGB color profile. The AdobeRGB (1998) color profile has a larger color gamut, which results in fewer colors being clipped and the original appearance of your images being better preserved. The ProPhoto RGB color gamut is even larger, capable of representing any color from the original raw image. However, to correctly display images using the AdobeRGB (1998) or ProPhoto RGB color profiles on screen you need an image editing application capable of reading these color profiles. You'll also need to turn color management on and calibrate your computer display. Without taking these measures, your images will look bad on screen with the AdobeRGB (1998) color profile—and even worse with ProPhoto RGB.

4   Choose PSD from the Format menu. Choose 8 Bits/Component from the Bit Depth menu. Unless you have a particular need to output 16 bit files as part of your workflow, 8-bit files are smaller and compatible with more programs and plug-ins, but do not preserve fine tonal detail as well as 16-bit files. Lightroom actually operates in a 16 bit color space but by the time you're ready to export images you've usually already made any important corrections or adjustments that were necessary, so you won't loose much in terms of editing capability by converting the files to 8 bits for export.

► **Tip:** Choose your preferred external editor, file format, color space, bit depth, compression settings, and file naming options on the External Editing tab of the Preferences dialog box. In the Lightroom workspace, choose Photo > Edit In, and then choose your preferred external image editing application from the menu. Lightroom will automatically export an image in the appropriate file format, open it in the external editor, and add the converted file to the Lightroom library.

5   In Image Sizing, disable Resize To Fit; to preserve all the image information for further editing, we wish to export every pixel of the original image.

6 Leave the Output Sharpening and Metadata settings unchanged. If you have Adobe Photoshop CS2/CS3/CS4/CS5 installed on your computer, choose Open in Adobe Photoshop CS2/CS3/CS4/CS5 from the After Export menu in the Post-Processing options. Alternatively, choose Open In Other Application, and then click Choose to select your preferred image editor. Click Export.

7 Wait until the export is complete and the photo has opened in the external editor. The image has been exported with the BW Creative - Cyanotype preset that you applied in the Quick Develop panel. Its dimensions are the same as those of the original Raw image—4288 by 2848 pixels.

8 Quit the external editor, delete the file from the Export folder in Windows Explorer / the Finder, and then return to Lightroom.

Exporting as Original or DNG for archiving

1 In the Grid view, make sure that the photo 4_Winter.NEF is still selected.

2 Choose File > Export. In the Export dialog box, leave the Export Location and File Naming settings unchanged.

● **Note:** When you choose to export images in DNG file format you have additional options that affect the way the DNG files are created, but the original image data remains essentially unchanged.

3 In File Settings, choose Original from the Format menu. Note that there are now no other File Settings, Image Settings, or Output Sharpening options available; Lightroom will export the original image data unaltered.

4 In the Post-Processing options, choose Show In Explorer / Show In Finder from the After Export menu; then, click Export.

5 Wait until the export process completes and the Export folder inside the Lesson 10 folder opens in Windows Explorer / the Finder. In the Windows Explorer / Finder window, note that an XMP sidecar file has been saved together with the copy of the original RAW image. This XMP sidecar file contains editing settings and any additional metadata, such as the rating you applied to the image.

6 In Windows Explorer / the Finder, delete both files from the Export folder, and then return to Lightroom.

Using export presets

Lightroom provides presets for commonly performed export tasks. You can use a preset as is or as a starting point for creating your own.

If you find yourself performing the same operations over and over again you should create your own presets to automate your workflow.

1 In the Grid view, select one of the other images in the Lesson 10 folder and then choose File > Export.

2 In the list of presets on the left side of the Export dialog box, choose For E-Mail from the Lightroom Presets.

3 Note the export location settings associated with this preset. Under Export Location, choose Specific Folder from the Export To menu, and then click the Choose button, if necessary, to reinstate the Lesson 10 / Export folder as the destination. Make sure the Put In Subfolder option is activated, and then type **To E-Mail** as the name for the new subfolder.

4 Examine the rest of the settings associated with this preset. With the current File Settings, an exported file will be an sRGB JPEG file with a Quality setting of 50%. Under Image Sizing, the exported image is set to be resized so that its longest side will be scaled down to 640 pixels. In the Metadata options Minimize Embedded Metadata is activated, and under Post-Processing, Show In Explorer / Show In Finder is selected from the After Export menu. These are all reasonable settings for images to be viewed as email attachments. If you prefer different settings for any of the options, adjust them now.

5 In the list of presets on the left side of the Export dialog box, click to select the Burn Full-Sized JPEGs export preset.

6 Note the changes in the export settings. The Export Location settings are no longer available; CD / DVD is now selected in the Export To menu at the top of the Export dialog box, instead of Hard Drive. Under File Settings, the JPEG Quality setting has been set to 100%.

7 Scroll down in the Export dialog box to examine all the preset options. Under Image Sizing, the Resize To Fit option is disabled. In the Metadata options, Minimize Embedded Metadata is disabled. You can adjust any of the settings in the preset if you wish. Note that for this preset there are no Post-Processing options; If you go ahead and click the Export button, Lightroom will automatically open the Choose Burner / Burn Disc dialog box, where you can nominate your disk burner and specify the burn speed before clicking Burn.

Setting up post-processing actions

You can streamline your export workflow by setting up an automated post-processing action. For example, when you export an image to be used as an e-mail attachment, you could have Lightroom automatically launch your e-mail application and prepare a new message with the exported image attached.

1   Choose For E-Mail from the Lightroom Presets. Set up the Export Location as you did in step 3 on the previous page. Adjust the other settings to your liking.

2   In the Post-Processing options, choose Go To Export Actions Folder Now from the After Export menu.

Lightroom opens a Windows Explorer / Finder window with the Export Actions folder already selected. The next step in setting up your automated export is to place a shortcut or alias for your e-mail application into this folder.

3   Open a second Windows Explorer / Finder window and navigate to the folder containing your e-mail application. Right-click / Control-click the e-mail application, choose Create Shortcut / Make Alias from the context menu, and then drag the new shortcut or alias into the Export Actions folder. When you're done, return to the Export dialog box in Lightroom.

4   In the Post-Processing settings, choose the new shortcut or alias to your e-mail application from the After Export menu.

With the current settings you could export an image as a small JPEG file and Lightroom would automatically launch your e-mail application and open a new message with the image already attached. But first, there's one more step that can help automate the process even further.

Creating user presets

You can save your customized export settings as a new user preset. Export presets
are always available from the File menu (File > Export With Preset) where you can
start your export without having to open the Export dialog first.

1   Click the Add button in the lower left corner of the Export dialog box. In the
    New Preset dialog box, type **For E-Mail And Attach** as the name for your new
    preset, choose User Presets from the Folder menu, and then click Create.

In the Export dialog box, your new preset is now listed under User Presets.

2   Click Cancel to close the Export dialog box without exporting any images.

3   Select one or more images in the Grid view and choose File > Export With
    Preset > For E-Mail And Attach.

The export process will begin immediately. When exporting is complete, your
e-mail application will be launched automatically and will open a new message
with your exported photo or photos already attached; all you need a to do is to
enter the recipient's e-mail address and you're ready to send.

Review questions

1 What are the two basic components of your photo library that need to be backed up?

2 How can you move a selection of images or your entire image library with all the associated catalog information from one computer to another?

3 How can you do an incremental backup of your photo library?

4 How would you choose between file formats for exporting your photos?

5 What is a post-processing action?

Review answers

1 The two basic components of the image library are the original image files (or master files) and the library catalog file, which records all the metadata and the complete editing history for every image in the library as well as information about collections, user templates and presets, and output settings.

2 On one computer, use the Export As Catalog command to create a catalog file together with copies of the original images and the available previews. On the other computer, use the Import From Catalog command.

3 Once you have created a full backup of the library using Export As Catalog, you can switch to the backup catalog regularly and use the Import From Catalog command to update it. You can configure the import settings so only those images that have been modified since the last backup are imported from the main catalog. In this way, you can keep your existing backup catalog updated incrementally—avoiding the more time consuming process of making a full new backup.

4 The appropriate choice of a file format depends on the intended use of the exported images. To export images for on-screen viewing as e-mail attachments, you'd use the JPEG file format and minimize the file size. To export an image to an external image editing application you'd use PSD or TIFF and export the image at full size. For archival purposes, export the images in their original format or convert them to DNG.

5 A post-processing action is a preset that can help to automate your workflow. You can choose a preset that will automatically burn your images to a CD or DVD after export, or one that will launch your e-mail application and attach your exported images to a new message. You can save your own action presets, which will be listed beside the Lightroom presets in the Export dialog box.

INDEX

Clone mode, 182
collapsing panels, 67–69
collections, 27, 145–148
    rearranging images, 29
Collections panel, 28–29, 43, 67, 129,
    146, 222, 244–245, 265–266, 281
color adjustments, 203, 204
color cast, 188
color corrections, 185
color fringes, 199
color gamut, 189, 319
color labels, 26, 157–158
color management, 319
    by Lightroom, 264
    by printer, 263
    using, 263
Color Palette panel, 287
ColorSync, 263
color temperature, 186, 189
Color Wash option, 227
color wheel, 203
Compact Cells option, 121
Compare view, 30–32, 31, 62–63, 73,
    119, 124–126
comparing photos, 30–34, 124–126
compatibility problems
    avoiding when naming files, 302
Contact Sheet layouts, 246
contrast, 191
    adjusting, 192
cool colors, 189
copying
    Classroom in a Book files, 2
    lessons files from CD, 2
crop overlay rectangle, 176
Crop Overlay tool, 37–39, 176–178
cropping images, 176
Crop To Fill slideshow template, 224
Custom Name option, 91
Custom Package layouts, 246
    creating, 259

D

data loss, preventing, 308
daylight, 189
Default Columns option, 163

Default slideshow template, 224
Delete Selected Snapshot button, 179
Deselect Photo icon, 32, 126
Detail panel, 196
Develop module, 18, 34–40, 174–212,
    262
develop presets, 15, 19, 33, 36, 172, 175
Digital Negative (DNG) file format, 93
dimming lights, 76
Distortion slider, 40
Don't Enlarge option, 316
Draft Mode Printing option, 248, 262
duotone effects, 203

E

editing
    using external editor, 14
EXIF Metadata slideshow template, 224
Expanded Cells option, 121
expanding panels, 67–69
Export As Catalog dialog box, 312
Export Containing Keywords
    export option, 151
Export dialog box, 316
exporting images
    as catalog, 312
    as e-mail attachment, 323
    as JPEG, 315
    as original or DNG, 320
    as PSD or TIFF, 318
Export PDF button, 235, 236
export presets, 321
Export Synonyms option, 151
Export With Previous
    menu command, 319
Exposure settings, 42
external editor
    preferences, 14, 214
    working with, 214

F

file formats, about, 93
Filename Template Editor
    dialog box, 92
Fill Light controls, 41, 173, 190

Thumbnail Badges option, 121,
    146–149
TIFF file format, 93
tint, 188, 204
Tint Grid Cells With Color Labels
    option, 121
Tint Grid Cells With Label Colors
    option, 73
Tint slider, 189
Title option, 293
Toggle Zoom View command, 72
tokens, 92, 232
tonal corrections, 185
tonal ranges, 186, 193
tone, 204
Tone Curve panel, 192
Tone Curve Target mode, 194
Toolbar, 15
    customizing, 16, 71, 119
    showing and hiding, 58, 71
Top Label option, 121
top panel, 15
Transform sliders, 40
Treat JPEG Files Next To Raw Files As
    Separate Photos option, 86

U

undoing changes, 178
Unrated option, 163
Unsaved Metadata option, 121, 310
Upload button, 302
Upload Settings panel, 301
upsampling images, 316
Use Defaults button, 75
Use Defaults option, 121
Use Second Monitor button, 60

V

vibrance, 191
video files, 93
View Gallery button, 291, 299
view modes, 70, 119
view options, 73
View Slideshow button, 291
virtual copies, 30, 105, 180, 266, 311

W

warm colors, 189
watched folder, 107
watermarking, 295
Watermark Editor dialog box, 295, 303
web galleries
    customizing, 285
Web module, 21, 43
white balance, 173
    about, 188–189
    adjusting, 185
White Balance Selector tool, 189
white point, 188
Widescreen slideshow template, 224
work area, 15, 70
workflow, 22
workspace
    customizing, 16
    overview, 14

X

XMP metadata, 149, 159
XMP sidecar file, 310

Z

zoom levels, 123
Zoom To Fill option, 248

Production Notes

The *Adobe Photoshop Lightroom 3 Classroom in a Book* was created electronically using Adobe InDesign CS3. Art was produced using Adobe InDesign, Adobe Illustrator, and Adobe Photoshop.

References to company names in the lessons are for demonstration purposes only and are not intended to refer to any actual organization or person.

Team credits

The following individuals contributed to the development of this edition of the *Adobe Photoshop Lightroom 3 Classroom in a Book*:

Project coordinators, technical writers: John Evans & Katrin Straub

Production: Manneken Pis Productions (www.manneken.be)

Copyediting & Proofreading: John Evans & Katrin Straub

Designer: Katrin Straub

Special thanks to Torsten Buck, Victor Gavenda, Connie Jeung-Mills, Lisa Brazieal, and Christine Yarrow.

Typefaces used

Adobe Clean, Adobe Myriad Pro, and Adobe Warnock Pro are used throughout the lessons. For more information about OpenType and Adobe fonts, visit www.adobe.com/type/opentype/.

Photo Credits

Photographic images and illustrations supplied by Torsten Buck, John Evans, Katrin Straub, and Adobe Systems Incorporated. Photos are for use only with the lessons in the book.

Contributors

John Evans has worked in computer graphics and design for more than 20 years, initially as a graphic designer, and then since 1993 as a multimedia author, software interface designer, and technical writer. His multimedia and digital illustration work associated with Japanese type attracted an award from Apple Computer Australia. His other projects range from music education software for children to interface design for innovative Japanese font design software. As a technical writer his work includes software design specifications, user manuals, and more recently copy editing for *Adobe Photoshop Elements 7 Classroom in a Book*, *Adobe Photoshop Lightroom 2 Classroom in a Book*, and *Adobe Creative Suite 4 Classroom in a Book* and authoring for *Adobe Photoshop Elements 8 Classroom in a Book*.

Katrin Straub is an artist, a graphic designer, and author. Her award-winning print, painting, and multimedia work has been exhibited worldwide. With more than 15 years experience in design, Katrin has worked as Design Director for companies such as Landor Associates and Fontworks in the United States, Hong Kong, and Japan. Her work includes packaging, promotional campaigns, multimedia, website design, and internationally recognized corporate and retail identities. She holds degrees from the FH Augsburg, ISIA Urbino, and The New School University in New York. Katrin has authored many books, from the *Adobe Creative Suite Idea Kit* to Classroom in a Book titles for Adobe Photoshop Lightroom 2, Adobe Creative Suite 4, Adobe Soundbooth, and several versions of *Adobe Photoshop Elements Classroom in a Book* and *Adobe Premiere Elements Classroom in a Book*.

Torsten Buck has been involved in the development of software for the design and desktop publishing industries in Japan, China and the United States for almost 20 years. A Masters in Computer Science combined with a passion for typography have shaped a career that took Torsten from the development of ground-breaking Asian font technology in Hong Kong to a position as Head of Type Development at Adobe Systems in the USA. As director of Manneken Pis Productions he has authored a wide range of design software training books including several versions of *Adobe Photoshop Elements Classroom in a Book* and *Adobe Premiere Elements Classroom in a Book*, *Creating a Newsletter in InDesign*, and more recently *Adobe Photoshop Lightroom 2 Classroom in a Book* and *Adobe Creative Suite 4 Design Premium Classroom in a Book*.

AdobePress

Learn Adobe Photoshop CS5 by Video:
Core Training in Visual Communication
(ISBN 9780321719805)

Learn Adobe Flash Professional CS5 by Video:
Core Training in Rich Media Communication
(ISBN 9780321719829)

Learn Adobe Dreamweaver CS5 by Video:
Core Training in Web Communication
(ISBN 9780321719812)

The **Learn by Video** series from video2brain and Adobe Press is the only Adobe-approved video courseware for the Adobe Certified Associate Level certification, and has quickly established itself as one of the most critically-acclaimed training products available on the fundamentals of Adobe software.

Learn by Video offers up to 19 hours of high-quality HD video training presented by experienced trainers, as well as lesson files, assessment quizzes and review materials. The DVD is bundled with a full-color printed book that provides supplemental information as well as a guide to the video topics.

Up to 19 hours of high-quality video training

Tutorials-to-Go! Transfer selected movies to your iPhone, iPod, or compatible cell phone

Table of Contents never more than a click away

Watch-and-Work mode shrinks the video into a small window while you work in the software

Video player remembers which movie you watched last

Lesson files are included on the DVD

Additional Titles

- **Learn Adobe Photoshop Elements 8 and Adobe Premiere Elements 8 by Video** (ISBN 9780321685773)
- **Learn Photography Techniques for Adobe Photoshop CS5 by Video** (ISBN 9780321734839)
- **Learn Adobe After Effects CS5 by Video** (ISBN 9780321734860)
- **Learn Adobe Flash Catalyst CS5 by Video** (ISBN 9780321734853)
- **Learn Adobe Illustrator CS5 by Video** (ISBN 9780321734815)
- **Learn Adobe InDesign CS5 by Video** (ISBN 9780321734808)
- **Learn Adobe Premiere Pro CS5 by Video** (ISBN 9780321734846)

For more information go to **www.adobepress.com/learnbyvideo**

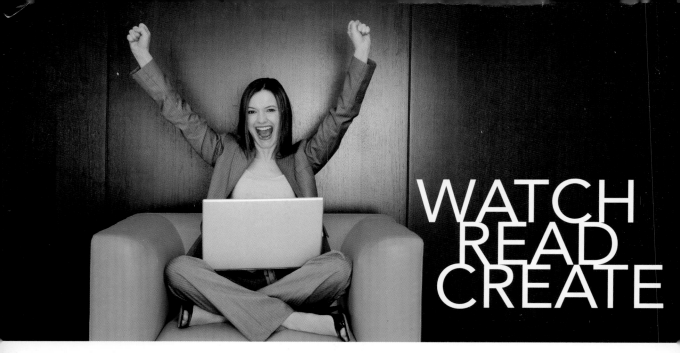

WATCH
READ
CREATE

Meet Creative Edge.

A new resource of unlimited books, videos and tutorials for creatives from the world's leading experts.

Creative Edge is your one stop for inspiration, answers to technical questions and ways to stay at the top of your game so you can focus on what you do best—being creative.

All for only $24.99 per month for access—any day any time you need it.

creative
edge

creativeedge.com